President Truman

Jonah Goldberg

"It is amazing what you can accomplish if you do not care who gets the credit."

- Harry S. Truman

Contents

Chapter One

From Missouri to the White House

Harry S. Truman was thrust into the Oval Office on April 12, 1945. Less than three months earlier, Truman had been a member of the United States Senate, one of ninety six men who served in that body. In fact, he was even the junior member from Missouri, indicating his lack of seniority within the chamber. Having been chosen as a compromise running mate for Franklin Delano Roosevelt at the Democratic National Convention in July of 1944, Truman campaigned with the incumbent President for an unprecedented fourth term in office. Due to Roosevelt's ill health, it was well known among the Washington political establishment that Truman would likely be called upon to serve as the nation's president. Nonetheless, few believed that he would become the nation's chief executive after a mere three months as the thirty fourth Vice President of the United States. The Roosevelt-Truman ticket soundly defeated their Republican rivals, Governor Thomas Dewey of New York and Senator John Bricker of Ohio, in the 1944 Presidential election. Having won the election largely on Roosevelt's overwhelming popularity, many Americans knew little about the man who would become their thirty third President.

Harry Truman was an improbable President. He did not exhibit any overwhelming charisma or charm, and had an ordinary background that contrasted sharply with President Roosevelt, who had spent years studying at universities. Truman had never pursued any post-secondary education, and his only non-political experience was in the military, farming, and running a number of unsuccessful small businesses. In fact, Truman was the first President since Grover Cleveland to not have attended a college or university. Nonetheless, Truman was a quiet man who was known as a smart student, avid history reader, hard worker and a trusted ally. For years he would be constantly trying to live up to the aura and stature of President Roosevelt, perhaps America's most successful President in the twentieth century.

Harry Truman came from Independence, Missouri, a small town not too far from Kansas City, although he was born in nearby Lamar. His parents, John Anderson Truman and Martha Ellen Young, had three children, their oldest being Harry, who was born on May 8, 1884.

A passionate student with impressive skills on the piano, Truman pursued a series of service and clerical jobs after completing high school, later returning to rural Missouri to farm until America joined the First World War. While training in advance of his military deployment to France, Truman met Eddie Jacobson and James Prendergast, both of whom had a profound effect on his business and political future. After a decorated record during the war, serving as a lieutenant and captain, Truman returned home to Independence where he married Bess Wallace. The couple would have only one child, a daughter named Margaret.

Truman's wartime connections would prove to be crucial in his foray into politics. In 1922 he was elected as a judge on the county court with the backing of Tom Prendergast, the head of the legendary Prendergast Democratic political machine. Prendergast was the uncle of Truman's friend James Prendergast from his military days, and it was James who put the two political activists in touch with each other. Truman nevertheless lost that position during the 1924 Republican wave that saw the re-election of President Calvin Coolidge of Massachusetts. In 1926, however, he returned to politics as the county's presiding judge, overseeing and supporting a wealth of infrastructure projects throughout Jackson County.

While Truman found considerable success in local politics, he had long desired to cultivate a career in Washington. In advance of the 1934 midterm elections, Truman wanted to pursue the Democratic Party's nomination to challenge incumbent Republican Senator Roscoe Patterson. Tom Prendergast, however, was skeptical about Truman's ability to hold his own on Capitol Hill, and sought to find other candidates to support. Nonetheless, after Prendergast failed to find an alternative candidate, he elected to support Truman, who won the primary and the general election, defeating Senator Roscoe Patterson in a landslide. Truman ultimately bested his Republican opponent by more than two hundred and fifty thousand votes.

When Truman arrived in Washington, many assumed that he, like many of his predecessors, was simply a foot soldier for the Prendergast family in Congress. Nonetheless, Truman was determined to prove them wrong, often railing against the interests of large corporations, a theme he would frequently return to during his time in the White House. His rise to fame came during the preparation of America's war effort during the early years of the Second World War. After encountering numerous abuses in taxpayer funds for military purposes, Truman called for the formation of a special Senate committee to investigate the country's defense program. When it was formally created in 1941 it came to be known as the Truman Committee, named after the man who chaired its proceedings and came to dominate the investigation. It was ultimately suggested that the Truman Committee found up to $15 billion of wasted and abused funds allocated for government defense spending, and the Committee's recommendations saved the American taxpayers a significant expense. Time Magazine would call the Truman Committee one of the government's most important agencies in the period covering the Second World War.

It was the success Truman had in leading his special committee that really propelled him to political prominence, and it eventually earned him a place on the Democratic ticket headed by President Roosevelt during the 1944 Presidential election. Roosevelt's Vice President during his third term had been Henry Wallace, the son of a former Republican Secretary of Agriculture, but many considered him to be too liberal to become President in the event of Roosevelt's death. With Roosevelt determined to choose either Truman or Supreme Court Justice William Douglas to be his running mate, and with the majority of grassroots supporters indicating their preference for Truman, the Senator for Missouri was selected to be the party's nominee for Vice President.

While the Democratic ticket won handily in the November 1944 Presidential election, many Americans only knew Truman for his work on the Truman Committee, and he was therefore a largely unknown quantity. After being sworn in as Vice President on January 20, 1945, Truman was rarely contacted by Roosevelt and was left out of policy decisions altogether.

When Roosevelt was found dead on April 12, 1945, Truman had been Vice President for only eighty two days, and had little knowledge of the intricacies of the Presidency or America's war effort. Nonetheless, Truman was called on to lead the nation during a time of crisis, and he met the challenge head on. Truman learned of Roosevelt's death after being summoned to the White House following an afternoon of presiding over a session in the Senate. It was Roosevelt's wife, Eleanor, who broke him the news.

Roosevelt's death would have a profound effect on the Second World War. The Japanese imperialists saw the event as a major stroke of luck, preferring to face off against an untested politician rather than a weathered statesman. Back home, the whole nation stood at a standstill. Many grieved about the death of America's longest serving President, and were equally concerned that Truman, as a man of such small stature, was to be his replacement. Thus, the eyes of observers around the world were on Washington when Truman took the oath of office just after 7pm in the Cabinet room at the White House. With Bess at his side and their daughter Margaret looking on, Harry Truman took the Presidential oath to become the thirty third President of the United States, simultaneously becoming arguably the most powerful man in the world.

After being sworn in by Chief Justice Harlan Stone in the Cabinet room, Truman assembled Roosevelt's Cabinet. He told his colleagues that his administration would continue to implement President Roosevelt's program, and that he hoped to do so with the help of his entire Cabinet. His first decision as President was to instruct government officials to ensure that the United Nations founding meeting in San Francisco went ahead as planned. As the first President to have served in the United States Senate since Warren G. Harding's death in 1923, Truman benefitted by strong connections to Congress, but was also hampered by the institution's reputation. The general trend throughout the twentieth century was the election of former Governors to the Presidency, with giants such as Franklin Roosevelt, Woodrow Wilson, and Theodore Roosevelt having all served as the Chief Executive in their respective home states. Harding's Presidency had been controversial at best, and Truman was faced with the task of overcoming his legacy.

Although most people worried about Truman's ascension to the Presidency, others were rather confident in the new President's abilities. John Nance Garner, who had served as Roosevelt's first Vice President for eight years, regarded Truman as a man of courage and conviction. Even Republicans such as Arthur Vandenberg, one of the most powerful members of the Senate at the time, saw Truman as up to the task. Vandenberg himself claimed that Truman was a man with "high honesty of purpose," someone who was prepared to lead America during a major war. While many were initially worried about Truman being America's first change in leadership in over twelve years, most would later reflect that Roosevelt had made an excellent choice in effectively nominating his own successor.

Like many of his detractors, Truman was quite solemn about his swift rise to the Presidency. He worried of his inexperience, and the difficulty of succeeding a man of Franklin Roosevelt's stature, someone who was recognized as one of the world's numerous giants throughout the twentieth century. As he would later say to the press while visiting Capitol Hill, Truman felt "like the moon, the stars, and all the planets had fallen on me."

On his first full day in office, Truman was fully briefed on the state of America's war effort and the situation in Europe. Secretary of State Stettinius outlined the deep divisions that were beginning to appear between the Americans and their Soviet allies. But Truman had never been actively involved in foreign policy, nor had he met any of the world's other major leaders, including those of the Allied nations. Nonetheless, Truman, like President Roosevelt before him, was provided with useful summaries of the major events that were happening around the world on a daily basis, which helped the new President orient himself with the current situation. He also immediately requested from Secretary Stettinius an outline of the major problems now confronting the United States in every region of the world. The briefing suggested that Great Britain's foreign policy was based almost exclusively on maintaining a sound relationship with its American ally, and recommended that the American government do all that it could to help France rebuild. In a statement that would foreshadow the difficulties to come, Truman's briefing noted that "the Soviet Government has taken a firm and uncompromising position on nearly every major question that has arisen in our relations." On interactions with Germany's Nazi regime, the State Department outlined American policy goals, including the "destruction of

National Socialist organizations and influence, punishment of war criminals, [and] disbandment of the Germany military establishment." Liberated areas in Europe would also have to be supplied with essential goods for citizens of the region, as restoring their morale would be the only way to maintain political stability, and re-establish overthrown democratic governments. Several other more minor objectives were also included in the briefing. On his first full day as President, Truman found that he had a lot to learn when it came to fully understanding the intricacies of American foreign policy.

When the President's military advisors assembled in the Oval Office for their first official meeting with the new President, they discussed frankly the state of the war in Europe and Asia. The party included Secretary of War Henry Stimson, Secretary of the Navy James Forrestal, Army Chief of Staff George Marshall, Chief of Naval Operations Ernest King, commander of the Air Force Barney Giles, and the President's Chief of Staff, William Leahy. The group collectively predicted that the Nazis would not be defeated for another six months or more, and that Japan would be able to hold out for more than a year and a half. Everyone at the meeting agreed that no further action or major decisions should be taken until President Truman spoke before Congress. As the President's military advisors left the Oval Office, Truman asked Leahy to stay behind, and requested that he remain in his post as the chief assistant to the President. Leahy gladly accepted.

President Truman also decided on his first full day in office who he would like to serve as his first Secretary of State. Edward Stettinius had already indicated that he would like to retire and Truman wanted to nominate James Byrnes, President Roosevelt's Director of the Office of War Mobilization, to take his place. Byrnes was summoned to the White House and was informed by the President that he would likely nominate him as Secretary of State once the United Nations conference in San Francisco had ended, which would only be in a few weeks' time. Truman wanted

Byrnes in the State Department for his valuable expertise, but also for his political experience. Without a Vice President, Truman's Secretary of State would be the next in line for the Presidency should anything happen to the President. Thus, he wanted a Secretary of State who had experience in the realm of politics, something that Stettinius clearly lacked. Byrnes had been a member of the House, Senate, and a Justice on the Supreme Court, so he was certainly qualified to take on high office. Two years later, under Truman's leadership, Congress would pass the Presidential Succession Act in 1947, placing the Speaker of the House of Representatives, a prominent elected official, next in line for the Presidency after the Vice President. Truman worried after taking office about the dangers of the 1886 Presidential Succession Act, which had placed the Secretary of State second in line for the Presidency.

On April 14, 1945, the day of President Roosevelt's state funeral, Truman received two cables from Prime Minister Churchill of Great Britain, who informed the President that the Soviet army in the east marching west, and the American and British armies in the west marching east, would meet in the next several days in Eastern Germany. Churchill suggested that he, Truman, and Stalin all release a joint announcement of the impending event, something that might benefit people across the world who would be reassured by an Allied victory in Europe. Truman readily agreed, pending Stalin's approval. Churchill also told Truman that, despite plans made by the Roosevelt administration, some of the bombing offensives that were scheduled to target German industrial areas were no longer necessary, and that any retaliation would further endanger the city of London. The President, after conferring with the Joint Chiefs, agreed with Churchill on that point as well.

When Roosevelt's funeral was finally held in the late afternoon, the new President played a relatively small part in the ceremony, as Mrs. Roosevelt had requested that no eulogies be made at the service. President Truman, Bess, and Margaret then accompanied the Roosevelt family on a train to New York, where Franklin Roosevelt was buried the following morning. Truman, returning to Washington later that afternoon, spent his time on the train putting the finishing touches on the speech he was to deliver to Congress on the following day.

After several days of mourning, Truman set out to make his own mark on American policy in his address to Congress on April 16, four days after he had assumed the Presidency. Earlier that morning, Truman had received word from Stalin in the Soviet Union that he would agree to having a joint statement released to announce the fall of Germany. Buoyed by the rather promising news from Europe, Truman met with British Foreign Secretary Anthony Eden before departing for Congress to make his speech.

When Truman arrived on Capitol Hill, he was greeted by old colleagues and friends from his time in the Senate, an institution he had left only three months earlier. He waited in Speaker Sam Rayburn's office, and spoke with Congressional leaders before leaving for the chamber to speak to the nation at one o'clock in the afternoon. When Truman entered the House of Representatives, he was greeted with thunderous applause. Members of the Supreme Court had even ensured that they were present for Truman's speech.

In beginning his first official address to Congress and the American people as their Commander in Chief, President Truman declared unequivocally that he intended to carry out the actions of his administration in the way that Roosevelt would have wanted him to, and pledged to carry the former President's ideals forward. Truman came out decisively and aggressively in the defense of world freedom, committing to defend the cause of freedom with all of his strength and ability.

Today, the entire world is looking to America for enlightened leadership to peace and progress. Such a leadership requires vision, courage and tolerance. It can be provided only by a united nation deeply devoted to the highest ideals.

With great humility I call upon all Americans to help me keep our nation united in defense of those ideals which have been so eloquently proclaimed by Franklin Roosevelt.

Like Roosevelt, Truman demanded an unconditional surrender as the only means of ending the Second World War, and spoke of the necessity of the United Nations as a means of keeping the peace following the current conflict. America, he said, must not repeat the same mistakes made after the First World War, in which the country returned to an isolationist mindset with the hope of remaining safe within its own borders. That dream had been shattered at Pearl Harbor, and Truman was determined to ensure that isolationism would never again become official United States foreign policy. Moreover, he distinguished involvement from interference, proclaiming that any good state seeks to serve others and not to dominate them, something he would emphasize throughout his term in office.

After receiving nearly unanimous praise for his address to Congress, Truman found that he had the support, albeit temporary support, of both parties in the Congress. They sought to help him with his transition into the White House, and even his Republican friends in the Senate genuinely wished him well, each speaking of the kind and warm colleague that had served among them until only months before.

Truman made some important steps during his first few days in office. He appointed Charlie Ross, a boyhood friend, reporter, and Pulitzer Prize recipient, as his new press secretary. He insisted on showing up for work by eight in the morning, rather than waiting until after 10am to arrive as Roosevelt had. Furthermore, unlike Roosevelt, Truman refused to utilize J. Edgar Hoover's FBI to obtain information for political purposes. The two men would come to severely dislike each other, with Truman insisting that he would only contact the FBI through his Attorney General's office. He even compared the FBI and its actions under Hoover to those of secret police. Truman had no use for blackmail or scandalous information, much to the chagrin of Hoover. Truman also received a delegation from the Senate Republican caucus on April 18, nearly all of whom had not set foot in the White House since the Hoover administration, as Roosevelt refused to invite them to visit his residence. After meeting with dozens of other guests and dignitaries in the White House over the following several days, Truman finally began to feel as though he was getting a grasp on the duties and responsibilities that accompanied the Presidency.

Truman also had extensive consultations with W. Averell Harriman, the United States Ambassador to the Soviet Union, who landed in Washington on April 20. It was Harriman who was presented with the task of familiarizing the President with the situation in Russia. Harriman noted that Stalin had two major objectives: cooperate with the United States and Great Britain, and gain more influence and control in Eastern Europe. As Harriman readily pointed out, these two policy goals clashed with each other. As concerns about the Soviet Union began to deepen in Washington, Truman pledged to take a fair but firm approach in bilateral relations. Many, including Harriman, worried that America's temporary ally, the Soviet Union, could prove to be a greater totalitarian adversary than even the Nazis and imperialist Japan. Even Roosevelt had come to realize that Stalin could not be trusted.

Harriman's arguments would foreshadow the Truman administration's approach to the beginning of the Cold War. As Harriman insisted, the Soviet Union could not be trusted. Their objective was to dominate Eastern Europe through a "barbarian invasion" and ignore the traditional parameters of international relations, as Stalin was already doing in Poland by establishing a government that would take its orders from Moscow, despite the fact that the Soviets claimed, and had promised, otherwise. Should this trend in Poland continue, Truman was certain that the Senate would never agree to ratify a treaty creating the United Nations. Nonetheless, Harriman was also convinced that the Soviet Union could be negotiated with.

President Truman first got a good look at the nation's finances after meeting with Treasury Secretary Henry Morgenthau on April 20. Morgenthau reported that the government's expenditures for the fiscal year 1944-5 were more than double its revenues. In sum, expenses came to $99 billion, but $88 billion of that was devoted to wartime expenses. Revenues were only an estimated $46 billion, although Morgenthau wanted to undertake an extensive campaign to fight tax evasion. Beyond domestic expenses, Allied nations from around the world were pleading with the American Treasury for help. China wanted more gold to reduce inflation, the British would need help after the war, France wanted funds to help finance reconstruction, and India was requesting help as well. The Treasury Department would clearly have very demanding days in the months to come. Positive news, however, came on April 21, when the President was informed that German resistance was collapsing throughout Europe, and Allied forces were rapidly approaching the heart of Nazi territory.

On April 22, nine days after Truman assumed office, Soviet Foreign Minister Vyacheslav Molotov made an official visit to Washington on his way to San Francisco to participate in the negotiations for the formation of the United Nations. The fact that Molotov himself came was very important: Stalin had long intended to send a junior official to the United Nations meeting to play down the organization's relative importance. Nonetheless, Ambassador Harriman had been able to convince Stalin to send Molotov as an expression of goodwill following the death of President Roosevelt.

The main point of contention was Poland. The Soviets were insisting on installing a Moscow friendly government in the Eastern European country regardless of previous commitments to free and fair elections. Moreover, the Soviet Union's approach to the situation in Poland was quickly becoming part of a much larger trend. The Russians appeared to be moving into several Eastern European nations, most notably Romania. Their previous commitments at the Yalta Conference in favor of free elections appeared to not be worth the paper it was written on. Truman and his advisors agreed that Washington would have to play hardball with the Soviet Union. One concern, however, was to ensure that the alliance between America and Russia remained intact in order for the latter to participate in the war against Japan.

Truman was blunt with Molotov. He suggested that the United States would not recognize any government in Poland that had not been elected in a fair contest. Molotov was instructed to tell Stalin that the United States expected the Soviet government to fully live up to their previous commitments. The United States was honoring its commitments made by President Roosevelt during his conference with Winston Churchill and Joseph Stalin in Yalta, and Truman expected Russia to do the same. Truman's determination and frustration with respect to the Soviet government would only deepen in the months and years ahead.

On April 23, the day after Molotov's arrival, Truman met with his close advisors in the Oval Office to discuss the implications of the previous day's conversations. The foreign ministers of Great Britain, Russia and the United States had met earlier that morning, and the Secretary of State reported that the Russians appeared to be fully intent on violating the agreement made at Yalta to hold free and fair elections in Poland. As President Truman told his advisors, only the United States and Great Britain seemed to be abiding by the agreements made by the three leaders. Despite their profound contribution to the war effort in Europe, the Soviets could not be trusted as a genuine ally.

Truman met with Molotov again later that afternoon. He emphasized to the Soviet Foreign Minister that the United States could not allow for a government to be installed in Poland that did not represent the interests of all of the nation's citizens. Truman furthermore declared that the United States would go forward in supporting the creation of the United Nations regardless of the state of American – Russian relations. President Truman gave Molotov a letter to relay to Stalin, one that outlined the possibility of a fundamental discord among the three Allied nations.

> The Soviet Government must realize that the failure to go forward at this time with the implementation of the [Yalta] decision on Poland would seriously shake confidence in the unity of the three governments and their determination to continue collaboration in the future as they have in the past.

President Truman was fully briefed on the Manhattan Project for the first time on April 25. The briefing was delivered by Henry Stimson, Roosevelt's Secretary of War, a veteran Republican politician, and distinguished public servant. Stimson had also served in the same position three decades earlier under President William Howard Taft, and was also Herbert Hoover's Secretary of State. In a meeting in the Oval Office attended only by the Secretary of War, General Leslie Groves, who was in charge of the Manhattan Project, and the President himself, Stimson revealed to Truman that the United States would have a nuclear bomb in its possession in about four months' time, and that the weapon would be the most deadly device created throughout the history of mankind. He also warned that Russia was likely working hard to build up similar capabilities. America's decision to pursue the construction of such a weapon had been made in the fear that Nazi Germany might gain nuclear capabilities, although they never did come close to fully assembling such a device. A nuclear weapon would furthermore provide the United States with a means of attaining an earlier conclusion of the war, saving thousands of American lives in the process.

After meeting with Stinson and Groves, Truman departed for the Pentagon to contact British Prime Minister Winston Churchill. The two discussed a secret overture made by the Nazis, who were looking to pursue some kind of negotiations. Heinrich Himmler had suggested that, while Germany was willing to deal with the Western alliance, he would not entertain the idea of surrendering to the Soviets. A German surrender would also mean the freedom of Italy, Norway, Denmark, Yugoslavia, and Holland, five occupied nations that were all situated west of Germany. Both Truman and Churchill felt that the Nazis would have to surrender to all three nations at once, and they agreed to alert Joseph Stalin of the communication and their decision.

As American and British forces in the west, and Soviet forces in the east, raced towards Germany, disagreements about occupational zones quickly emerged. The three powers had initially agreed to occupational zones that were outlined in London in January of that year. But as the armies marched towards Berlin, precise borders could not be upheld and occupation plans would have to be adjusted to meet the reality of the situation on the ground. The British government, along with the Truman administration, proposed that the previously agreed to borders be upheld as soon as the military situation would permit the armies to do so. Communication between the three major powers should also continue on a regular basis. Three weeks before his death, President Roosevelt had issued a directive regarding the treatment of an occupied Germany. He decided that General Eisenhower would operate as a military governor in the American-occupied territory, but a civilian should also be appointed High Commissioner for Germany in the coming months. Truman's advisors were also concerned by the possibility of mass starvation and homelessness. Great Britain and other Allied nations were suffering from massive food shortages as well. The President ordered that action be taken to aid America's wartime allies in their food supply crisis.

More tension between the Allied leaders on Poland emerged by late April. On April 29, Prime Minister Churchill sent a cable to Stalin expressing immense disappointment about the Soviet leader's failure to live up to the Yalta agreements. It had been agreed to that Poland should become whole and free, and its government should not be under the control of a foreign power. But Stalin, angry that Truman and Churchill wanted to dictate Soviet policy on Poland despite the fact that Poland was Russia's neighbor, was still in no mood to talk. In his telegram to his Russian counterpart, Churchill foreshadowed the dark possibility of a world divided into two blocs.

> There is not much comfort in looking into a future where you and the countries you dominate, plus the Communist parties in many other states, are all drawn up on one side, and those who rally to the English-speaking nations and their associate dominions are on the other.
>
> It is quite obvious that their quarrel would tear the world to pieces and that all of us leading men on either side who had anything to do with that would be shamed before history. Even embarking on a long period of suspicions, of abuse and counter-abuse and of opposing policies, would be a disaster hampering the great developments of world prosperity which are attainable only by our trinity.

Developments in Europe continued rapidly. Italy's fascist dictator, Benito Mussolini, was killed by rebels on April 28. The Nazi contingent in Italy officially surrendered to Allied forces on April 29. Because there were no Soviet troops in Italy, Nazi leaders were far less reluctant to surrender to Allied forces than they were elsewhere, fearing the Communist barbarism that would inevitably accompany Russian troops. Ultimately, their concerns about surrendering to Soviet forces elsewhere were largely proven to be correct. Truman used the statement he released upon the surrender of Axis forces in Italy to warn Germany and Japan that nothing other than an unconditional surrender could save them from utter destruction.

Hitler committed suicide on April 30, and Berlin fell under the control of the allies on May 2. Nonetheless, it was not until May 7, a week after Adolf Hitler had killed himself, when Germany officially and unconditionally surrendered to the Allied forces, although Truman had allowed Stalin to delay the official announcement until the following day. The Western Allies had received messages days earlier suggesting that Nazi forces would surrender to them, and not the Russians, but Truman and Churchill worried about the tension that would emerge should the Nazis not surrender to all three allies simultaneously, which finally happened on May 7. On May 8, 1945, President Truman, Prime Minister Churchill, and Comrade Stalin all announced the unconditional surrender agreed to by the German army. The new American President described the moment as "a solemn but glorious hour." After less than a month as President, Harry Truman had presided over the conclusion of the war on the European front. The final and official German authority surrender agreement was signed by the Allied commanders on June 5, surrendering control over the country to the four great powers.

Despite the end of the war in Europe, America's overall war effort was still very much alive. While the Germans and their Nazi allies in Europe had laid down their arms, Japan was still committed to continuing its war against the United States and its allies. While President Truman quickly called on Japan to surrender along with the other Axis forces, the Japanese leadership pointedly refused to entertain the idea. Truman targeted the Japanese leadership while holding an official press conference to confirm that the Nazis had surrendered, and issued a similar statement later that day in his official televised address to the nation.

> The longer the war lasts, the greater will be the suffering and hardships which the people of Japan will undergo - all in vain. Our blows will not cease until the Japanese military and naval forces lay down their arms in unconditional surrender.

With the war in Europe officially over, many in the United States immediately turned their attention to Japan. But Truman was still concerned with the European situation, as was his colleague from Great Britain. Churchill had urged Truman even before Germany's surrender to maintain a strong presence in Eastern Europe, apprehensive of the possibility that a pullback made by the United States might allow for the Soviet Union to swallow up parts of the eastern portion of the continent. Truman also indicated to Churchill that he was intent on forcing the Soviet Union to adhere to the borders agreed to at the 1944 Quebec Conference and finalized at Yalta. Nonetheless, Churchill remained very concerned with the European situation, suspecting that Stalin would do everything he could to expand Soviet territory into Europe, which is why the Prime Minister had continued to urge both Roosevelt and Truman to have the Western Allied forces push as far east as possible before the war came to an end.

While he had sought to keep Roosevelt's Cabinet largely intact, Truman made several changes early on in his tenure. Senator Lewis Schwellenbach was appointed to replace Frances Perkins as Secretary of Labor, while Tom Clark of Texas was chosen to replace Francis Biddle as Attorney General. New Secretaries were also appointed to the positions of Postmaster General and Agriculture. The new Postmaster General was Robert Hannegan, the Chairman of the Democratic National Committee, while Clinton Anderson was installed in the Agriculture Department. Truman had already decided to install Jimmy Byrnes as Secretary of State, and he was confirmed by the Senate in early July. In revamping his Cabinet, Truman had chosen to appoint loyal Democrats, many of whom had served in Congress. This was just another step in Truman's effort to restore relations between the executive and legislative branches.

Another personnel move Truman made soon after the end of the war in Europe would prove to be an even bigger break from Roosevelt's style than the Cabinet revamp. Herbert Hoover, the only former President who was still alive, was asked to come visit Truman at the White House. Hoover had been despised by Roosevelt, who constantly sought to degrade his reputation. But Truman believed that Hoover could prove to be very useful in managing the famine that was spreading across Europe given his experiences following the First World War. Hoover, happy to be of any assistance to the President and those suffering in Europe, readily accepted Truman's request that he help manage the food relief that would be needed desperately by America's allies in the coming months.

While Truman continued to settle into the White House, America was closer than ever to completing the construction of the world's first nuclear weapon. The committee placed in charge of overseeing the development of the device was headed by Henry Stimson, the Secretary of War. Truman also appointed his soon to be Secretary of State, Jimmy Byrnes, as his personal representative to the civilian body. The committee agreed on three major principles in late May. First, it was decided that a nuclear weapon should be used against Japan as soon as possible in the hope of quickly concluding the war and avoiding a costly ground invasion. Second, the eight men involved in the discussions concluded that the nuclear weapon should be used without any warning. Finally, it should be dropped on an area where it could inflict the most psychological damage on the Japanese people, and that included possibly thousands of civilian casualties. While none of the men on the committee could be sure how much damage a nuclear weapon could inflict, all were certain that it would be catastrophic.

As the war against Japan continued, the United States air force continued to bomb Japanese targets at an incredible rate. With the Japanese convinced of the need to fight to the very end, many believed that the use of a nuclear weapon was a necessity. But Secretary Stimson, among others, worried that because of the widespread bombings that had already occurred across the country, the United States would find it challenging to locate an area of Japan in which to use the nuclear weapon to demonstrate its full power. Moreover, such a target was essential because Truman and Stimson were convinced that the Japanese Emperor and his followers would only surrender quickly after being presented with such a high level of devastation.

Despite Churchill's warnings, the Truman administration decided to pull American forces back from the Soviet occupation zones to ensure that the United States adhered to the agreement made at Yalta. Truman officially informed Churchill of America's withdrawal from the Russian zones on June 21, and the process was to begin immediately. But signs were already emerging that suggested that the Soviets had no intention on meeting the commitments they had made at the very same meeting. With a decision not yet made on the future of Poland and the fate of Eastern Europe, the three Allied leaders decided to meet in Potsdam, Germany on July 15. Truman was anxious to try to maintain the unity that had existed between the so called Three Powers throughout the war.

Although fighting in Europe had ended, the Second World War was by no means over. Nonetheless, many in Congress sought to cut off financial aid to Allied nations who were still in desperate need of assistance. With concern mounting in Europe, Truman released a clarifying statement to ease concerns among America's allies, promising that there would not yet be an end to wartime monetary support. As he said in an open letter to the

Speaker of the House of Representatives, "the war against Japan, like the war against Germany, is a cooperative Allied effort...[therefore] we shall continue to pool our resources with those of our allies."

In the interim, preparations continued for a ground invasion of Japan. It had not yet been decided whether the United States would simply drop a nuclear bomb Japan or launch a full scale ground invasion. But Truman's advisors warned that a ground invasion from Okinawa would be incredibly costly. General MacArthur's advisors put their casualty estimate for the first thirty days at fifty thousand, an incredible sum that would be more than the number of lives lost during the invasion of Normandy in France the year before. When the Pentagon included other areas that might be invaded at the same time as Okinawa into their estimates, the total number of expected casualties topped two hundred and fifty thousand. Secretary Stimson feared that the Japanese would continue to fight until the bitter end, which would likely mean that up to one million American troops could lose their lives until the Japanese were finally defeated. The invasion plans suggested that the operation would begin in November of 1945 and carry on well into 1946. They were approved by Truman before he left for San Francisco to make a speech on June 26. Nonetheless, America's invasion plans could quickly change depending on whether or not the Soviet Union made a commitment to declare war on Japan.

Questions remained on the future of China as well. The Chinese were participating in the war on the side of the Allies, having been invaded and molested by Japanese armed forces. Truman spent a lot of time working with his advisors and Stalin to reach a consensus on the future of their Chinese allies. Ultimately, Truman, Stalin, and Churchill all agreed that China's anti-Japanese forces, led by General Chiang Kai-shek, should be placed in charge of a new government and given the tools necessary to unify the country after a Japanese withdrawal. Despite their commitment to support Chiang, it would be the Soviets who were largely responsible for undermining Chiang's Nationalist government in the years to come through their support of Mao Zedong's Communists. The agreement among the leaders also stipulated that the United States, Great Britain, the Soviet Union, and China would gain a trusteeship over Korea, another area that would later cause friction between the Soviets and their current Western allies.

Truman had insisted on flying to California to be present for the official signing of the United Nations Charter on June 26, 1945. It was his hope that the United Nations would succeed where the League of Nations had failed, and that meant active participation on behalf of the American government. The new President made a passionate address to the convention upon his arrival.

> It was the hope of such a Charter that helped sustain the courage of stricken peoples throughout the darkest days of the war. For it is a declaration of great faith by the nations of the earth – faith that war is not inevitable, faith that peace can be maintained.
>
> By their own example the strong nations of the world should lead the way to international justice. That principle of justice is the foundation stone of this Charter. That principle is the guiding spirit by which it must be carried out – not by words alone but by continued concrete acts of good will.
>
> I shall send this Charter to the United States Senate at once. I am sure that the overwhelming sentiment of the people of my country and of their representatives in the Senate is in favor of immediate ratification.

After returning to Washington, Truman called on the Senate to approve the United Nations Charter in an address delivered on July 2. It was the same institution that had blockaded President

Wilson's attempt to have the United States join the League of Nations more than two and a half decades earlier, but this time Truman had insisted on bringing Republicans as delegates to partake in the foundation of the new international organization. The President specifically brought along Senators Arthur Vandenberg of Michigan and Tom Connally of Texas, the ranking Republican and Democratic members of the Senate Foreign Relations Committee, to ensure that the Senate's most influential members would be prepared to support the United Nations initiative. Truman returned to the Senate to make a plea to his former colleagues to not make the same mistake that their predecessors had made decades earlier.

> This Charter points down the only road to enduring peace. There is no other. Let us not hesitate to join hands with the peace-loving peoples of the earth and start down that road, with God's help, and with firm resolve that we can and will reach our goal.

During the United Nations founding conference in San Francisco, a dialogue between the United States, Great Britain, the Soviet Union, and France had begun on the treatment of war criminals. Truman's White House Council, Samuel Rosenman, who had also served under Roosevelt, drafted the American proposal for the treatment of Axis war criminals, while Justice Robert Jackson of the Supreme Court was chosen to represent the United States during official discussions between the four nations. Those who had been identified as war criminals would be sent back to the nation in which they were accused of committing those crimes, and punished accordingly by that country's judicial system. The most prominent members of the leadership of the Axis nations would be tried by a military tribunal with representatives from the United States, Great Britain, the Soviet Union, and France as its officers. Evidence would be provided and criminals would be allowed to testify in their own defense. Those war criminals who could not be fully identified with solid proof would instead be tried by their membership to specific organizations, such as the Gestapo or other secret police units.

After returning to Washington from the United Nations conference in San Francisco, Secretary Stettinius left for Berlin in advance of Truman's departure for the Potsdam Conference. It was Stettinius who was most adamant about the need to rebuild the German economy to ensure the peace and stability of Europe, an idea that Truman would champion throughout the latter years of his presidency. Treasury Secretary Hans Morgenthau, who was resolute about accompanying Truman on his trip to Europe, submitted his resignation to the President over his being left out of the three power conference. Truman decided to appoint Fred Vinson, a veteran member of Congress and long-time government official under President Roosevelt, as Morgenthau's replacement. Although he was reluctant to leave the country after having assumed office only three months prior, Truman understood the grave importance of the conference he was about to attend. At issue would be not only the future of Europe, but also the future of the world order itself. Never before had Truman been faced with such a difficult test of his resolve and he was determined, if also hesitant, to rise to the occasion.

Days before Truman's departure for Europe, an agreement about the future of Poland was struck on July 5, when the United States and Great Britain jointly announced that they would officially recognize the new Polish government, which represented a mix of Communist supporters and those more favorable to democratic powers. The Soviets had previously announced that those who were labeled as democratic leaders would be arrested and tried, but a compromise was worked out in order for the government to be composed of national unity supporters. Truman had instructed the State Department to recognize the independence of Poland following the addition of several moderates to the Soviet friendly government, which essentially fulfilled the treaty that the Roosevelt, Churchill and Stalin had struck at Yalta.

Chapter Two

Winning the War

When Harry Truman arrived in Europe, he saw the full extent of the devastation that now plagued Germany. Roads, cities, and factories were in ruins. Thousands were without homes and meals. Disease and death was rampant. As he made his way to the Potsdam Conference, Truman was accompanied with a large delegation of representatives from his administration. This included his Secretary of State and the American Ambassador to the Soviet Union. Doctors, cooks and a chauffeur were brought along as well.

All three leaders would stay in Babelsberg, a small town outside of Potsdam. The town was surrounded by Soviet, American and British soldiers to guard Stalin, Truman, and Churchill. Truman's goal was to settle some of the issues that had remained unsettled in the aftermath of the Yalta Conference and to get acquainted with his counterparts. The leaders were to talk about the situation in Eastern Europe and Russia's contribution to the war against Japan. It was the latter issue that Truman was the most eager to deal with. He had rigorously prepared for these meeting for weeks, spending dozens of hours studying with his close foreign policy advisors. Truman was determined to ensure the continued influence of the United States in world affairs, especially in the face of replacing such a prominent leader in Franklin Roosevelt.

Truman first met Winston Churchill on July 16. As a veteran politician and stalwart leader of the British Empire throughout the Second World War, Churchill, like Roosevelt, was very familiar with Joseph Stalin, and with dealing dozens of foreign leaders on a personal basis. All of this was new for Truman. Possibly because he had a wealth of experience in dealing with international political issues, Churchill had not prepared for the meetings nearly as extensively as Truman had, nor was his delegation as large. When the two leaders met for the first time, Churchill was only accompanied by his Foreign Secretary, Anthony Eden, and his permanent Under Secretary, Alexander Cadogan.

Although Churchill was an experienced world leader, he was still faced with a nearly bankrupt Empire and personal fatigue. Even more important was the British general election, which had been held on July 5, although the results would not be known for a few weeks, after the votes from members of the military were counted. Although few expected it at the time, Churchill would lose the Prime Minister's office only ten days after he first met Truman. Thus, it would turn out, Truman was not the only world leader who arrived handicapped at the conference.

At their first meeting, Truman and Churchill spoke for more than two hours, and Churchill emerged from the meeting confident in the ability of the new American President. Truman, however, was not as impressed with his British counterpart. Although he believed that Churchill was a fine leader whose intelligence was quite evident, Truman felt that the British Prime Minister had attempted to flatter him too much. This impression of Churchill, however, would not last throughout the entirety of their partnership.

Joseph Stalin, it would turn out, was a day late for the Potsdam Conference due to a mild heart attack. Thus, Truman elected to tour the city of Berlin on the afternoon of July 16. Truman met with American soldiers who were still camped out in Berlin in the American sector. As he continued his tour, Truman saw the full extent of the damage done to Berlin itself. One of the most preeminent cities in the world lay in ruins, with millions of people left without homes and loved ones. Fifty thousand civilians had been killed by Allied bombings, and thousands more had been raped and assaulted by Soviet forces once they had driven out the Nazis. As Truman would later write in his diary, he "never saw such destruction" before his tour of Berlin.

July 16 was an even more important date in American history because of events that were happening in New Mexico. That morning, scientists working on the Manhattan Project exploded their first nuclear bomb, marking the first time in human history that a nuclear weapon was successfully constructed. Truman and the man in charge of the project, Secretary of War Henry Stimson, learned of the news that evening, although it would take days for the full details of the explosion to be relayed to Potsdam.

Truman first met Joseph Stalin the following day when the Soviet leader, accompanied by Foreign Minister Molotov, came to his quarters. Truman hoped to treat Stalin as a friend, but the dictator would soon become an adversary. Good news, however, preceded any quarrels. Stalin told Truman that he was committed to following through on the promise he made to President Roosevelt at Yalta, that being to have the Soviet Union declare war on Japan. Stalin pledged to do so sometime in August. Truman, who was quite pleased, was also informed that the Russians intended to attack Manchuria, which they saw as occupied Chinese territory, meaning that the Soviets intended to take a very active role in the war in the Pacific. At the outset, Truman felt that his relations with his Soviet counterpart could be cordial and productive.

Truman was not the only one drawn in by Stalin's charm. Churchill, Jimmy Byrnes, and even Dwight Eisenhower had been impressed. One factor allowing for the positive impression many powerful world figures had after first meeting Joseph Stalin was that little was known of the atrocities he was committing domestically. Only months and years later would Western leaders realize the full extent of Stalin's brutality, especially on his own citizens. The deliberate starvations, Katyn Forest Massacre, sheer brutality of his secret police, and millions put into labor camps were temporarily hidden, veiled behind Stalin's personal charm and his military alliance with the Western powers. As the war came to a close, more attention would be paid to Stalin's actions at home.

At the first official meeting to kick start the Potsdam Conference on July 17, all three leaders brought with them a number of aides and members of their Cabinets. Churchill brought Clement Attlee with him, his Labor Party opponent in the election and his eventual successor, as well as Anthony Eden. Truman brought Secretary Byrnes and former United States Ambassador to the Soviet Union Joseph Davies. Stalin brought Molotov and his future Foreign Minister, Andrey Vyshinsky. Both Churchill and Stalin suggested that Truman chair the conference. Although little was accomplished at that first meeting, the leaders agreed to delegate most of the controversial discussions to their Foreign Ministers. At the end of the meeting Stalin suggested that that the three countries should divide the German fleet, which was quickly agreed to by Churchill, but Truman refused to make a final decision. Despite Truman's anxiety, the leaders were able to work together and become acquainted on the first day of the conference, and reached some decisions, albeit minor ones. Many items, such as Truman's suggestion of creating a Council of Foreign Ministers representing the major powers, were delegated to the foreign ministers to deal with. Beyond that, Stalin had confirmed his intention to declare war on Japan.

Truman informed Churchill the following morning of America's success in testing a nuclear bomb. After having lunch with Churchill, Truman then proceeded to visit Stalin at his quarters, who also invited Truman to join him in eating lunch. When the three leaders resumed their meeting that afternoon, tensions rose as Stalin sought to make the results of the war more permanent. The first controversy was over the German question. Churchill and Truman sought to define German territory as what it held in the prewar era, whereas Stalin was convinced that they should recognize Germany as it was presently constituted, therefore allowing for more territory to be annexed by the Soviets. Despite a lively debate, nothing on the subject was resolved during the first full day of meetings.

As the Conference reconvened the following morning, President Truman told the other leaders that he was not willing to commit to the immediate division of the Germany navy. Truman announced that he was in favor of dividing it three ways, as Churchill and Stalin had suggested, but only after the defeat of Japan. Moreover, after debate among the foreign ministers, Truman suggested that because his counterparts had reservations about allowing China to immediately become a member of the Council of Foreign Ministers, only the United States, Great Britain, Russia, and France should be included, with the possibility of China joining the group at a later date. Both Churchill and Stalin agreed.

The next topic on the agenda for the second day of the conference was, once again, Germany. It was agreed that any discussion of Germany would begin with the understanding that the country's pre-1937 borders were to be considered to encompass the nation of Germany, meaning that any territorial gains made by Hitler's Nazis would not factor into the equation. Any further decisions would be put off until a later date, and the leaders then began to discuss the future of Poland. Stalin proposed that all funds and military assets that were in the hands of Poland's government-in-exile in London be transferred to the provisional Warsaw government, which happened to have been established under the influence of the Soviet Union, although he failed to admit that reality. The Soviets clearly wanted to get the property and tools of the more than one hundred and fifty thousand men in the Polish army representing the government-in-exile, despite the fact that its troops had been supplied by British and American forces. Churchill immediately launched into his own monologue, reminding his colleagues that Great Britain had accepted a heavy burden through providing a home for Poland's government during the war, and all of the financial resources of the government were frozen as the property of the prewar state of Poland. Churchill had furthermore promised Polish soldiers that had fought alongside the allies an offer of British citizenship, something that he could not undo. The three leaders again decided to leave the issue in the hands of their foreign ministers.

The third day of meetings began with a presentation made by Anthony Eden on the progress the foreign ministers had made on establishing points of agreement. He provided the leaders with a final version of Truman's initial German proposal, which was agreed to by everyone. Prime Minister Churchill then raised the issue of Spain, whose fascist regime was one of the last surviving governments formed in the tradition of Hitler's Germany and Mussolini's Italy. Great Britain, Churchill proclaimed, was disgusted by the brutality of the Franco regime, but rejected the idea of breaking off relations with a regime that had done nothing to harm any of the Allied nations. Moreover, doing so would set a dangerous diplomatic precedent that could harm future generations. He was more than happy to call attention to Franco's domestic atrocities, but relations should not be broken off altogether. Truman sided with Churchill, wary about the possibility of setting off another civil war in a nation that had been through so much internal strife in the previous decade and a half. Stalin claimed that the Franco fascist regime had been imposed on the Spanish people by Mussolini and Hitler, and wanted Churchill and Truman to commit to reprimanding the regime, if not ending relations entirely. Churchill and Stalin had reached an impasse and the issue was therefore put off again until a later date.

Truman again returned to Berlin on July 20, this time to speak to the crowd in the American sector as the nation's official flag was raised, the same flag that had flown in Washington on the day of the bombing of Pearl Harbor. The flag was a symbol, Truman declared, of an American victory over a determined adversary, an event that he hoped could prove to be the beginning of a pursuit of a more peaceful world order. The war, he said, was a means of fighting for peace, something the Americans were still pursuing aggressively in Japan. Unlike the Russians, the United States did not expect to gain any territory from winning the war, but rather to ensure peace and prosperity in Europe and across the world, something he hoped could prevent such a devastating conflict in the future.

> We are here today to raise the flag of victory over the capital of our greatest adversary. In doing this, we must remember that in raising this flag we are raising it in the name of the people of the United States who are looking forward to a better world, a peaceful world, a world in which all the people will have an opportunity to enjoy the good things in life and not just a few at the top. Let's not forget that we are fighting for peace and for the welfare of mankind.

General Eisenhower was asked to accompany Truman on his visit to Berlin, and the President startled the Allied commander by offering to support him should he make a bid for the Presidency in 1948. Truman adamantly believed, until 1952, that Eisenhower was a Democrat. His eventual disappointment in Eisenhower's choice of party would later sour their relationship. On that trip, however, Eisenhower ruled out challenging Truman for the Presidency in 1948, pledging that he wanted to ensure that the President sought re-election.

The following morning brought news of the full extent of the success of the nuclear bomb that had been exploded in New Mexico days earlier. Its sheer power and force was much greater than most scientists had dared to anticipate. The explosion had been seen almost two hundred miles away from the test site and heard for up to one hundred miles. Truman was extremely pleased with the news, as both he and Secretary Byrnes believed that their possession of a nuclear device would strengthen their hand in negotiating with the Russians immensely. They were also quite relieved that the $2 billion that the government had poured into the Manhattan Project had been well spent. Moreover, because of the successful testing of the nuclear bomb, America was now in possession of a weapon that had the capability of forcing the surrender of Japan without American troops having to invade the country. Churchill, who learned of the full extent of the bomb's success the following day, was equally enthused.

When the leaders returned to the negotiating table, they quickly became divided on issues such as the puppet Soviet governments in Romania, Bulgaria, and Finland, and the question of Germany's borders. Truman was dismayed that Russia had unilaterally changed the borders between Germany and Poland without any consultation with the other Great Powers. Truman wanted to use Poland's 1937 borders, as had been done with Germany, but Stalin insisted that all of the Germans near the old border had fled west, meaning the territory should therefore go to Poland, which was then occupied by the Soviet Union. Stalin also argued that the disputed region had advantageous areas that had once helped to power the German economy, and it should therefore be given to the Poles to prevent the Germans from ever regaining significant power in the region. Churchill argued that such a decision would give away arable land that the Germans needed to avoid mass starvation and Truman wholeheartedly agreed. Despite the animated conversation, the major issues were again left unresolved, although Stalin conceded that the Soviets might be persuaded to allow the press to observe the next Polish election.

On July 22, while still at Potsdam, Truman was confronted with further decisions that had to be made about using nuclear weapons on Japan. Secretary Stimson sought to have the President choose the military's targets and his first suggestion was Hiroshima, which Truman agreed to. The following day, Truman decided on drafting a warning declaration, otherwise known as the Potsdam Declaration, calling on Japan once again to agree to an unconditional surrender, which was issued by the Allied leaders on July 26. The President and his advisors made a final decision that a nuclear bomb would be used on Japan the day after they had written the declaration, which was July 27, but the details were still not yet decided. Truman was convinced that the bomb would have to be used to spare America from incurring hundreds of thousands of casualties through a ground invasion. Churchill and all of Truman's advisors pushed for the use of the bomb, including the majority of America's scientists who had worked on the device.

Truman officially informed Stalin of the existence of the nuclear weapon on July 24, although he was rather vague about exactly what the weapon was, and of his intent on using it to attack Japan. That same day, debates among the leaders flared when Stalin insisted on asking the Americans and British to recognize the legitimacy of the Russian puppet governments in Eastern Europe. But Truman was adamant that the United States could not recognize the legitimacy of the governments in Romania, Bulgaria, and Hungary because representatives had not yet been allowed to enter the countries and observe the situation. America would recognize those governments only after winning access to the countries, and Truman insisted on them being democratic, something Stalin objected to despite the fact that it had been agreed to at Yalta. Only a democratic government would be allowed to join the United Nations, although Stalin argued that other members, such as Argentina, were just as undemocratic as some of the Soviet Allied governments in Eastern Europe. Churchill wanted an agreement to admit Italy into the organization, but no settlement was forthcoming.

As the President's discussions with his advisors about using a nuclear weapon continued, Truman decided that a nuclear bomb would be deployed against Japan at the beginning of August, but that it should also be dropped on an area in which there were at least some military targets, and not just civilians. In the meantime, Truman, Churchill, and Stalin once again returned to the negotiating table, revisiting the issues of Italy and Eastern Europe on July 25. Truman and Churchill both spoke in favor of admitting Italy to the United Nations, as well as other former Nazi allies in the Baltics. They also once again insisted that Romania, Bulgaria and Hungary, which were all under Russian control, could not be admitted to the United Nations until they had established democratic governments, which had been agreed to at Yalta. Stalin countered this position by noting that Italy had not yet chosen a democratic government either, so Truman's point about only admitting Soviet occupied nations to the United Nations after they had elected a democratic government was moot. Secretary Byrnes, however, clarified the American and British position, reminding Stalin that Italy had open borders, whereas the Soviet occupied nations would not allow Western Allies into their country.

One major problem that spanned the entire conference was that Truman and Stalin disagreed about what a democratic government was. Truman insisted that a democratic government was one that was chosen by the people in free and fair elections. Stalin simply claimed that any government that was not fascist was democratic. Thus, he insisted that the Soviet Union and its satellite nations were all governed by democratic governments. This difference of opinion would not be resolved between the two world powers until the Cold War ended more than forty years later.

Truman then turned to his proposal for the internationalization of waterways across the world, which would grant all nations access to every major waterway. Churchill appeared to agree with the President's proposal, but Stalin was not willing to commit to such an arrangement.

Winston Churchill left the Conference on the evening of July 25 to return to London to learn of the results of the British general election that had been held earlier that month. Churchill expected to win handily, and promised the other two leaders that he would return to the Conference in a few days. After the other world leaders learned of Churchill's stunning defeat, Stalin again put the Conference on hold, reluctant to have to deal with a new counterpart in Clement Attlee. With the departure of Roosevelt and Churchill from leadership roles in the three Great Power wartime alliance, only Stalin was left as the lone holdover from a generation that was quickly being replaced in political circles. Once Attlee arrived back at the conference on July 28 to replace Churchill in the meetings between the Allied leaders, Truman was far from impressed by Churchill's successor. Ernest Bevin had also been appointed to succeed Anthony Eden as the British Foreign Secretary.

Truman decided to release the Potsdam Declaration on July 26, just hours after a nuclear bomb had been delivered to American forces in the Pacific for its eventual usage. Moreover, it was of great importance that Truman, Atlee, and Chiang Kai-shek, the Chairman of China's government, all signed onto the statement, suggesting that the Japanese were doomed to failure with the world's Great Powers, along with the Chinese, united in pursuit of Japan's unconditional surrender to Allied forces. In the aftermath of a Japanese surrender, the Great Powers announced that they would call on Japan to allow for the freedom of speech, reinstate a policy of religious tolerance, and elect a peaceful government, after which invading forces would withdraw from the country. Papers were dropped by American planes across Japan detailing the declaration to the population at large, as the Japanese military forces controlling the government were unlikely to inform the nation's citizens of the ultimatum posed by Allied forces. Ultimately, Japan's Prime Minister decided to ignore the threat posed by the allies. The statement was nonetheless a powerful one.

> The time has come for Japan to decide whether she will continue to be controlled by those self-willed militaristic advisors whose unintelligent calculations have brought the Empire of Japan to the threshold of annihilation, or whether she will follow the path of reason.

President Truman learned of the vote that had taken place in the United States Senate on the ratification of the United Nations treaty on July 28. The support for the United Nations charter was overwhelming, with eighty nine Senators voting in favor of joining the organization, and only two opposed. This was a major victory for President Truman, for he had managed to do something that had eluded President Wilson's grasp decades earlier. Truman was thrilled that the organization he and President Roosevelt had long championed was finally becoming a reality. In a brief statement released to the press, Truman proclaimed that "it is deeply gratifying that the Senate has ratified the United Nations Charter by a virtually unanimous vote. The action of the Senate substantially advances the cause of world peace."

Truman's final approval of the use of a nuclear weapon against Japan, and the weapon's specific target, was issued on July 31.

The Potsdam Conference was expected to end on August 2, but, as the meetings were winding down in the last few days of July, Truman was left with few successes. Beyond securing Stalin's promise to declare war on Japan, he had failed to resolve the German and Polish questions, and had still not received a new commitment from the Soviets to hold free and fair elections in Eastern Europe. Despite the lack of progress, there was a general consensus that Truman had performed admirably in his dealings with the other two Allied leaders, although relations between the United States and Russia appeared as though they would soon deteriorate. As Stalin had told Truman early on, it would be much harder for the two nations to remain as allies in peacetime. Nonetheless, the leaders did manage to agree that the German state should be fully demilitarized, and that, in the interim, it would continue to be occupied by Allied forces.

Truman and Stalin agreed to hold the Nuremburg war crime trials in Germany itself, and designated some reparations for the Soviet Union because of the sacrifices the country had made in fighting the Nazis during the war, or at least the conflict's latter four years. The Russians would maintain their ominous presence in Eastern Europe, as the reality of the situation on the ground meant that the Western powers had little choice but to accept the current situation. The three leaders did manage to agree on the share of German reparations that the Soviets would receive, and on the final border of Poland's western frontier.

Truman had come to dislike Stalin by the end of the conference. He saw the Soviet Union as a police state, and even told his mother that he believed Stalin to be barbaric. And yet he could not escape Stalin's charm, and predicted that he was the type of man who would keep his word. As Truman would later find out, this type of thinking was incredibly naive on his part, although countless others had been fooled by Stalin's friendly demeanor. Only after he had left office would Truman remark about the many mistakes he made at the conference, first among them his inherent trust of the Soviet dictator to keep his word.

Truman left Potsdam for Washington on August 2. On his way back home, he dined with King George VI en route to the Augusta near Plymouth. The Augusta was to take Truman back home across the Atlantic Ocean. Once at sea, Truman informed the press of the existence of a nuclear weapon. One of his biggest worries was that other nations would soon acquire nuclear capabilities, although most thought that the Soviet Union would take possibly more than a decade to produce one for themselves. Ultimately, they would explode their first nuclear bomb in 1949, well into the beginning of the Cold War.

Hiroshima was bombed on August 6, 1945, although the date was still August 5 in Washington. After the first use of a nuclear weapon in the history of mankind, Truman was informed of the development while having lunch with some colleagues and members of the crew. Secretary Stimson informed Truman and Secretary of State Byrnes that the nuclear weapon had been even more successful than those in the military had hoped. Truman was euphoric, hoping that this would be the shock the Japanese would need to finally agree to an unconditional surrender, saving the lives of hundreds of thousands of American men who would certainly become casualties as a result of ground forces invading Japan itself. Truman and his advisors were still not fully aware of the extent of the physical damage done to their adversaries, but they released a statement threatening to bombard the Japanese with even more nuclear weapons should their government not capitulate. Most believed, however, that the Japanese would quickly reassess their policies in the face of such a horrible military threat. Statistics would ultimately show that more than eighty thousand residents of Hiroshima were killed upon the bomb's impact, with tens of thousands more severely affected by the by-products of radiation.

Not everyone was ecstatic. Many feared that the use of a nuclear weapon would bring the world into a new age of more dangerous warfare. The idea that major cities could be destroyed instantly by one bomb was frightening to say the least.

In a speech broadcast from the cruise ship over the radio to the American people on the same day that the nuclear bomb was dropped on Hiroshima, Truman attempted to justify his use of such a dangerous weapon. He told Americans listening across the country that the bomb had been used "to shorten the agony of war, in order to save the lives of thousands and thousands of young Americans." The United States, Truman proclaimed, would continue to drop nuclear bombs on Japan until they surrendered unconditionally.

Truman returned to the White House on August 8. He had been gone for nearly a month, and was glad to be back home in the United States. When a second nuclear bomb was used against Japan in the city of Nagasaki, Truman was in the White House to follow the proceedings much more closely. The death toll in Nagasaki would prove to be nearly as high as the losses suffered in Hiroshima. Truman, privately grieving over the deaths of thousands of civilians, recognized that his actions were necessary to force the extremist Japanese government and military to finally surrender. He eventually called on Japanese civilians to try to leave sites of major industry to help protect themselves. The Japanese government had been issued a grave warning on August 5, but they had refused to capitulate. The release of a second nuclear bomb in the heart of Japan would prove to be of greater psychological effect.

On the same day that Truman returned to Washington, August 8, word came from the Russians that they were prepared to declare war on Japan the following day. The message had come through Ambassador Averell Harriman, who had spoken with the Soviet Foreign Minister, Vyacheslav Molotov, who came to inform the American Ambassador of Stalin's decision. Truman chose to notify the American people of the Soviet government's commitment at a press conference from the White House.

News came of a settlement overture made by the Japanese leadership on August 10. It had been sent through the neutral states of Switzerland and Sweden. The point of contention appeared to be the role Emperor Hirohito would play following the war. The Japanese sought to keep the Emperor in place, and this appeared to be the only thing standing in the way of a full Japanese surrender. While Truman, Churchill, and Stalin had all agreed that an unconditional surrender was their prime objective,

Truman began to ponder whether or not to allow the Emperor to stay in place. As hundreds of thousands of Russian soldiers were invading Manchuria, Secretary Stimson supported the idea of making peace with Hirohito left in place, while others, including Secretary Byrnes, were unwilling to yield on that point of contention. Many Americans still saw Emperor Hirohito as a central part of the militaristic Japanese government that they had committed to destroy. Ultimately, however, it would be up to the President to decide on a course of action.

Truman decided that the Emperor could be allowed to remain in place, but that his role in the country would be tightly controlled by the United States. He would effectively become the head of state in name only. Truman's initiative won the support of the British, Australians, Chinese, and the Soviets. It appeared as though the United States would not be forced into employing the use of another nuclear bomb, and Truman hoped that a quick surrender would mean fewer Soviet troops making incursions into the region, as their track record of wreaking havoc in Europe, and their expansionist policies throughout the world, were by then well known. General Douglas MacArthur was chosen to serve as the Supreme Allied Commander for the Allied Powers in Asia, and was charged with taking control of the situation in Japan. In China, however, fears were already focusing on what the impending withdrawal of Japanese troops would mean for the hope of installing and stabilizing a new government. The international position was that Chiang Kai-shek's forces should take control of the country, but Communist rebels threatened to plunge the country into a civil war. The Soviet Union already appeared to be prepared to back the Communist forces in China rather than pursue a moderate and stable government, which the allies had formerly agreed to.

The Japanese issued an unconditional surrender to the Allied forces on August 14, and Truman quickly briefed the press of the news that the war was finally over. He then issued a televised statement to the American people to confirm that the war had officially ended. Truman and his wife Bess then left the White House to wave to supporters on the front lawn, celebrating the victory with their fellow citizens. Harry Truman, the everyday American who had come from a farm in rural Missouri to the White House, had won the war. Speaking to supporters, Truman hailed the moment as a great day for freedom across the globe and the time in which "fascism and police government ceases in the world."

By the time the war officially ended on August 14, Truman had been in office for a mere three months and two days. In that time, he had met with two of the most powerful men in the world to discuss the fate of Europe, presided over the creation of the United Nations, oversaw the successful completion of the Manhattan Project, and issued the order to drop nuclear bombs on two Japanese cities, the first and so far only time in history that such a weapon was used. Harry Truman was the man who made what might have been the hardest decision in human history, agreeing to allow such a profound level of devastation to occur through the use of just one military weapon. And yet Truman would be the first to say that he was simply an ordinary American who had been placed in an extraordinary circumstance. But he rose to the occasion, and oversaw the ascension of the United States into the role of the most powerful nation in the world.

Conflict with the Soviets, however, would continue. Truman and Stalin bickered about the future of the Kurile Islands, then a part of Japan, before the war had even officially ended. Truman agreed to the Soviets taking control of the territory, but asked in return to be allowed to keep an American landing area on one of the islands for wartime and commercial purposes. Stalin eventually agreed to let the United States maintain a temporary base in the region, but these kinds of disputes were set to become the norm in the months and years ahead. Debates about Manchuria and the right of Russian troops to undercut General MacArthur's orders would continue to annoy the President throughout the reconstruction of Japan. The two sides did, however, quickly agree to divide the occupation of Korea along the 38th parallel, a border that would prove to be of great importance during Truman's second term in office.

The final and official Japanese surrender agreement was signed on the U.S.S. Missouri on September 2, 1945. Besides the four major Allied powers in the battle for the Pacific, those being the Americans, British, Chinese, and Soviets, other partners, including Canada, Australia, France, New Zealand, and the Netherlands were also signatories. Truman, like millions of other Americans and people from around the world, listened to the official ceremony over the radio. After the end of the ceremony, President Truman made an address to the American people from his office in the White House. At that moment, Harry Truman truly became the leader of the free world.

My fellow Americans, the thoughts and hopes of all Americans – indeed of all the civilized world – are centered tonight on the battleship Missouri. There on that small piece of American soil anchored in Tokyo Harbor the Japanese have just officially laid down their arms. They have signed terms of unconditional surrender.

God grant that in our pride of the hour we may not forget the hard tasks that are still before us; that we may approach these with the same courage, zeal and patience with which we faced the trails and problems of the past four years.

This is a victory of more than arms alone. This is a victory of liberty over tyranny.

It was the spirit of liberty which gave us our armed strength and which made our men invincible in battle. We now know that that spirit of liberty, the freedom of the individual, and the personal dignity of man are the strongest and toughest and most enduring forces in the world.

Chapter Three

A Year of Discontent

As the Second World War came to a close, Truman was able to turn his focus to domestic policy for the first time in his Presidency. Truman was in many ways a New Deal Democrat. He wanted a higher minimum wage, unemployment compensation, crop insurance, and a whole host of other liberal legislative initiatives. But Truman soon found out that politicians on Capitol Hill were much more cooperative and conducive in wartime, and that his first true opposition in the Congress was soon to arrive. Truman's agenda appeared to be even more ambitious than Roosevelt's, and he was quickly alienating many conservative Democrats.

Truman was also determined to avoid the chaos that had occurred in the aftermath of the First World War. Twelve million American soldiers were returning from the war in 1945, and most of them would need to find jobs. America's economy had flourished during the war, but many worried that its success could not be sustained with the end of wartime production. Because of all of the soldiers at war, unemployment had declined to a low of two percent at the end of the war, but twelve million new workers would surely allow the unemployment rate to skyrocket. Many, including members of Truman's own Cabinet, were convinced that Americans would be forced to return to the same problems that plagued the country before the war began in 1939.

Many of the worriers were right: workers went on strike across the country demanding higher wages, and many soldiers returned home to find a housing deficit. Congress was hesitant to act, but, although economics had never been Truman's strong suit, he was determined to do something to demonstrate his solidarity with the American people.

Many changes in government personnel were made in the months following the end of the war, foremost among them the retirement of Henry Stimson as Secretary of War. Stimson was by then nearly eighty and more than ready to retire after decades of public service. Truman awarded him with a Distinguished Service Medal. A similar honor was given to General George Marshall, who had been the army's Chief of Staff throughout the war. He too was retiring, although Truman would later ask him to return to public service as a liaison to China, Secretary of State, and later as the Secretary of Defense.

Disorganization and confusion began to plague the White House as Truman's inexperience finally began to show. He had dozens of priorities and was trying to get everything done at once, constantly frustrated by the Congress's refusal to act. More problems erupted on the labor front. After declaring his support for moderate wage increases, Truman was convinced by members of Congress to toughen his stance on unions, but his stern actions only delayed pending strikes for a month, frustrating everyone involved.

After the American Ambassador to China unexpectedly resigned because of what he argued was support in the State Department for the Chinese Communist rebels, Truman asked George Marshall to end his six day retirement and depart for China immediately.

The Council of Foreign Ministers, which had been set up at the Potsdam Conference to include the United States, Great Britain, and the Soviet Union, met for the first time in September of 1945. The three nations had originally decided that France and China could be part of the conference, but that they could only vote on matters that directly concerned their interests. The Soviet Union's Foreign Minister, Molotov, was now threatening to go back on his word and boycott the gathering if France and China were not excluded from all discussions that did not concern their own national interest altogether, rather than allowing them to participate but not vote. Secretary Byrnes called Truman from London eleven days after the conference had begun, and was forced to plead with the President to contact Joseph Stalin directly to prevent the Soviets from walking out of the meeting altogether. After Stalin refused to budge on Molotov's position, the conference was brought to an abrupt end on October 2, leaving most observers with the impression that the meeting had been an overall failure. Further problems with the council emerged when, despite an agreement among the major powers that all foreign troops would be withdrawn from Iran by early 1946, Russia was actually sending more troops into the country rather than pulling them out. Stalin's Soviets appeared to be very reluctant to ever keep their word.

Truman's honeymoon with the press and politicians came to an abrupt end only weeks after the war was over. Many suggested that Truman was unqualified for the Presidency, and had fallen into the position by accident. Truman felt that his Secretary of State, Jimmy Byrnes, was not keeping him sufficiently informed on international affairs. Truman's suspicion was that Byrnes secretly believed that his own intelligence far outweighed that of the President. At the end of a Foreign Ministers conference in Moscow in the fall of 1945, Byrnes had released his own policy statement without consulting his boss. He was furthermore planning to do radio interviews to brief the nation on the conference before even reporting back to the President. By the time Byrnes met Truman just before New Year's Day in 1946, the

President was furious with his Secretary of State, convinced that Byrnes could not be trusted to keep him in the loop. He also felt that Byrnes was being too soft on the Soviets.

President Truman sent a detailed message to the Congress on September 6, 1945, outlining the domestic goals that the he would pursue throughout his time in the White House. It included twenty one major proposals to help bring the nation forward and assist American workers, and would later become known as Truman's "Fair Deal," a play off of President Roosevelt's so called New Deal. Truman himself claimed that the speech delivered to Congress on September 6 marked the first time he really felt that the Presidential mandate had become his.

The President's twenty one point proposal was focused on eight main points of policy that Truman wanted to pursue: demobilize some of the armed forces, turn wartime production plants into peacetime production facilities, cancel war contracts, keep prices and rent charges at low and stable levels, remove wartime government controls, prevent a decrease in wage incomes, and uphold the consumer's purchasing power. More generally, the President wanted to pursue policies that would help to guarantee full employment and equal opportunity, although the unemployment rate remained quite low throughout Truman's years in the White House. Within weeks of the publication of Truman's proposal, members of the administration had the President add four more points to his agenda: new legislation for health insurance and medical care, the nationalization of atomic energy, forward movement on developing the St. Lawrence Seaway with Canada, and more federal spending allocated to education. The President would also battle the menace of inflation for the next several years, and was forced to do so without strong support from the Congress, which continued to pass legislation that failed to address the major problems that led to inflated prices in the first place.

President Truman was forced to deal with the fiscal problems that were plaguing the United Kingdom by the fall of 1945. Truman felt that temporary measures would not fix the underlying problem. Thus, to figure out a more long term solution to the British debt problem, officials from the American and British governments met in Washington on September 11, 1945, to enter negotiations. The British delegation was led by John Maynard Keynes, a brilliant economist and the father of Keynesian economics, creating the idea of business cycles and spearheading the formation of macroeconomic studies. The two delegations found themselves in intense negotiations for more than three months. Truman's representatives ultimately agreed to lend the British government $3.75 billion with an annual interest rate of two percent, although a five year grace period was included in the final package. The British in return promised to support the American government in the pursuit of a multilateral trade program to be negotiated in the near future. Truman immediately called on the Congress to approve the loan, claiming that it would help to cement the accomplishments of the Bretton Woods agreement of 1944. Congress ultimately passed the legislation and the President signed it into law the following July.

The beginning of 1946 was no kinder to the President than the previous autumn had been. Steel workers were threating to strike, which would essentially grind the nation's economy to a halt. The steel workers' union wanted a larger raise than the companies were willing to give them. After meeting with Truman at the White House, the unions, led by Phil Murray, agreed to delay their national strike for a week to allow for further negotiations. Truman suggested that the two sides compromise and allow for a wage increase much closer to the figure desired by the unions, but the companies refused. On January 19, the largest strike in American history began, and more than 800,000 steel workers refused to go to work.

More strikes began to pop up across the country. Workers at General Electric, other electric companies, and even meatpackers walked off the job. Truman would later reflect that dealing with strikes was perhaps the most difficult job he had to undertake as President. Housing was also a major problem: more than one million families were forced to share a home with another family because of a massive housing shortage. America's construction industry had spent several years putting all of their efforts into wartime production, meaning that little effort had been made since 1941 to expand housing availability. Hundreds of thousands of soldiers were coming home from Europe as married men and were hoping to start a family. All of them would need to have adequate homes. In the fall of 1945 President Truman had directed the Federal Public Housing Authority to sell more than three hundred thousand government owned homes that had been stationed around wartime production plants. But those homes were far from enough. In fact, Truman believed that construction industry would have to erect at least five million new homes in the immediate future. The construction industry certainly had their work cut out for them, especially after the President convinced members of Congress to allocate funds for the creation of nearly three million homes within two years.

Truman decided on a candidate to replace General Marshall as the army's Chief of Staff following his retirement, nominating General Dwight D. Eisenhower to the post in early 1946. Eisenhower had previously served with distinction as a Supreme Allied Commander in Europe during the war. Secretary Stimson was replaced by Robert Patterson in the war department. Harold Ickes, the Secretary of the Interior, quit in February. Truman had questioned Ickes's judgement because of his damning testimony on Truman's appointment of Ed Pauley, a Democratic fundraiser, to serve as the Under Secretary of the Navy. Truman was then forced to withdraw Pauley's nomination. Ickes accused Truman in a hastily called press conference of asking him to commit perjury by lying under oath and not reporting his knowledge of some of Pauley's shady dealings. Truman vehemently denied those allegations, but they proved to be very harmful to the President's reputation nonetheless. Ickes was hailed by the media and the public as a noble man who had served his country with distinction, while Truman was accused of returning to the corrupt days of Warren G. Harding's administration. Like President Harding, Truman's tendency was to appoint party loyalists and personal friends to government posts, although he did not do so to the same extent. Ickes was eventually replaced by Julius Krug as Secretary of the Interior. Krug was well known and respected in Washington for his role as former chairman of the War Production Board.

All was not lost in early 1946, however. Herbert Hoover, who Truman had sent to Europe to lead America's efforts to help reduce the food crisis that was occurring across the continent, as he had done so capably after the First World War, was doing a tremendous job. The food crisis in Europe, particularly in nations that had been devastated by Nazi occupation, was nonetheless threatening to endanger the fragile postwar order that had been cobbled together at Potsdam.

Despite all of the calamities that the administration had been experiencing over several months, Truman did make progress on a number of fronts, especially through urging Americans and the country's international allies to work together to increase food production and prevent mass starvation. Moreover, Congress also finally passed an Employment Act, although it was not nearly as far reaching as Truman had hoped.

President Truman delivered his first State of the Union address on January 14, 1946. During his speech, Truman laid the groundwork for his future atomic energy policies and signaled his intent of turning more of his attention to problems at home, while remarking on the accomplishments made in 1945. He spent much of the address talking about budget issues, but did take some time to reflect on just how important the last year had been as a moment in history.

> All those hopes, and more, were fulfilled in the year 1945. It was the greatest year of achievement in human history. It saw the end of the Nazi-Fascist terror in Europe, and also the end of the malignant power of Japan. And it saw the substantial beginning of world organization for peace.

> These momentous events became realities because of the steadfast purpose of the United Nations and of the forces that fought for freedom under their flags. The plain fact is that civilization was saved in 1945 by the United Nations.

Although the President's attention was largely focused on domestic issues, rapid developments around the world forced Truman to return his focus to foreign affairs. A speech made by Joseph Stalin on February 9, 1946, laid the groundwork for the Cold War between the Soviet Union and the United States that was soon to follow. In one of the most important speeches made during the twentieth century, Stalin declared that because capitalism and Communism were not compatible, a war between the West and the East was a forgone conclusion. He even suggested that the war could come as soon as the 1950s.

Concerns about Stalin's speech were amplified by a speech made by former British Prime Minister Winston Churchill, who came to Truman's home state of Missouri to speak about his views on the dangers of the Soviet Union. Truman himself had invited Churchill to come to Missouri and make a speech at Westminster College, and even discussed the content of the speech with the former Prime Minister at the White House in advance.

Churchill's speech was delivered on March 5, and he himself believed that it was one of the most important speeches he would ever deliver, conscious that only the United States could match any aggression made by the Communists. Churchill noted that Stalin still appeared to be ignoring his commitments made to both Roosevelt and Truman. His army was still in China, Iran, and Germany, all three areas in which the Soviets had pledged to pull back. Churchill, who had always been more hawkish about the threat posed by the Soviets than Roosevelt or Truman, felt that it was his responsibility to warn the American people of the dangerous times that lied ahead.

It was a unique circumstance in which the President of the United States introduced another speaker to an audience, but the move seemed only fitting for such a giant figure in world history. Truman himself understood Churchill's powerful legacy as much as any other. Had Great Britain fallen to the Nazis, they likely would have been able to gain control of all of Europe. But Churchill had rallied the British people to the cause of freedom, and the free world owed him their gratitude.

Churchill began the speech by speaking about the bravery and sacrifice of the Russian people during the war, and the prominent place the country deserved to have on the world stage. Nonetheless, Churchill warned, Stalin's actions necessitated a firm Western response. In one of the most famous lines in any speech delivered in the twentieth century, Churchill declared that an "iron curtain had descended across the continent" of Europe. The great cities and nations in Central and Eastern Europe were being subjugated to Soviet influence, and were often forced under the control of the Soviet politburo. The Soviets were pursuing an aggressive expansionist agenda, seeking to pull Eastern European nations into the Russian yolk. For Churchill, the response to Stalin's actions had to be a united opposition to the Soviet agenda among democracies in the free world, and that unity was particularly dependent on a close relationship between two of the three Great Powers: Great Britain and the United States.

While Truman appeared to approve of Churchill's speech, which for the most part he had seen beforehand, newspapers across America were outraged, suggesting that Churchill's words were only making an already difficult relationship with the Soviets worse. But with the hindsight of history, Churchill was proved once again to be right. Nonetheless, Stalin saw the speech as some kind of indication that the West intended to go to war with the Soviet Union.

Truman was put under enormous pressure immediately. With such vehement opposition to Churchill's speech across the country, Truman claimed that he had not known the content of the speech in advance. But, for many Americans, it appeared as though the President was determined not to have a good relationship with Stalin's Russia. Many in Truman's administration approved of the speech, including Under Secretary of State Dean Acheson, who would later serve as President Truman's fourth Secretary of State. Secretary Byrnes's reaction, however, was not nearly as positive, and he insisted that Truman distance himself from Churchill's comments.

Dean Acheson and some of Truman's other colleagues in the White House were not the only ones to welcome Churchill's speech. George Kennan, who worked in the American Embassy in Moscow and would later become famous for his telegram to Washington about American – Russian relations, warned Truman that any hope of a collaborative relationship with the Soviets was unrealistic. Stalin, he claimed, felt that there could not be a long term positive relationship between his nation and the United States because of his disdain for capitalism. The Soviet Union's long term goal was to destroy the American way of life, a system that was incompatible with Bolshevik Communism. Moreover, the Soviet regime's insecurity was largely responsible for their imperialist policies in Eastern Europe and elsewhere abroad. Kennan's message, which was first delivered to the State Department in February of 1946, would later become the basis of the policy of containment that the Truman administration would adopt in the government's approach to American-Soviet relations.

More trouble was brewing with the Russians by March of 1946, this time in Iran. The Soviet and British governments had reached an understanding with the government in Iran that their troops could be stationed in the country for no more than six months after the end of the war, which meant March 2, 1946. Despite the agreement, Soviet troops began pouring into Iran, rather than out of the country, in the weeks leading up to the beginning of December of 1945, and the Soviet government declared that a revolutionary government had been established in parts of Iran, essentially suggesting that the country be split into two separate entities with two governments. The Iranians were outraged, and took the issue of Russia's political interference in their domestic affairs to the United Nations Security Council. The organization, however, suggested that the two countries engage in bilateral talks. The Iranians charged that the Soviets had essentially created their own puppet rebel regime to help further their Communist crusade. Moreover, despite the agreement made by the Soviets with the British and Iranian governments, Russian troops remained in Iran past the March 2 withdrawal deadline, and representatives in Moscow announced that the Soviets would have a troop presence in the country indefinitely.

As the situation in Iran became more serious, Truman instructed Secretary Byrnes to inform the Soviet government that his administration viewed the situation as dangerous and a gross violation of international relations protocol. The Soviet government failed to even reply to the letter sent to the Foreign Ministry by Secretary Byrnes, instead deflecting pressure by attacking Winston Churchill for his so called Iron Curtain speech. After another strongly worded warning was issued by President Truman himself, Stalin announced that all Soviet troops would in fact be withdrawn from Iran, preventing a situation that could have easily turned into a regional crisis by endangering Turkey's independence.

When Truman marked the end of his first year in the White House, coal miners were on strike across the country, and editorials in various newspapers were critical of his performance as America's thirty third President. Without coal, businesses across the country were forced to close their doors or put production on hold. United Automobile Workers had gone on strike against General Motors, which ultimately lasted for nearly four months. Inflation was rampant, and everyone seemed to be calling for a significant raise in pay. The President had spent months trying to get labor and management to agree to a new bargaining approach, but his efforts were to no avail. On Wednesday, May 22, Truman ordered the government to seize control of the coal mines.

Even more damaging than the coal miner strike was conflict within the railway industry. Railroad workers were threatening to strike, and, although eighteen of the twenty major unions had agreed to management's new proposal, the two biggest unions were holding out. After delaying the strike on multiple occasions, the Truman administration failed to convince the union bosses to accept a deal. Passenger and freight trains stopped operating, and production across the country was forced into a full halt. It was a strike of enormous consequence, and a significant burden to economic growth. Many blamed Truman for not being effective and assertive enough to force the other two unions to accept a compromise.

The consequences of the railway strike were not just felt in the United States. Grain shortages could lead to the starvation of millions across Europe who relied on American assistance, largely through grain. Produce was left to rot.

Truman called a Cabinet meeting for May 24, the morning after the railway strike had begun. As those who attended the meeting would later reveal, Truman was livid, something rarely seen from a President who was well known for his calm and positive demeanor. Truman announced his plans to address the nation and Congress, and to draft railway workers into the army to force them to return to work. Members of the Cabinet were stunned. Truman had a new assistant, Clark Clifford, draft a copy of his speech.

Truman said to viewers on television, and those listening on the radio, that he was addressing them in a time of danger and consequence. The President was concise and spoke his own mind: the leaders of some of the unions, he claimed, were putting their interests ahead of those of the nation. It was only two men representing two unions, Alexander Whitney and Alvanley Johnson, who were holding the entire nation hostage. Moreover, Truman announced his intention of using the army if the railway workers did not return to work the following day. One way or another, Truman insisted that the strike would be brought to an end.

Truman's speech to Congress was set for four in the afternoon on May 25, 1946. As he made his way to the Capitol, news came to Truman that negotiations were becoming more fruitful. The President entered the House chamber to a standing ovation, and declared that Congress and the administration had to work together to ensure that these kind of paralyzing strikes were brought to an end. He called on Congress to pass drastic measures to save the nation from a major crisis. Even after only two days of strikes, the nation's economy had taken a big hit. He asked Congress to pass legislation to allow him to draft railroad workers into the army on an emergency basis, and members of the House of Representatives and the Senate rose to applaud the President's bold initiative.

> The disaster will spare no one. It will bear equally upon businessmen, workers, farmers and upon every citizen of the United States. Food, raw materials, fuel, shipping, housing, the public health, the public safety—all will be dangerously affected. Hundreds of thousands of liberated people of Europe and Asia will die who could be saved if the railroads were not now tied up.
>
> As I stated last night, unless the railroads are manned

by returning strikers I shall immediately undertake to run them by the Army of the United States.

As he was nearing the end of his speech, a Senate aid ran into the House chamber and came up to the podium to speak with the President. Truman immediately told the Congress that the strike had been settled on the terms he had insisted on from the beginning. Truman finally appeared decisive and courageous, something that had been missing for many months. The public and members of the legislative branch overwhelmingly supported the President's initiative, and the House passed a bill to allow striking workers to be drafted into the army just hours after Truman's speech.

Not everyone was pleased. Truman's hardline attitude towards the striking workers alienated many liberals who were closely affiliated with the unions. Many conservatives felt that Truman had proposed something that was blatantly unconstitutional. Nonetheless, Truman was supported overwhelmingly by those who did not see themselves as extremists on either side of the political spectrum, and Truman had no concerns that his actions might hurt his chances of re-election. Moreover, with Truman's new bellicose attitude, he chose to target the coal industry as well. After allowing the bitumen coal miners to go on strike for forty five days, the President decided to have the federal government run the facilities on a temporary basis. Another coal strike flared up in the fall for seventeen days, this time when workers chose to walk out on the government, costing the American economy millions of tons of coal.

President Truman announced his nomination of Fred Vinson to serve as the Supreme Court's next Chief Justice after the death of Harlan Stone in June of 1946. Vinson, a former member of the House of Representatives who was serving as the President's Secretary of the Treasury at the time, had been a close Truman ally since they served together on Capitol Hill. Both were Democrats from mid-Western states: Truman from Missouri, and Vinson from Kentucky. But Vinson's nomination was met with a firestorm of protest. Most saw him as too political, having been a prominent member of the Democratic Party for decades. Many Americans took the nomination as just another sign of Truman's tendency to reward loyal Democrats with cushy government jobs. Despite widespread opposition, Vinson was confirmed by the Democrat dominated Senate, and was sworn in as America's thirteenth Chief Justice on June 24.

President Truman was questioned by the press about a speech the Secretary of Commerce was set to deliver in New York in September of 1946: an early draft had already been seen by reporters. When Truman claimed that he endorsed the speech, members of the press were flabbergasted. Truman, of course, had never read the speech, although he claimed that he had. In the speech, Secretary Henry Wallace, the former Vice President, began by claiming that America wanted world peace, and that its government had no special friendship with any nation, which was what Truman and Secretary Byrnes had been trying to communicate to the public. But Wallace also condemned what he saw as British imperialism, and appeared to suggest that the American government should accept the idea of a Russian sphere of influence. America, he claimed, also had no role in dictating a policy for Eastern Europe. To make matters even worse, Wallace added a few lines to his speech during its delivery, claiming that imperialism was more of a danger to America than Communism, which seemed to suggest that Wallace, and thereby the Truman administration, had sympathies for Soviet style expansionist Communism.

Truman was furious at himself for having endorsed a speech he had never read. Although he had claimed that the administration's policies were no different than those furthered by Wallace in his speech, they could not have been further apart. Unlike Wallace, Truman saw Communism as the world's greatest danger, and did not believe that Russia should have a sphere of influence in Eastern Europe, instead advocating for a tough approach to American-Soviet relations. Truman's comments at that press conference turned into a disastrous scandal that the administration was forced to deal with.

Secretary Byrnes, who was at a conference of Foreign Ministers in Europe, was livid. He felt that Wallace, the Secretary of Commerce, was out of line in making comments on foreign affairs, and even more so because of his attack on the administration's actual foreign policy. A private letter that Wallace had sent to the President dated two months earlier also ended up in the press, and the Secretary of Commerce had been even more critical of Truman's foreign policy in private. For many in the public, it appeared as though the President couldn't win over the support of members of his own administration, another sign that he was way out of his depth in the White House. Truman asked Wallace to stop making speeches on foreign policy, but he refused to do so.

Possibly because of Wallace's decision to attack his foreign policy, in tandem with Truman's reluctance to fire his Secretary of Commerce, Byrnes requested that the President accept his resignation. Byrnes had been trying to resign for months, but each time the President had refused to consider it. Wallace, Byrnes claimed, had destroyed his credibility and that of the President on foreign affairs. Faced with Byrnes's threat to quit, Truman requested Wallace's resignation in late September. As the last New Deal holdover from the Roosevelt administration, Truman had been reluctant to break with the left wing of the Democratic Party. But Wallace's independence was becoming far too costly. He was later replaced by Ambassador Harriman, who returned from his short stint as the American Ambassador to Great Britain.

Despite the controversies, America's postwar economy had rebounded from some early struggles, unemployment was still very low, most of the strikes had subsided, and the paychecks of the majority of Americans were on the rise. But Truman could not shake the impression that he was bumbling around in the White House. The midterm elections were drawing near, and nearly everyone expected the Republicans to win control of Congress for the first time since their defeat in 1930. Because of his unpopularity, Democratic congressional leaders specifically asked the President to avoid making any campaign appearances.

Republicans were in the meantime accusing Truman of being soft on Communism, and the so called Red Scare became a reality across the country. But Truman was worried about the spread of Communism as well. Secret surveillance was approved, and the President was just as determined as Republicans to take on and beat any Communists that were in the United States.

The results of the 1946 midterm elections were devastating for Democrats. The Republicans received a net gain in the House of Representatives of fifty five seats, and Joseph Martin, rather than Sam Rayburn, was to be the next Speaker of the House. Martin, a Congressional veteran and close friend of President Calvin Coolidge, had served in the House for more than twenty years. The Republicans picked up eleven seats in the Senate, returning the party to majority status for the first time since the election of Franklin Roosevelt in 1933. Even in Truman's district in Kansas City, the Republican candidate defeated the Democratic candidate that Truman had wholeheartedly supported.

With a landslide victory for the Republicans in 1946, pundits and politicians across the country declared Truman to be a sitting duck. Observers believed that Truman had a very slim chance, if any, of being elected to a second term. Many even speculated that Truman wouldn't run for re-election at all because of his unpopularity. Nevertheless, Harry Truman had never been a quitter, and the Republican victory in the midterm elections only made him more determined than ever to fight for the Presidency in 1948.

Chapter Four

Truman Bounces Back

While many saw the midterm drubbing of congressional Democrats as a major setback for the Truman administration, the President himself appeared to be far more comfortable in the Oval Office now that the midterm elections had provided for a new mandate for America's elected leaders. Some attributed the election of a new Congress as having given Truman a clean slate, enabling him to finally see his administration as the Truman administration rather than a holdover from the Roosevelt era. Whatever the cause, Harry Truman finally took control over the agenda, and took ownership of the record created by the executive branch. Truman's Press Secretary, Charlie Ross, summed it up perfectly when he declared that "the real Truman administration began the day after the elections."

Despite Republican control in the Senate, Truman still found allies that he could work with. He old friend Arthur Vandenberg, a Republican from Michigan who had served since 1928, remained loyal to the President on issues dealing with foreign affairs. As Chairman of the Senate Foreign Relations Committee, one of the most powerful Senate committees, Vandenberg would side with the Truman administration on several important issues, including the Marshall Plan, the formation of the North Atlantic Treaty

Organization, and a broad policy of internationalism. Senator Robert Taft would also have a lot of influence over his Republican colleagues, although he spoke primarily on domestic affairs. The son of former President and Chief Justice William Howard Taft, Robert had served in the Senate for less than ten years, but still held considerable influence within the Republican caucus. Nonetheless, Truman found it much harder to find common ground with Taft than he did with Vandenberg. Taft was an ardent isolationist when it came to foreign affairs.

Truman found that Republicans in the House of Representatives were willing to partner with him as well. Republicans were tired of President Roosevelt's tendency to marginalize the congressional institution altogether. Thus, in Harry Truman they felt they finally had a President who believed in reasserting a more prominent role for the Congress in American politics. Joe Martin, the new Speaker of the House, publicized his intent on fully cooperating with the Truman administration. Martin had always abided by the policy of supporting whatever was in the best interest of his district, and what was in the best interest of his district he saw as in the best interest the nation. Never much of a partisan, Martin promised Truman that his number one priority would be to find common ground with the Democratic President.

On January 6, 1947, Harry Truman delivered his second State of the Union address. As he reported to Congress, unemployment was low and dropping, and household income was rising at a record rate. America was in an unprecedented position to succeed more than at any time in the nation's history.

> If in this year, and in the next, we can find the right course to take as each issue arises, and if, in spite of all difficulties, we have the courage and the resolution to take that course, then we shall achieve a state of well-being for our people without precedent in history.

In his lengthy address, President Truman specifically called on members of Congress to pass a form of government run health insurance, a theme that would become common in Truman's rhetoric. Nonetheless, despite his painstaking efforts, the President was unable to make any progress with the Congress on that issue. Reflecting on the damaging strikes that had occurred the year before, Truman also sought new legislation to improve the negotiating process between the unions and management to avoid further strife in the future. Price control legislation was part of the President's agenda as well, but the Republican Congress would make little progress on that front.

Truman's speech was well received, but his performance was soon overshadowed by an announcement the following day that Secretary of State Jimmy Byrnes would be replaced by George Marshall, the army's former Chief of Staff, who was popular and well respected by voters across the nation. Republicans even lauded Truman's choice for Secretary of State, speeding up the nomination process to have him confirmed on an expedited basis. Marshall would soon become well known as the savior of Europe because of the plan that would later become known as the Marshall Plan, which delivered aid to European nations to help them rebuild and avoid the tide of Communism.

Weeks earlier, and after less than two years on the job, the President had decided that he would have to fire his Secretary of State. Byrnes, who had been Truman's first appointment to the State Department, believed that he possessed a more sound judgement on foreign affairs than the President did, and made that clear to his boss. As Truman would later say in his memoirs, Byrnes "was beginning to think of himself as an Assistant President in full charge of foreign policy." Truman believed that some of Byrnes's foreign policies were too lenient on Moscow, and the Secretary of State continuously made decisions without even consulting the President. Truman had been anxious to have Byrnes quit for months, but delayed the departure until General

Marshall was able to return from an important diplomatic mission in China.

Truman's appointment of General Marshall marked the first time someone from the military was called on to serve in the Secretary of State portfolio, but many future Presidents followed his lead. Most recently, President George W. Bush appointed General Colin Powell to serve in the same position. Marshall brought a sense of calm and reassurance to the Truman administration. Those who thought of the President as inexperienced, and were worried about his ability to handle foreign affairs, felt that American policy was in safe hands with the presence of General Marshall.

Truman also tapped David Lilienthal to serve as the civilian head of the newly created United States Atomic Energy Agency. In deciding to create the agency, Truman was determined to have the institution under the control of citizens rather than the military, and sought to have the new institution cooperate with its counterparts in Canada and Great Britain. The President hoped that the new organization could ultimately pursue the potential of placing nuclear power under international control, although this line of thinking was incredibly controversial, especially because the Soviets were deemed very untrustworthy. Nuclear energy, Truman told the Congress in his energy proposal that created the agency, had the potential to unleash vast scientific discoveries, but was also accompanied by grave responsibilities. The President therefore proposed the creation of the Atomic Energy Agency to leave any work on nuclear power in the hands of the government. The Atomic Energy Agency would be responsible for all nuclear research, development, and the production of nuclear devices. Nonetheless, the President would still be responsible for the testing of any nuclear weapon, meaning that the Commander in Chief would have to give a direct approval for any new testing that might occur.

When President Truman invited British Prime Minister Clement Attlee and Canadian Prime Minister Mackenzie King to Washington in the fall of 1946, all three leaders were anxious to discuss the future of nuclear energy, and the extent to which nuclear secrets might be shared with other nations. They were also excited, however, about the possibility of unleashing the potential of nuclear energy for peaceful purposes, which was one of the reasons President Truman had turned to David Lilienthal, the former Chairman of the Tennessee Valley Authority, to chair the new Atomic Energy Agency, which was largely responsible for pursuing that objective. Lilienthal, along with four other Presidential appointees that had to be confirmed by the Senate, would make up the new agency's decision board. Truman summed up the meeting's importance during a speech given at a state dinner for the two leaders, alluding to the policies that had been agreed upon between Attlee, King, and himself. The basic principles that were established at that meeting would become the basis of the modern international nuclear energy policies.

> I am hoping that the United States of America can implement a foreign policy which will be the policy of the people of the United States and not the policy of any political party.
>
> The Prime Minister of Great Britain and the Prime Minister of Canada are here to discuss with the Secretary of State and the President of the United States a program that will be world-wide and continuous, and that will include every nation in the world without exception.

Lilienthal had previously chaired multiple government organizations during the war. He born to Jewish immigrant parents in Morton, Illinois, but, due to his heritage in Czechoslovakia, Senators at his confirmation hearings questioned his dedication to the country, and accused him of having a soft stance on Communism. Although Lilienthal defended himself admirably, Senator Robert Taft of Ohio, a member of great influence, chose to oppose his nomination, holding up the process for weeks. Many other Republican Senators felt that the Lilienthal nomination would be the last chance for conservatives to stop the control of America's nuclear program from falling into liberal hands permanently. Most believed that the program should be in the control of the army, who had more expertise in that area. The decisive turn in the Lilienthal debate occurred when Senator Vandenberg addressed the Senate chamber and defended Lilienthal against the Communist sympathy accusations made by his colleagues. He also recommended that the Senate endorse Truman's nomination, and Lilienthal was swiftly confirmed by a vote of fifty in favor and thirty one against. Truman's nominee had been confirmed by managing to win substantial Republican support, which was another major victory for the administration.

The Lilienthal nomination only further encouraged Republicans to raise the issue of Communism, and try to successfully paint the Democratic Party as soft on Communism. Truman was forced to agree to new measures recommended by the Attorney General, and the Federal Bureau of Investigation, to assess any sign of communist sympathies among important Americans. Truman therefore authorized the creation of the Federal Employees Loyalty and Security Program. For the President, this move was necessary to protect those who were not guilty of communist sympathies from unwarranted suspicion, and to root out any disloyal public servants. In reality, it was a solution to a political problem, neutralizing accusations from conservative Democrats, and almost all Republicans, that the administration had not been vigilant enough on facing the domestic threat of Communism.

One of the major issues that the Congress did act on in late 1946 and early 1947 was labor legislation. People across the country were still angered by the coal and railway unions that had given a beating to the American economy, and the Republicans introduced legislation that would effectively cripple the role of unions in the negotiation process. Truman supported reigning in the power of union bosses to a certain extent, but also saw labor organizations as an essential part of the business process. The Republican bill, championed by Representative Fred Hartley of New Jersey, would make industry wide strikes illegal, and also eliminate the National Labor Relations Board, sympathy strikes, and government worker strikes, as well as forcing unions to provide greater financial transparency. Hartley partnered with Senator Robert Taft to craft legislation that could be approved in both houses of Congress, and their Labor-Management Relations Act, otherwise known as the Taft-Hartley Act, was approved by Congress in June of 1947. President Truman felt that the bill went too far in curtailing the role of unions and provided too much power for those in management, and therefore vetoed the bill. Nonetheless, the bill had enough support in Congress for Truman's veto to be overridden, and the Taft-Hartley Act was signed into law by the end of the month.

After having served as Secretary of State for only a month, George Marshall was notified by the British government of an impending crisis. Great Britain's financial situation was in significant peril, and their government could therefore no longer afford to give financial aid to Greece and Turkey, two nations that were receiving help to try to stave off communist influence in the region, and therefore avoid a possible Communist takeover of those governments. In the specific case of Greece, the Attlee government in London informed General Marshall that the British government would have to stop all aid to the Mediterranean nation as of March 30, 1947. Worse still, the British were planning to pull their troops out of the country altogether, providing Communist forces with an easier path towards a revolution. As President Truman poignantly observed, "the alternative [to aid] was the loss of Greece and the extension of the iron curtain across the eastern

Mediterranean." Without American help, freedom and liberty would be put into retreat in the entire Mediterranean region.

General Marshall, President Truman, and Under Secretary of State Dean Acheson all agreed that the United States would have to step up to the plate financially, and help prevent chaos from taking hold and putting Allied governments in Greece and Turkey at risk of collapse. Greece, many predicted, would fall to the Soviets if their government did not receive substantial aid from the West. Moreover, Turkey was a nation that Russian leaders had long coveted to add to the Soviet bloc, which would have made the Russian sphere of influence far more extensive than it had already become. President Truman and those in his administration were determined to contain Bolshevik expansionism.

In meeting with congressional leaders, General Marshall predicted a Soviet expansion into Central Europe and the Middle East if something was not done about the situations in Greece and Turkey. When the House and Senate Republican leadership told Truman that he would have to come before the Congress and make his case to his fellow elected officials, Truman quickly agreed. Although Truman's endorsement of aid to Greece's democratic government was the right move, he worried that it could only lead to further American involvement in European politics, a spectre that outraged Republican isolationists. But there was little time to ponder the consequences: American had to act, and it had to do so quickly.

As the crisis in Europe and the Middle East mounted, Truman was also told by officials in his administration that the Soviet Union was trying to stall postwar peace negotiations to try to occupy even more territory in Europe. Moreover, as time went by, the feasibility of forcing the Soviets to withdraw from these areas declined, as the Russians increasingly gained a foothold in the region. White House Counsel Clark Clifford's analysis of American-Soviet relations that was given to the President during this period insisted that the United States had to adopt a policy of actively supporting any and all democratic nations in their fight to oppose Communism. Russian expansionism would have to be countered by American support for the opposing domestic forces. The Soviets were already in charge of much of Eastern Europe, and in 1947 the threat of a significant Soviet expansion was very much a reality. The United States would therefore have to maintain a strong and active military to help blunt Soviet tendencies of aggression. As President Truman himself declared, "victory had turned a difficult ally in war into an even more troublesome peacetime partner."

Harry Truman laid out what would later become known as the Truman Doctrine in a speech to a joint session of Congress on March 12, 1947. It would set the stage for America's foreign policy that endured throughout the Cold War. The United States, Truman declared, needed to help create conditions in which people could make their own political decisions without force or coercion. Wherever peace or international security was threatened in the world, Truman proclaimed that the United States would get itself involved in the situation. The time had passed when America could stand idly by while other states pursued policies of aggression. He requested funds to aid Greece to the tune of $250 million, and a further $150 million to help Turkey. Only the United States could help prevent Communist expansionism. Truman himself called his own doctrine "America's answer to the surge of expansion of Communist tyranny."

> I believe that it must be the policy of the United States to support free peoples who are resisting attempted subjugation by armed minorities or by outside pressures.
>
> One way of life is based upon the will of the majority, and is distinguished by free institutions, representative government, free elections, guarantees of individual liberty, freedom of speech and religion

and freedom from political oppression.

The second way of life is based upon the will of a minority forcibly imposed on the majority. It relies upon terror and oppression.

Should we fail to aid Greece and Turkey in this fateful hour, the effect will be far reaching to the West as well as the East.

We must take immediate and resolute action.

This is a serious course on which we embark. I would not recommend it except that the alternative is more serious.

The seeds of totalitarian regimes are nurtured by misery and want. They spread and grow in the evil soil of poverty and strife. They reach their full growth when the hope of a people for a better life has died.

We must keep that hope alive.

If we falter in our leadership we may endanger the peace of the world, and we shall surely endanger the welfare of this nation.

Truman found overwhelming support from newspapers and politicians across the country. The speech had jolted Americans and awakened them to the threat of Soviet expansionism, and they found decisive leadership in President Truman. Truman's passionate plea to the American people was perhaps the most important speech of his political career. It would also set the stage for the Marshall Plan that was soon to follow.

The Senate approved Truman's aid package to Greece and Turkey by an overwhelming majority by the end of April 1947. The House of Representatives passed the bill by an even larger margin in early May. Truman's speech had won over Democrats and Republicans alike. Nonetheless, Truman sought to reassure skeptics that his foreign policy was simply an evolution of the policies laid out at the postwar peace conferences, and in the tradition of the Monroe Doctrine.

Despite the ratification of the aid package, General Marshall was becoming deeply concerned about Soviet actions elsewhere in Europe. Peace talks were grinding to a halt. Stalin wanted to avoid making an agreement on the future of Germany. His regime favored a climate of indecision and chaos, hoping to win over parts of Eastern Europe, and even China, in the process. On a tour of Western Europe following his talks with Stalin, Marshall realized just how urgently the Allied nations needed help from the American government.

President Truman knew that something had to be done to improve the economic situation throughout Western Europe. Despite the great expense that would accompany any economic assistance, a thriving Europe would certainly be a boost to the American economy. Ever since the end of the war in 1945, the question of economic aid from the United States to its European allies had largely been left unanswered. Nonetheless, along the lines of the newly pronounced Truman Doctrine, the President was determined to help spread and uphold the cause of freedom around the world. And that meant saving Western Europe economically.

Rather than simply providing economic relief to Europe, the Truman administration was convinced that America had to provide European states with the tools to build successful economies on their own. That meant a revitalized agricultural industry, new industrial developments, and commercial relations with other nations around the world. That kind of help would not only benefit Europe, but also the United States by serving as an engine for international trade. Without action, a total economic collapse in Europe would surely occur, therefore damaging the American economy, and leading to the starvation of hundreds of thousands of people. Clearly, America had to step up to the plate and lead the free world.

General Marshall was sent to Harvard University in June of 1947 to deliver the basic tenants of what would become known as the Marshall Plan. He claimed that the government's goal was not to fight Communism or to support democracy, but rather to aid people in need and revitalize Europe. Marshall wanted European leaders to deliberate on what kind of support they needed from the American government, and to design their own relief programs. Rather than simply dictating how financial aid would be spent, Marshall and Truman wanted the Europeans to decide where and how to spend the aid money themselves. More importantly, however, Marshall cleverly suggested that nations in the Soviet sphere of influence would be eligible for funding as well, hoping to pull some of Russia's satellite states out of the firm control of the Soviet politburo. Although Marshall and his advisors in the State Department doubted that Stalin and the Soviet Union would agree to participate in such a program, they decided to extend the overture all the same.

In justifying the great expense his plan was to place on American taxpayers, Marshall reminded his fellow citizens that a strong Europe was essential for the wellbeing of America, and that without American assistance hundreds of thousands of people could die of starvation. Politicians in Europe were taken aback by the extreme generosity of the support the Truman administration was offering, and pledged to quickly compile a program that could be sent to the American government for approval. Nonetheless, Truman would also have to win the support of the Republican Congress for the initiative to succeed. Because of that, Truman decided that the plan would have to be called the Marshall Plan. Marshall, unlike Truman, was universally held in well regard by politicians across the political spectrum. The Marshall Plan would furthermore began the process of European economic integration, another goal of the Truman administration, with the European Coal and Steel Community, the forerunner to the European Union, forming in 1951.

The Republican Congress had been hoping to restrain spending and foreign aid rather than increase it exponentially, which was what the Marshall Plan entailed. Up to $7 billion dollars in additional funding in the coming months would have to be sent to Europe on top of the $6 billion already spent. Politicians of every stripe, including Republican Arthur Vandenberg and Sam Rayburn, the former Democratic Speaker of the House, thought that the plan was far too expensive and would surely fail to win over the support of their colleagues, but they supported the President's initiative nonetheless.

In Europe, a conference was held in Paris to negotiate the details of the European proposal. The meeting was led by the British government under Prime Minister Clement Attlee and his Foreign Secretary, Ernest Bevin, but a total of sixteen countries attended, including a large Soviet bloc contingent as well. Nonetheless, Soviet satellite states' representatives stormed out of the meeting, accusing Truman of wanting to buy his way into control over the European continent. Despite the billions of dollars' worth of authorized aid with few strings attached, Stalin convinced the leadership of the Soviet satellite states to reject the American overture.

The program turned out to be far more expensive than even Truman or Marshall had imagined when they originally discussed and proposed the initiative. Primary estimates following the European conference pegged the cost at $17 billion, an extraordinary level of funding. Nonetheless, Truman saw it as a necessary expense that would prevent another depression and save hundreds of thousands of Europeans from starvation.

The Marshall Plan caught the Soviet leadership completely off guard when it was first proposed in the fall of 1947. The Russians had been relying on economic chaos and poverty as a pretext for Communist expansionism, but the threat of peace and prosperity in Western Europe would make it nearly impossible to extend the Soviet sphere of influence further west. Stalin's alarm after learning of Truman's plan was one of the primary reasons that the Soviets would soon blockade the city of Berlin.

Just as Secretary Marshall was in the process of configuring the Marshall Plan, another one of Truman's initiatives was ratified by Congress in June of 1947. The National Security Act made major changes to the military and intelligence services in Washington, and for the first time created the Cabinet post of Secretary of Defense. It abolished the position of Secretary of War, and Truman chose to appoint James Forrestal, the former Secretary of the Navy, as the first man to hold the post.

Truman had been determined to find ways to make government more efficient and organized since his inauguration, and the new Defense Department was a central part of that plan. Truman had long felt that the national defense system in the United States was archaic, and that unifying the army and the navy under one department was simply common sense. He had found enormous amounts of waste across the military establishment as Chairman of the Truman Committee, and the President adamantly believed that a more unified and streamlined national defense system could better protect the country, and at the same time reduce excessive government expenses.

Leaders in both the Navy and War Departments were reluctant to allow the President to make such a drastic change, but Truman ultimately left them with little choice. The President sent a letter to Congress as early as December of 1945 to request the creation of a unified National Defense Department, but it took more than a year for the President to fully convince members of his own administration to pursue the initiative, and Congress finally passed the National Security Act in July of 1947, officially creating the Department of National Defense. The bill also created the Central Intelligence Agency and the National Security Council. Beginning in 1947, and continuing until the present day, the director of the Central Intelligence Agency reports to the President as his first visitor every morning to brief the Commander in Chief on a whole range of international intelligence issues. Roscoe Hillenkoetter, a rear admiral from Missouri, was appointed to be the agency's first director.

The National Security Council also became a very important governmental institution in the aftermath of the passage of the National Security Act in 1947. The council was designed to provide a forum in which military, diplomatic, and intelligence issues could be discussed among the President's appointees and provide multiple courses of action for the President. Truman first created the National Security Council as an institution that had seven members: the President, Secretary of State, Secretary of Defense, Secretary of the Army, Secretary of the Navy, Secretary of the Air Force, and the Chairman of the National Security Resources Board. By 1949, however, Truman was convinced that the council's membership would have to be altered to include fewer members. The President's newly redesigned National Security Council was composed of the President, Vice President, Secretary of State, Secretary of Defense, Chairman of the National Security Resources Board, and any temporary member the President might want to include on an ad hoc basis.

Despite being a southern Democrat, many of whom in Truman's era were largely known for their support for segregation, the President delivered a passionate speech on June 28, 1947, in front of the Lincoln Memorial that called on all Americans to do their part in advancing civil rights. Whether black or white, every American, Truman declared, was equal under the law, and should therefore be equal in society. Biased standards for employment opportunities and segregated schools had to go. Although Truman's aides told the President that addressing the civil rights issue could hurt him politically, especially in the south, he did so anyway. Truman was always proud to claim that his decisions were made in the interest of the United States and without regard to his political fortunes. While any President is bound to make decisions that are at least somewhat political, Truman did take many unpopular steps to secure for the country what he thought was right. Civil rights was one such issue.

Truman's attention, however, would soon return to Western Europe. George Kennan, the Deputy Chief of Mission for the United States in the Soviet Union, published an article in the Foreign Affairs journal in the summer of 1947 entitled "The Sources of Soviet Conduct." In it, Kennan argued that the expansionist Soviets had to be contained, meaning that they had to be prevented from annexing new countries or regions that might allow their power and influence to grow. The report had been authored in January for the Secretary of Defense, and was then published anonymously, but the author was soon revealed to be Kennan.

The Kennan report caused quite a stir, but President Truman had already realized that negotiations with the Russians would lead nowhere. Secretary Marshall concurred. The Soviets were happy to continue the stalemate in Europe to suit their own purposes and leave Europe in shambles. With the Marshall Plan, the Truman administration had already signalled that the United States would counter Soviet obstructionism by helping to rebuild Western Europe. With that shift in policy, Truman realized all too well that the Cold War had begun.

The Truman administration had tried to work with the Soviets for more than two years, but finally gave up hope in the first half of 1947. The President's desire for cooperation and peace among the world's great powers now appeared to be all but impossible. The Marshall Plan was seen by Truman as something that was absolutely necessary for the survival of Europe and for the economic interests of the United States. The Soviet Union had left Truman with no option other than to break away from Soviet obstructionism and go at it alone in reconstructing Europe.

Despite widespread concern that the United States could not afford to pay for every aspect of the Marshall Plan, Congress approved General Marshall's initiative in the spring of 1948, four months after Truman had personally appeared before a joint session of Congress to urge for the legislation's passage. The House of Representatives approved of the plan, known as the Economic Cooperation Act, in March of 1948, and the Senate quickly endorsed the deal by an overwhelming margin. On April 3, 1948, President Truman signed the Marshall Plan into law. The final cost estimate was said to be $13 billion, less than the $17 billion that European officials and Truman's advisors had initially projected. As Truman later reflected, the United States was the first nation in history to give food and monetary aid to nations that they had defeated during a war only a few years prior. But America was now in a very different situation than it had been in the past, and, with a Communist menace seeking to expand abroad, the United States was faced with the task of protecting the free world from Soviet aggression.

Chapter Five

Preparing for the 1948 Election

Harry Truman had always claimed that he did not want to be President. He hated the attention and constant scrutiny, and wanted to have more privacy and time with Bess and Margaret. By the time of next election, Truman would be more than sixty years old. President Coolidge, who, like Truman, hated nearly everything that came along with the Presidency, had stunned the nation and declined to seek re-election in 1928. But Truman ultimately decided to campaign for four more years in the White House. After investigating whether or not he could find a suitable candidate to replace him, Truman, who always enjoyed a spirited political contest, was determined to be re-elected, if only to keep the presidency out of the hands of the Republicans. His most preferred candidate, General Dwight Eisenhower, claimed that he did not want to go into politics. Four years later, Truman would be shocked to learn that Eisenhower was in fact a Republican.

Politics was Truman's lifeblood, and he had never found great success in any other arena. After losing both houses of Congress to the Republicans in 1946, Truman was determined to keep the White House in Democratic hands, and even win back the Congress. Many believed that the Republicans would end up winning Congress and the White House, but Truman was determined to prove them wrong. His politician persona, however, often proved to be a problem with American voters, who were used to grander presidential personalities along the lines of Franklin Roosevelt or Woodrow Wilson. Nonetheless, as a wartime leader who clearly rose to the occasion, Truman had proven himself to be much more than the average career politician, which was what many of his opponents painted him to be.

President Truman kicked off his re-election bid with his State of the Union address on January 7, 1948. He once again emphasized the need to expand progressive programs, calling for better housing provisions, more funding for education, a healthcare program, a hike in the minimum wage, and tax reductions for the lower classes. It was a typical liberal progressive speech, and it was delivered by a man who embodied those ideals. But the Republican dominated Congress quickly rejected most of Truman's ideas, as did many conservative Democrats. The civil rights agenda delivered to Congress weeks later was more progressive than nearly everyone had anticipated, further angering southern conservative Democrats. Truman called on Congress to pass new civil rights legislation that could be enforced by all three branches of government. Truman was far less willing than Roosevelt had been to make unilateral moves without the support of the legislative branch, and claimed that he could only act on civil rights with the support of the Congress.

The fact that Truman acknowledged publically the second-class treatment African-Americans were receiving across America was nothing short of extraordinary. No President had ever been as open or honest in addressing the issue, nor had any of his predecessors proposed legislation that could help to reverse the trend. One initiative that was especially close to Truman's heart was to enact new legislation to better protect all voters who sought to participate in the democratic process. Fair employment treatment in the segregated south was also a high priority. But many believed that Truman was once again endangering his re-election bid, putting policy ahead of politics, and even threatening his support among Democrats in Congress. Nonetheless, Truman and some of his close supporters believed that his civil rights stance was morally right, and that it would be well received by many voters, especially in the more progressive northern states. As one of his closest aides, Clark Clifford, was fond of saying, Truman's principled civil rights agenda would allow the White House to occupy the moral high ground as a contrast with their Republican opponents.

Claiming the moral high ground, however, would prove to be much harder with the likelihood of Thomas Dewey leading the Republican ticket. Although Dewey had been defeated by Roosevelt and Truman four years earlier, it had been Roosevelt's unprecedented third re-election effort, and the nation had been at war. This time, the war was over, and it would be Truman who faced the New York Republican governor, and the President was seen as much more beatable than his predecessor. Dewey, who by 1948 had served as the Governor of New York for more than five years, was now much more experienced in politics than he had been four years earlier, and had taken many lessons away from his landslide loss to the Roosevelt ticket.

Truman's aides told him that Democrats would have to pull out all the stops to win in 1948. The party would be seeking a fifth term in the White House, which had only occurred once before in the nation's history, and that had been under Republican rule. Truman would have to fire up Democratic labor allies, maintain support in the segregated south, win the rural farm vote, and gain support in the inner cities and among minorities. One particularly vocal minority group, urban Jewish voters, would be hard to win over, but their influence in the crucial state of New York was significant, especially because Truman would be handicapped in facing the state's Governor in the Presidential contest. But no President had won the White House without New York in more than thirty years, so the President would have to make a conscious effort to gain support in the Empire State. Moreover, not only did Truman have to win over the segregationists in the south, but also the black voters who were subject to that segregation. The Democratic ticket definitely had their work cut out for them.

A strong line against the Soviet Union was also important for Truman's re-election effort in 1948, as many voters wanted to see their President as someone who could be tough in dealing with other leaders on the world stage, especially communists. It was very important that the Republicans not be able to paint Truman as soft on Communism, which was largely the reason for the President's decision to back a loyalty investigation program. Furthermore, in times of crises or discontent abroad, Presidents are more likely to be re-elected at home. One such example was Roosevelt's extended Presidency, with the incumbent seeking an unprecedented third and fourth mandate under the rationale of having an experienced head of state during a world war.

The most important advice Truman was given by his political advisors was to travel the country. While he could not actively campaign for re-election too early in the calendar year, Truman could begin connecting with voters by giving speeches and remaining active in crucial bellwether states. On March 8, 1945, Truman officially announced his candidacy for re-election. But his bid for the White House was quickly opposed by many southern Democrats, including Governor Strom Thurmond of South Carolina, who would later leave the Democratic Party to oppose Truman as a separate Presidential candidate under the Dixiecrat banner. Progressive Democrats felt alienated as well.

President Truman was confronted in 1947 and early 1948 with another controversy, this one in foreign affairs. Following the devastation of the Holocaust, Truman and millions of Americans sought to secure a safer future for Jewish people around the world. His firm belief in the Bible also led him to support the idea of a Jewish homeland. But to support the creation of a Jewish homeland also meant angering Palestine's Arab neighbors, many of whom supplied the United States and its industries with oil. Truman was determined to make a decision based on what was morally right, but the State Department continuously voiced concern about the reaction that would result among America's Arab allies should the President support the Jewish state initiative.

Truman's reluctance to support the creation of what would later become known as the nation of Israel was largely centered around the idea that Palestine was still overwhelmingly occupied by Arabs, and that any hope the new Jewish state might have of survival would almost certainly mean military involvement on the part of the United States. He faced substantial pressure at home from political, religious, and cultural groups and their prominent figures to side with the Jewish people, not to mention Republicans, which only seemed to anger him further. Truman had long stood for an increase in the number of Jews allowed to immigrate to the state of Palestine, but the British had been reluctant to do so.

Government officials within the Truman administration were largely torn about what the country's Palestinian policy should be. Some, led by Secretary of State George Marshall, Secretary of Defense James Forrestal, and others in the State Department, sided with the Attlee government in Great Britain in calling for the United Nations to gain trusteeship over the country when British forces vacated the territory in the spring of 1948. Others, led by Clark Clifford, insisted that the President should recognize the legitimacy of Palestine becoming a Jewish state, reminding Truman of the legacy of the Holocaust. The President remained largely non-committal for months.

The United Nations voted in the fall of 1947 to partition the territory and allow for the creation of a Jewish state. According to many working within the Truman administration, it had been the President's lobbying that proved to be the difference with nations around the world. Truman decided that turning the state of Palestine into two separate entities would be the ideal way of pursuing a compromise, and allowed that opinion to be known to the American public. But the approval of the United Nations was by no means a guarantee for the maintenance of a new Jewish homeland. A Jewish state in Palestine would have a hard time establishing itself with Arab neighbors threatening to attack the area as soon as a new state was declared, as many nations continued to amass military forces on their Palestinian borders.

A number of high ranking members within the Truman administration continued to speak out against helping to create a Zionist state. General Marshall worried that losing the support of America's Arab allies could prove to be devastating should a war with the Soviet Union erupt. The Central Intelligence Agency suggested that the establishment of a Jewish state would be met with hostility across the region, and that such animosity would quickly overrun the new country. They therefore suggested caution: America had voted in favor of partition, but did not have to support the immediate creation of a Jewish state. State Department officials claimed that partition was unrealistic, and that it could never work in reality. Moreover, it was the British who oversaw the governance of Palestine, and a decision over the future of the Middle East was not one that the Truman administration could make alone. The State Department assumed that the President had been convinced by Marshall's argument and therefore believed trusteeship was the government's official policy, an assumption that would come to plague the administration in the coming days. What Marshall believed to be Truman's new policy was also kept out of the press due to its unpopularity.

It was his old friend Eddie Jacobson, whom he had met and befriended in the military, who finally convinced Truman to end his waffling and put his full weight behind the Jewish cause. Jacobson, who was neither religious nor a Zionist, had been contacted by Chaim Weizmann, a prominent Zionist leader and future President of Israel, and members of his inner circle to try to convince the President to stand fully behind their cause. Jacobson asked Truman to consider seeing Weizmann again, but the President claimed that nothing had changed and there was therefore nothing new to discuss: Weizmann had already plead his case to Truman months earlier. Jacobson then decided to fly to Washington and speak to the President directly, barging into the White House without an appointment.

After discussing their personal lives and other events in the news, Jacobson forced Truman into a discussion about Palestine. The President was momentarily filled with anger at having to once again participate in such a discussion. Truman claimed that he was sick and tired of Jews trying to bully him into a decision, coming very close to espousing anti-Semitism. Jacobson then turned to the statue of Andrew Jackson that Truman had in the Oval Office, and told the President that Chaim Weizmann was his hero just as much as President Jackson was for Truman. Moreover, Truman was trying to avoid the Zionist leader simply because he was being insulted by some American Jews at home. Truman, Jacobson claimed, was trying to paint all Jews with one brush. After a long pause, Truman relented: he would see Weizmann one last time.

Eddie Jacobson's visit to the White House was on March 13, 1948. Less than a week later, on March 18, Weizmann returned to the White House without the knowledge of the press. Truman and Weizmann agreed that a Jewish state was fundamentally necessary, and that the United States stood firmly behind the immediate partition proposal, contrary to the advice of General Marshall. Weizmann told the President that he was pleased, and departed. On March 19, however, Truman had yet to inform the State Department of the meeting, or about his apparent change of heart on the administration's policy in the Middle East. Acting on what he thought to be Truman's official policies, the American Ambassador to the United Nations, Warren Austin, proposed that the General Assembly delay its support for partition, and therefore leave Palestine under the guise of the United Nations on a temporary basis.

Austin's announcement stunned the American public, as the move was an about face on the administration's United Nations vote in favor of the pro-partition policy, and the opposite of what he had agreed to with Weizmann the night before. Jewish groups across the country were stunned, and understandably irate. Members of Congress slammed the White House for selling out to the Arabs. Most in the Democratic caucus were ashamed by Truman's move.

Truman learned of the discord in the administration's policy the following morning. The President's staff members were surprised to learn that such an important announcement had been made without Truman's explicit confirmation. Secretary Marshall had immediately come out to champion the administration's United Nations trusteeship proposal, declaring at a news conference that the President fully supported the State Department's request to leave Palestine in the hands of the United Nations. Truman was fuming, as no one in the State Department had informed him of Austin's speech or its contents, nor had he spoken with Secretary Marshall, who still seemed to believe that his arguments had won over the President. Furthermore, Truman had told his entire administration not to include anything in the speech that could be taken as a walk back from the partition plan. Because of the move the United States delegation made at the United Nations, Weizmann effectively issued Truman an ultimatum, remarking that the Jewish people faced a future with either their own homeland, or no future one at all.

As the debacle over Palestine was going on, Truman addressed a joint session of Congress on March 16 to discuss other aspects of foreign affairs. There were rumors that the Soviets were on the march, and Truman proclaimed that, in addition to the Marshall Plan, Congress would have to act to legislate a universal military training program, and issue a brief reinstatement of the military draft. The blame for the necessity of those actions was placed by Truman squarely on the Kremlin in Moscow.

Despite Truman's passionate address to Congress, leaders in the House of Representatives and the Senate failed to act on Truman's initiatives. Moreover, Republicans were overjoyed with Truman's request to draft young Americans in an election year, and by his administration's insult to Jewish voters across the country.

As Truman was faced with an unresponsive Congress, he once again turned his mind back to Palestine. After the United Nations debacle, Eddie Jacobson returned to the White House to confront the President in early April. In their meeting, Truman promised Jacobson that he would fully support the creation of a Jewish state.

Jewish leaders in Palestine were set to declare the independence of what would later become known as the new state of Israel in mid-May. As the date came closer, Truman found himself under pressure from all sides, as he had yet to announce his intention of supporting the independence of a Jewish state in Palestine. While he had decided on a course of action, Truman sought one last time to convince General Marshall, who was by now fully aware that he had not won over the President on the subject of trusteeship, to support the initiative. It was Marshall's State Department that was responsible for the United Nations declaration against partition two months earlier, and Truman was adamant about getting his Secretary of State onside. Marshall, who had days earlier remarked that Truman had never made a decision that was not in the best interest of the United States abroad, was reluctant to support partition. But Truman wanted to try one last time to convince him otherwise.

The British were set to withdraw from Palestine on May 14, so Truman called Marshall, along with other administration officials and aides from the State Department, to the White House on May 12 to discuss the region's future. Clark Clifford, one of the President's closest advisors, was presented with the task of arguing in favor of the creation of a Jewish state, along with America's immediate recognition of its validity. One of Marshall's aides at the State Department, Robert Lovett, presented the case for leaving the region in the control of the United Nations on a temporary basis. Lovett was asked to go first. After he had made his case, Clifford was asked to respond. Clifford called on the administration to recognize the new Jewish state before the Soviets did, and that meant as soon as the following day. Marshall immediately objected, claiming that Clifford was playing politics. But the President intervened, and asked Clifford to continue. The Jewish people, he claimed, would create their own state in Palestine whether the United States endorsed its creation or not. After six million European Jews had been murdered in the Holocaust, they would wait no longer.

Marshall and his aides responded that America could not support the creation of a state without even knowing its final boundaries. The General even suggested that the administration was considering supporting the state's creation for political purposes, and that such a decision was below the dignity of the office of the President. The meeting was then called to an end, and Truman told the press that he had not yet made a decision on the matter.

As a rift between Truman and Marshall looked as if it was nearly inevitable, Clifford and Lovett met privately to try to work out a compromise. Truman could not afford Marshall's resignation politically, but he was by now determined to support the creation of a Jewish state. Marshall would have to be convinced to support the plan without leaving the administration. On the afternoon of May 14, General Marshall told the President that he disagreed with his position, but that he would not say so in public. Truman was ecstatic. He would be able to support the creation of a Jewish state and keep Marshall in the State Department.

The creation of the state of Israel was declared at midnight in Jerusalem, which was 6pm in Washington. Only eleven minutes after the declaration, the Truman administration released a statement to the press announcing that the United States recognized the de facto creation of the new state of Israel, therefore supporting its independence. The United States was the first nation to do so. But after the crisis that had followed the fiasco at the United Nations in March, politicians and statesmen around the world were flabbergasted by Truman's wholehearted support for the new Israeli government. Ambassador Austin was embarrassed to say the least, as was the entire American delegation to the United Nations who had weeks earlier opposed what Truman was now declaring his support for. Although President Truman would refuse to arm the Israelis when they were attacked by neighboring Arab states in the coming months, he was still largely responsible, along with the Soviets, for the international legitimacy afforded to the new Jewish state. Newspapers across the country that had been critical of Truman's handling of the Palestinian file largely praised him for his final decision to wholeheartedly support Israel's creation.

Many in the State Department were also surprised by Truman's decision, but they had always been far more reluctant to support the Jewish state initiative. Israelis held their first democratic election on January 25, 1949. Following the election of David Ben Gurion's government, the Truman administration again released a statement to the press, this time officially recognizing the state of Israel. The reaction among Arab states to the Truman administration's decision was of immense anger, and a coalition of Arab states immediately invaded the new state of Israel to uphold the old Middle Eastern order. A United Nations mediator was sent into the conflict zone, but an official presence failed to prevent a full scale military conflict from erupting across the region. Once again, President Truman's controversial decision has been

vindicated by history, and, in a rare instance, Secretary Marshall
was proven to be far too cautious.

Chapter Six

The Do-Nothing Congress

After the Israel decision was made by the middle of May, Truman turned his attention back to domestic politics. The economy was strong, inflation was mostly under control, and unemployment was nearing a record low. Nonetheless, Truman was not very popular, with only a thirty six percent approval rating, and was widely seen as the 1948 election's underdog candidate. But Truman was convinced that he could win, and was reminded of the doomsday predictions in his 1940 Senate race when he faced off against the state of Missouri's popular incumbent Democratic Governor in the primary but managed to come out on top. If he could beat Governor Stark, Truman thought, he could definitely best a Republican opponent. Just like in 1940, Truman would win over the electorate by personally campaigning and meeting with voters. Truman had always been a strong campaigner, and the Democrats were relying on his barnstorming appeal to give them four more years in the White House.

Truman's family had wanted him to retire and move back to Independence, but the President felt that his job was not yet finished. Progressive forces, led by former Vice President Henry Wallace, advocated Soviet appeasement, and conservative forces were pushing to roll back elements of President Roosevelt's New Deal program. Truman believed that there was no other qualified Democrat who was willing to take his place, and that he therefore had to take it upon himself to defend the Democratic accomplishments of the last sixteen years.

Truman left Washington on June 3 to begin his cross-country tour to interact with voters. Never before had he been more desperate to engage with voters than after spending four tumultuous years in the White House. Although he could not actively campaign before the Democratic convention, there were significant electoral benefits to simply being seen by voters across the country, who wanted to see their President reach out to them. For a statistically unpopular President, Truman drew enormous crowds, including an audience of more than one hundred thousand supporters at a stop in Chicago. Even in Omaha, Nebraska, over one hundred thousand voters came out to greet the President.

Harry Truman was at his best when he was campaigning against something. Thomas Dewey, his likely opponent, was a centrist Republican with little in his record to criticise. But as the underdog, Truman needed to find a way to run against the Republican nominee in a way that could scare swing voters who were tired of having Democrats in the White House. Ultimately, Truman decided to seek his re-election by running against the Republican led Congress rather than Dewey himself. Congress, he claimed, had been stonewalling his agenda for two years, an agenda that was in the best interest of the American people. Truman failed to mention that the Republicans supported almost all of his foreign policy initiatives, thereby enabling him to still accuse them of being a party of isolationists. Nevertheless, foreign policy had never been a strong campaign rallying point regardless of the election year. The eightieth Congress, according to the President, was the worst Congress in American history. America needed more social security, price controls, a new housing bill, health insurance, and support for farmers. The Republican Congress had delivered none of that, and were therefore working against the welfare of the people. Insulted Republicans, however, fired back that Truman was the worst President.

At a stop in California, Truman delivered a commencement speech at the University of California, where he was to receive an honorary degree. In addressing foreign affairs, Truman claimed that it was the Soviet Union that was standing in the way of the peace that the world so desperately needed. Unlike the Soviets, Truman reminded the graduates, the United States only pursued expansionism insofar as it supported the expansion of freedom and liberty. The speech was very well received, and days later the President was met by more than one million supporters in Los Angeles.

Truman believed that the media was against him, and he was right: the vast majority of newspapers and radio hosts endorsed the Republican Presidential ticket. He was therefore determined to reach out to voters across the country by coming to them, leading to the most relentless re-election campaign ever undertaken by a sitting President.

Truman returned to Washington on June 18, and the Republican convention in Philadelphia began three days later. As many had already anticipated, Thomas Dewey, the Governor of New York and the 1944 Republican Presidential nominee, was chosen to be the Republican candidate. Governor Earl Warren of California, who would later serve as the Supreme Court's fourteenth Chief Justice, was chosen as his running mate. Both were popular liberal governors of two of the most populated states in the country. Republicans felt as if the Dewey–Warren ticket was virtually invincible.

One of the most significant crises of the Truman administration broke out in Europe on June 24. The Soviets blockaded the train, truck, and boat routes into and out of Berlin. They were attempting to take full control of the city, including the

American, British, and French districts, and force the Western allies into retreat. Stalin had continuously rejected American and British efforts to try to unify the country, and was now signalling that he wanted to do so, but as a Soviet satellite state. The blockade was the hallmark of the expansionist Soviet threat, and it woke many American voters up to that reality. It also demonstrated that President Truman's gloomy forecast of bilateral relations had been correct. If nothing was done, millions would starve and freeze to death, as the city only had enough food supplies for a month and coal supplies for no more than a month and a half.

Just six days before the Russian blockade, the American, British, and French governments announced the creation of a new German currency to replace the Reichsmark, which was plagued by rampant inflation. The Russians had the ability to make new copies of the old currency, and had used it to try to deliberately cause inflation to stymie any recovery efforts that were underway in the American, British, and French sectors. The American representatives and their British and French allies had announced the creation of a new currency in order to provide western Germany with a stable monetary system that could facilitate interaction with Western economies. The Russians resisted American efforts to allow the new currency to be used in all of Germany, preferring to keep the Reichsmark as a means of manipulating the German economy. When the Russians officially blockaded Berlin, Stalin announced that transportation routes would only be reopened if the Western allies canceled the creation of a new German currency. President Truman, however, believed that it was of very high importance that the German people obtain a new currency to help rebuild the nation's economy. Thus, a stalemate ensued.

President Truman declared that he was not about to be bullied out of Berlin by anyone, least of all the Russians. He ordered all American troops in the city to remain at their posts until the administration came up with a plan of action. The four victorious

World War Two allies had agreed to divide Berlin amongst themselves, and the Soviets had no right to try to occupy other areas of the city. The only solution, Truman decided, was to send in any and all supplies needed in Berlin through the air. It would be very expensive, and may not deliver all of the necessary supplies, but America and its allies began a full-scale airlift into western Berlin. Truman had intended for the airlift to be only a temporary solution until a diplomatic agreement could be formed, but the air force would ultimately deliver an average of four and a half thousand tons of goods to the city of Berlin on a daily basis. Several dialogues with the Russians resulted in little progress, as the Soviets continued to insist on a withdrawal of Germany's new currency from the market as the pretext to lifting any part of the blockade. Truman decided to bring the issue up at the United Nations Security Council, although the Soviets had a permanent veto. The Russians were trying to force Western forces out of Berlin for political purposes, having been embarrassed by the Marshall Plan's success in areas that had previously been primary targets for Communist expansionism, including in Italy, France, and Finland. If Stalin could force Truman out of Berlin, he would likely be able to obtain control over the rest of the country.

The boldness of Truman's airlift initiative later won him respect and admiration around the world, and with voters across the country. It lifted the spirits of nations across the world who were fighting to contain communist forces and their expansionist goals, but these reactions came only months and years after the President's decision. Truman's resolve and his actions on the Berlin issue likely played a role in his surprise victory in November, but few recognized the decision as a game changer right after it had been made. Nonetheless, Truman made the decision because he had no intention of backing out of Berlin. The political implications were largely an afterthought, or simply did not play a role at all. Truman had always prided himself on making decisions in the best interest of the country rather than in the interest of his

Presidency. The Berlin airlift could have failed to achieve its desired goals, and millions of Berliners might have been left starving, so the President's support of the initiative was almost entirely apolitical. Ultimately, the Russians would back down, although this would not occur until after Truman's re-election.

Truman's November prospects looked rather grim during the summer of 1948. Many within the Democratic Party wanted to nominate someone else, preferably General Eisenhower. Even President Roosevelt's sons wanted Eisenhower to replace Truman. Although the General had said he would not enter the field of politics, no one even knew whether or not he was a Democrat. As it would turn out, Eisenhower had no intention of partaking in the Democratic Party at all. Nonetheless, to quell the momentum, General Eisenhower once again announced on July 9 that he had no interest in being the Democratic candidate for President in 1948, and that he would not accept any kind of political nomination. With the hope of Eisenhower supporters dashed, it became all but certain that Harry Truman would easily win the party's nomination. To revive interest in his candidacy, Truman sought to have Supreme Court Justice William Douglas, a young and popular personality with the American people, run as his Vice Presidential counterpart. Many had considered Douglas to be a better alternative than Truman. Douglas told the President that he would consider the offer.

The Democratic convention was also in Philadelphia, and it began on July 11. The mood was grim. Traditional supporters who had flocked to previous conventions to see Franklin Roosevelt were staying home in the tens of thousands. Even the convention hall was largely vacated. Days earlier, Justice Douglas informed Truman that he did not want to join the Democratic ticket in order to remain on the Supreme Court, a move that many saw as disrespectful of the President. Like millions of Americans, Douglas expected Truman to lose, and did not intend to give up his seat on the nation's highest court only to be unemployed in early November. Truman, devastated, chose to watch much of the convention on a small black and white television in the Oval Office, preferring to remain alone rather than depart for Philadelphia at the beginning of the gathering.

Senate majority leader Alben Barkley brought the crowd to its feet on July 12 with a rousing address in which he attacked his Republican opponents. He reminded delegates of the bright legacy of the New Deal, which he felt was being capably carried forward by the Truman administration. He viciously attacked Republicans for leaving the country weak and divided in 1933, and warned Democrats that they could expect more of the same if their party failed to win in November. Barkley's performance made him the immediate frontrunner for the Vice Presidential nomination.

Senator Barkley, a Senate veteran who had first been elected to Congress in 1913, was an old stalwart in the Democratic Party, and had served alongside President Truman during his decade long stint in the Senate. Truman knew Barkley quite well even from his time in the White House, as Barkley had been the Senate minority leader since 1947. Like Truman, Barkley was from rural America. He was raised on a farm in Kentucky in a circumstance similar to Truman's upbringing in Missouri. The two men liked each other and came from similar backgrounds, and they appeared to be the perfect fit for running mates. Truman had never requested that Congress ratify a successor to serve as his Vice President after the death of President Roosevelt and his ascension to the White House, and the post had therefore been vacant since 1945. When Democratic leaders asked Truman what he would think of having Barkley as his Vice Presidential candidate, the President replied that he would be thrilled if that was what delegates were in favor of. One drawback was the Senator's age: he was already 71 years old. Moreover, unlike the Republican ticket, neither of the two Democratic candidates came from a populous or progressive state.

As Truman waited to learn whether or not Barkley would be confirmed as his running mate, his attention turned back to the agenda at the Democratic convention. Hours before Truman was set to deliver his acceptance speech on July 14, a fight broke out over civil rights. One wing of the party demanded more action on civil rights reform, while another more conservative flank threatened to leave the convention if such a move took place. Truman, worried about losing southern support, was hesitant to make the platform's civil rights language any more firm. Nonetheless, this angered the northern and more progressive members present at the convention.

Hubert Humphrey, who would later serve as Lyndon Johnson's Vice President and the Democratic Party's Presidential nominee in 1968, led the charge towards civil rights reform. He told the convention that now was the time for action. Humphrey declared that his progressive wing of the party was not trying to hastily settle the issue of civil rights. Rather, the debate that was occurring should have occurred more than a century ago. The Democratic Party, which had long championed states' rights, needed to put the interests of all citizens ahead of electoral fortunes in the south, and could no longer use the issue of states' rights to shield them from taking action. The convention rose to its feet when Humphrey concluded his speech, and the progressive wing of the party made it clear that they were no longer willing to wait for their party to take urgent action on the civil rights issue. Major elements of Humphrey's civil rights agenda were resolutely approved by the delegates, but the move set in motion a conservative break from the Democratic Party altogether.

Back at the White House, Truman was horrified to learn that Humphrey's resolutions might tear apart his already thinning coalition of support across the country. But what the President failed to realize at the time was that the party's civil rights platform, the first substantive reform proposal in the Democratic Party's history, would prove to be exactly what Truman needed to rally support for his party in the north, and ensure that he had enough support in some of the swing states to squeak out a victory in

November. Nonetheless, the Alabama delegation, led by former Lieutenant Governor Leven Ellis, walked out of the convention before Truman had even arrived.

After arriving at the convention, Truman was surprised to learn that voting was behind schedule, meaning that he would have to wait several hours before making his acceptance speech. He had taken the Presidential train up from Washington with Bess, Margaret, and some close advisors. In the interim, Truman spent some time with Alben Barkley, who was soon to be confirmed as his running mate. It was not until the early hours of July 15 that President Truman was officially nominated as the Democratic candidate for President of the United States. He handily defeated Georgia Senator Richard Russell, who had run against the President and the party's civil rights policies. After the vote, Barkley was unanimously chosen by delegates to be the party's Vice Presidential candidate. It was not until well after 2am that Truman finally made his acceptance speech, by far the most important and best speech of his political career.

Few Democrats expected Truman to be able to deliver a strong and passionate acceptance speech. But he did, and he did so by coming out swinging at the Republicans. Right at the beginning of the speech, Truman emphatically declared that "Senator Barkley and I will win this election and make these Republicans like it!" Then, touching on a theme that would become a cornerstone of his campaign, Truman declared that the Democratic Party would win over the people because it was the party of the people, while the Republicans were the party of vested interests and the wealthy establishment. Party unity was essential. Conservative and liberal Democrats would have to come together to beat their common enemy.

Income for farmers, Truman declared, had increased by more than $15 billion since 1932. Farmers owed their recent successes to the policies of the Democratic Party, and they were ungrateful if they did not support the party in November. National income had increased by five hundred percent since the election of Franklin Roosevelt, and wages had increased by more than $100 billion. If the working man did not support the Democratic ticket, they too were labeled as ungrateful. Furthermore, without the Roosevelt and Truman administration's handling of foreign policy, America would still be isolated in a dangerous world. The United States, Truman claimed, could not afford to go back to the days of Republican isolationism.

The Republicans were the party of obstructionism, and voters needed to look no further than the record of the eightieth Congress, Truman's primary campaign target. The Republican Party "favors the privileged few and not the common, everyday man. Ever since its inception, that party has been under the control of special privilege, and they proved it in the eightieth Congress." Truman had recommended the extension of sound price controls, and Congress did not deliver. He had proposed ten methods of improving welfare and called a special session of Congress to deal with the matter, but Congress did not deliver. A bill had been introduced to erect housing in urban slums, but Congress did not deliver. Truman asked Republicans in the House and Senate to enact legislation to strengthen the relations between unions and management, but Congress did not deliver. The President had asked for a medical care reform package, but Congress did not deliver. The President had requested progress on civil rights legislation, but Congress did not deliver. He had asked for surpluses to be used to pay down the national debt, but Congress passed an across the board tax cut instead, a move that primarily benefited the wealthy and was finally passed by overriding Truman's veto. Rather than supporting Truman's call for stable tax rates and surpluses to help pay down the national debt, Republicans in Congress instead preferred to drastically reduce taxes and put less money towards debt relief.

The Republican platform was full of "poppycock" promises. They called for something to be done about high prices, more funding for housing and slum clearing, and increased social security benefits. But Congress had failed to act in any of these areas when Truman had called on them to do so.

When Truman paused at this point of his speech, he prepared to deliver one of the shrewdest political gambits in history. If the Republicans claimed they wanted action in a whole host of areas in which Truman too sought action, he would call them back into a special session of Congress to deliver productive legislation for the American people. Knowing that the Republican promises were nothing more than token gestures, Truman declared that he was "therefore calling this Congress back into session July 26." Republicans would return to Washington and Truman would ask them "to pass laws to halt rising prices, to meet the housing crisis – which they are saying they are for in their platform." By this time everyone in the convention hall was on their feet cheering for the President. As he reached the climax of his address, Truman issued the final blow.

> Now, my friends, if there is any reality behind the Republican platform, we ought to get some action from a short session of the eightieth Congress. They can do this job in fifteen days, if they want to do it. They will still have time to go out and run for office!
>
> They are going to try to dodge their responsibility. They are going to drag all the red herrings they can across this campaign, but I am here to say that Senator Barkley and I are not going to let them get away with it!

Truman knew full well that Congress was unlikely to pass any of the legislation that the Republicans claimed they were in favor of in their platform. But he wanted to demonstrate to the American people that, no matter how much the Republican Party claimed it had changed, it was still the party of special interests, a party that refused to act in the benefit of the American people on almost every welfare issue. Beyond that, should the Republicans in Congress fail to produce any legislation whatsoever during the special congressional session, Truman would have enough ammunition to run his campaign against the "do-nothing" Congress rather than Governor Dewey himself, therefore targeting a more unpopular faction of the Republican Party.

Truman's aggressively direct attack on the Republican Party was the most spirited Presidential challenge issued in decades. The idea of a Presidential nominee basing his campaign on running against his opponents rather than on his agenda for the future was a novelty in American politics at the time. Nonetheless, Truman's campaign style is one that has become mainstream in politics today. He ended his speech with a call to arms and a reflection on the last decade and a half.

> In 1932 we were attacking the citadel of special privilege and greed. We were fighting to drive the money changers from the temple. Today, in 1948, we are now defenders of the stronghold of democracy and of equal opportunity, the haven of the ordinary people of this land and not of the favored classes or the powerful few. The battle cry is just the same as it was in 1932...give me your help, not to win votes alone, but to win in this new crusade to keep America secure and safe for its own people!

Republicans in Congress painted Truman's move to call a special session in the middle of an election campaign as desperation. Both sides knew that the move had been entirely political, but it was important for Truman to prove his point and call the opposition out on their bluff. Thomas Dewey was also left in a quagmire. He was one of the members of the progressive wing of the Republican Party that favored most of the reforms that Roosevelt and Truman had undertaken in the previous sixteen years. But he was also a Republican, and would be left defending an unpopular and obstructionist Congress rather than talking about his own liberal agenda.

Despite Truman's creativity and his brilliant electoral ingenuity, the President faced his own electoral setback in the Deep South. Breakaway Democrats who had left the party's convention after Humphrey's civil rights initiatives were ratified were meeting in Birmingham, Alabama. Under the guise of supporting states' rights, Alabama's Governor announced that Truman was trying to force the south into becoming an "inferior race." Calling themselves the Dixiecrats, delegates voted to select South Carolina Governor Strom Thurmond as their Presidential candidate, and Governor Fielding Wright of Mississippi as their Vice Presidential candidate. Thurmond declared that he was leaving the Democratic Party now, as opposed to earlier, because Truman was the first Democratic leader who actually intended to follow through on the civil rights agenda that was included in the party's platform. Franklin Roosevelt had never really been serious about doing so. Truman alluded to this fact in his memoirs, suggesting that "every Democratic platform since 1932 has stressed the devotion of our party to civil rights. But what aroused many Southerners now was that I meant to put this pledge into practice." President Truman had asked the Congress to abolish segregation in the transport industry, provide new laws to protect against lynching, help protect the right to vote for minorities, and settle financial claims made by Japanese Americans because of their treatment throughout the war. He also urged more self-governance for the territories, which led to Americans 49th and 50th states, Alaska and Hawaii, to be admitted to the union on August 21, 1959.

Further problems began to develop on the party's other dissatisfied wing. Progressive Democrats held their own nominating convention, and selected Henry Wallace, Roosevelt's former Vice President and Truman's former Secretary of Commerce, to be their candidate for President, while Senator Glen Taylor of Idaho would serve as his running mate. African Americans were present and played a major role in the convention, as did hundreds of women. One positive sign for Truman was

Wallace's ready acceptance of communist support, although he himself was not a communist sympathizer. Their platform rejected almost all of President Truman's foreign policy initiatives, particularly his confrontational attitude towards the Soviet Union, while Wallace placed the blame on America for all of the world's present problems. Although Wallace's Progressive Party was yet another opponent for Truman's Democrats, the nature of the party's support and its foreign policy agenda ensured that Wallace would remain marginalized. Wallace and his allies appeared to be in favor of finding a peace with the Russians at any price, and this policy was far outside of the mainstream in American politics.

Back in Washington, Truman was bombarded with further news of the growing crisis in Berlin. Supplies were being flown into the city in more than one hundred daily deliveries, while planes landed in as little as four minutes after the last one. After meeting with Cabinet members, Truman once again declared that he had no intention of pulling out of Berlin. The future of the continent, and of Truman's Presidency, was at stake in Stalin's high stakes Cold War games. There was a significant fear, however, that the stalemate might turn into a war if Stalin grew too impatient with Truman's tactics.

Despite the apparent success of the Berlin airlift, there were still too few supplies being flown into the city, and even more would be needed as the cold weather approached. Truman's advisors informed him that Berliners would be with the West every step of the way, all of them loathing the possibility of falling under Soviet control. To better help the people of Berlin, Truman ordered that even more of America's air force be redirected from other parts of the world to increase supplies being flown into the city. More landing areas would have to be cleared in Berlin, and the people of the city happily obliged, working day and night to clear more area for pilots to land. Come hell or high water, Truman was determined to have American forces remain in Berlin.

Truman's robust attitude towards the Soviet Union in the face of the Berlin crisis was well received by voters across the country. His decisions were now being seen as strong and decisive, and, although he had yet to experience a bump in the polls, Truman and his campaign aides were happy with the positive publicity, and began to feel some political momentum. The President did note, however, that the burden of the Presidency coupled with the need to campaign for re-election was incredibly taxing. Voters were to go to the polls during a very turbulent period in international relations.

An important meeting was organized at the White House for July 21 to allow members of the administration to confer with the Joint Chiefs of Staff over the possibility of handing control of the nation's nuclear weapons over to the military. Truman, who had always supported the idea of civilians remaining in control of the nuclear program, entered the meeting incredibly skeptical. Representatives from the military argued that because they would be the ones to actually employ the use of nuclear weapons, they should be the ones to have custody over them. David Lilienthal, Truman's appointee to head the United States Atomic Energy Commission, rebutted the military's argument by suggesting that the President alone should have authority over the weapons, and that it was dangerous to have anyone else play that role.

In a rather candid moment, Truman admitted that he hoped never to have to order the use of a nuclear bomb again. He believed that the weapons should only be used if the situation demanded them as an absolute necessity. While members of the military argued that they should be in control of the weapons because they would be the ones to deal with them, Truman felt that these weapons should never have to be used in the first place. Thus, the military should have no pressing need to have custody over them. As Truman argued, a nuclear bomb was not just another weapon. It had the ability to annihilate of hundreds of thousands of people.

While America had still been at war with Japan, Truman had been far more willing to accept the idea of a nuclear weapon simply being a military tool. But once one had been used, and the President was able to see the full extent of the danger of such a weapon, he had reconsidered. Even the government's top military and scientific advisors at the time had greatly underestimated the extent of the damage a nuclear weapon could inflict. Hundreds of thousands of women and children, the elderly and the sick, had perished. For Truman, it was time for the military to stop treating a nuclear bomb as a weapon like any other.

While the meeting broke up without any firm decisions, Truman met with his Secretary of Defense, James Forrestal, two days later. Against the wishes of Forrestal and those in the military establishment, Truman was absolutely convinced that nuclear weapons would have to remain under civilian control. Lilienthal would therefore continue to lead the Atomic Energy Agency that was tasked with doing just that.

Republican and Democratic lawmakers returned to Washington on July 26 to open the special congressional session that Truman had called for. But before the lawmakers had even begun their work or meet with their colleagues, Truman issued a surprising executive order to end racial discrimination in the military, and another one to end such practices in government hiring and personnel management. The President was once again infuriating his southern Democratic colleagues who championed segregation.

Truman delivered a speech to Congress on July 27 outlining the numerous goals that he wanted the special session to address: civil rights reform, credit controls, a profits tax, rent and price controls, education funding, support for farmers, a higher minimum wage, and a modified version of the discriminatory Displaced Persons Act. While Thomas Dewey encouraged his Republican colleagues in Congress to think seriously about the President's proposals, the party's congressional leaders had no intention of supporting the President's initiatives, despite the fact that many of them had been mentioned in the Republican platform.

Congress was in session for only two weeks, and its members accomplished nothing in furthering Truman's program. Truman had known all along that no action would be taken, but it demonstrated the hypocrisy of the Republican platform. His opponents made token gestures to support important welfare initiatives, but Republicans, Truman claimed, were only trying to fool American voters. They were still the party of the wealthy and special interests, and the party's members of Congress had clearly demonstrated that reality.

In speaking to reporters after Congress had departed from Washington, one reporter asked President Truman if he thought the eightieth Congress had been a "do-nothing" Congress. Truman agreed, and later realized that he had found the ideal campaign slogan for attacking his Republican opponents. The Republican Congress, Truman would charge, was the "do-nothing Congress."

Chapter Seven

The Final Stretch

After the special session of Congress had achieved virtually nothing in the two weeks members spent in Washington, politicians returned home to their districts to begin their campaign for re-election. Truman decided that he too would finally depart from Washington and undertake his first official campaign tour. The one in the late spring had not officially been part of his campaigning, but it certainly gave him valuable insight into the realities of pursuing votes across the country. This time Truman was convinced that he was ready to go.

Only days before Truman's departure, a scandal erupted in Washington. The House of Representatives had formed a Special Committee to investigate Un-American Activities. It was essentially a committee tasked with investigating signs of Communism among government officials and important national figures. On August 4, Time Magazine's editor in chief, Whittaker Chambers, testified before the Committee and charged that Alger Hiss, who had been a member of both the Roosevelt and Truman administrations, and was deeply involved in the formation of the United Nations, was a communist. Chambers, himself a former member of the Communist Party, was alleged to have been a high ranking communist official within the United States. The fact that

Hiss had served in government, and at the State Department, for over fourteen years led to an eruption of hysteria across the country. For his part, President Truman tried to stay away from the controversy, calling the investigation a Republican red herring that was meant to distract Americans from the important issues of the election campaign. If that was true, the Republicans were certainly successful in that regard.

Harry Truman left Washington on a private railway car to tour across the country. President Roosevelt had the car refurnished to Presidential standards when he campaigned across the country during his final years in office. It was fitted with the Presidential Seal on the outside for supporters to see while the President was en route to his next destination. The car was more than luxurious, with bedrooms for the President and his guests, and a private washroom with a working bath and separate shower.

Truman was thrilled. He had always loved trains when he was growing up in Missouri, and was more than happy to be living in one while barnstorming across the nation. Incidentally, it was the same railway car that Churchill had stayed in while the two men traveled to Missouri for the former Prime Minister to deliver his infamous "iron curtain" speech. The President departed on September 17 for what would prove to be a nearly twenty two thousand mile campaign trip, by far the most substantial effort undertaken by an incumbent President to campaign for re-election.

After sustaining beatings from the press and his opponents in Washington that had led to his thirty six percent approval rating, Truman was determined to interact with American voters and make his case without being analysed by the media or attacked by opposition commentators. Voters across the country doubted that Truman could recapture the White House, but Truman set off a thirty three day whirlwind tour to try to prove them wrong. Despite his rather advanced age of 64, Truman was as robust as ever. He had always relished campaigning and interacting with voters, and he would once again finally have his chance to do so.

Truman left Washington through Union Station, bringing along with him a number of aides and his daughter Margaret. Bess would join them several days later. Almost fifty reporters came along with the President on his tour. Truman's running mate, Senator Barkley of Kentucky, was at Union Station to see the President off as well. As he boarded the train to leave Washington, Truman pledged to his supporters that he was "going to give 'em hell!" The remark would prove to be one of the most prominent slogans of the President's campaign.

Truman knew that he would have to work incredibly hard if he had even a chance of returning to the White House. He was relatively unpopular across the country, and voters were ready for a change after sixteen years of a Democrat in the Oval Office. Two factions of the Democratic Party, northern progressives and southern segregationists, were running their own separate tickets. Most of all, Governor Dewey was popular and well respected by many across the country. Public opinion pollsters announced before Truman had even left Washington that they were suspending their operations. For many in the industry, the outcome seemed almost inevitable.

Despite the negative predictions, Truman found that an incredible amount of supporters came to greet him at nearly every stop his campaign tour made. As Truman crossed through Iowa, a traditionally Republican state, crowds turned out to greet Truman in the thousands. In Dexter, Iowa, Truman stopped to make a speech to the region's farmers. He reminded them of the situation farmers had been in the last time the Republicans occupied the White House. Truman argued that during the Great Depression more than two hundred thousand farmers had lost their farms, and all of their savings, because of Republican misrule. It was the Democratic Party that had been working for a decade and a half to restore adequate welfare for farmers across the country. The Republicans, members of the party of special privilege, would undo that progress, and the eightieth Congress had already begun to do so. Farmers did not need to vote for him, Truman declared, but rather they should vote for themselves, and that meant keeping a Democrat in the White House. In 1946 voters had stayed home and they were stuck with the eightieth Congress. Truman called on them to show up at the polls and fix the mistake that voters made two years earlier.

Truman made nine stops across Iowa in a single day, and spoke to local farmers about their experiences and his days on the farm before he had entered politics. According to the Des Moines Register, the crowd at each stop amounted to a higher number of people than the population of the towns themselves. Moreover, unlike Thomas Dewey, Truman had a real feel for rural America. He was the one who would represent farmers in Washington because he had been one himself.

Truman toured Missouri on the following day, and spent the day after that visiting his friends and family in Independence. By the end of the day Truman's train had departed once again, this time to Kansas. Once he got to Colorado, the President told his supporters that Republicans in Washington were not the same kind of people as their Republican neighbors. Most Republicans were nice people, but the policies of the party itself were very different. Once Republicans get into power, Truman argued, they ignore the needs and the wishes of the American people. They become corrupted by special interests and big businesses, and have little regard for the voters who elected them to their offices. Truman almost always spoke with few or no written out talking points, preferring to connect with voters directly rather than delivering the same speech at dozens of stops across the country.

Truman left Colorado and went through Utah and Nevada, calling on Americans not to let Republicans take the nation backwards. In California he lambasted the "do-nothing" Congress, and blamed the state for electing Republicans to

Congress and the Governor's residence. Voters, Truman declared, are the government, and no polling group or newspaper column could make it otherwise. Truman would only lose if voters wanted a Republican government, but that would mean undoing all of the New Deal progress that had been made under Democratic leadership. The people, rather than special interest groups, should remain in firm control of the government.

After promising Senator Barkley that he would give the Republicans hell on the campaign trail, supporters at almost every stop Truman's tour made yelled "give 'em hell Harry!" The President attacked Republicans for their inaction on high prices, their lack of support for western states and infrastructure projects, their tax cut for the wealthy, and their disdain for the progress made through New Deal policies. Across the nation, Truman found the most traction when he spoke to voters of the negative actions Congress had taken since Republicans had come to power. Voters, he claimed, could fix all that in November.

Another frequent theme during Truman's cross country tour was his consistency. While Republicans promised voters in their platform things they had opposed in Congress, voters, Truman declared, would always know where he stood. In his classic rural Missourian accent, the President declared that Americans "don't get any double talk from me." Nonetheless, despite his claims, voters need only to have looked back to Truman's wavering on the Palestinian issue to see that the Truman administration was not necessarily always consistent. Despite the facts, however, it was a very powerful message for the Truman campaign to be delivering across the nation: Republicans could not be trusted to keep their electoral commitments.

The President sought to frame the election campaign around one central theme: Republicans favored special interests while the Democratic Party was the people's party. This explained why the "do-nothing" Congress had never acted on its supposed support for a strengthened welfare state, and why Governor Dewey failed to campaign on specific issues. Americans ended up with a Congress that failed to respond to the people's needs because they allowed the Republicans to take control of the legislative branch. Truman warned them that this time the stakes were even higher. Should they win the Presidency, Republicans would surely dismantle the central tenants of President Roosevelt's New Deal.

As Truman traveled the nation, his wife Bess and daughter Margaret were frequently seen with the President as he campaigned at various events. Americans were able to see Truman as a family man, one who was deeply devoted to his wife and daughter. Truman's passion impressed even those who disagreed with him: Americans had not seen a sitting President campaign so forcefully in decades, perhaps not even in the nation's entire history. Most importantly, Truman came across to many Americans as their representative in the White House in a way President Roosevelt never had. Truman had never been wealthy or highly educated. He was just an ordinary man, one who graduated high school, served in the military during World War One, and farmed for a living. He did not go to a prestigious post-secondary institution like Harvard, as Franklin Roosevelt had. He was not a philosopher or a university professor, as was one of his favorite Presidents, Woodrow Wilson. Truman was the people's President. Unlike Governor Dewey, his Republican opponent, he was not a member of the upper class, nor had he ever had a job as prominent as a district attorney before becoming a Senator. Truman's image as an everyday American was perhaps his most significant asset during the campaign.

Once he arrived back in Los Angeles, California, Truman was met with wholehearted support from an actor and future Republican President, Ronald Reagan. Reagan, who had been an ardent Democrat and remained so until the early 1960s, would hold President Truman in high regard for the rest of his life. Together with other Hollywood stars, Reagan joined Truman in condemning the Wallace Progressive campaign. They warned wavering Democrats not to associate themselves with a party that was sympathetic to the Communists. A vote for Secretary Wallace would be a vote in favor of Communist forces around the world. Even worse, supporting Wallace would essentially mean electing a Republican President.

From Los Angeles, Truman continued south on his tour of California, stopping in San Diego, where he was greeted by thousands of supporters. The President's tour car then made the turn to head back east to reach out to voters in several more important swing states. As his tour went along, Truman made sure that his speechwriters include some campaign promises to play to more local issues.

As Truman continued on his cross country journey, Governor Dewey was making a similar, albeit much shorter, trip. His campaign was convinced that the Republicans would win in November, so Dewey acted as the front runner and made far fewer speeches and held far fewer campaign rallies than President Truman did. Even reporters believed that Dewey's win was set in stone, and they therefore decided to cover the Dewey campaign much more than the President's. Dewey was so confident about his chances of winning the White House that he named his campaign train the "Dewey Victory Express." The Republican campaign theme focused on national unity and reliable government. They rarely attacked or even spoke of Truman and their Democratic opponents, nor did they cater to the needs of specific sectors of voters in the way Truman did. Dewey made no effort to reach out to farmers or factory workers, preferring to run one national campaign rather than playing to regional issues. This decision was perhaps the biggest blunder of the Dewey campaign effort.

Truman was in many ways helped by Henry Wallace's association with Communist sympathizers, and his surprise decision to spend time campaigning in the segregated south, where Wallace's Progressive ticket had no chance of gaining significant support. He promised substantial action on civil rights reform that was far more ambitious than Truman's proposals, which angered southern Democrats, and also pledged to end the Cold War by negotiating with the Stalin regime, another unpopular point with many American voters. Even worse, Wallace, a long-time member of the Democratic Party, further alienated voters by claiming that Truman was no better than his Republican opponent. Liberal voters may have had a few quarrels with Truman, but Wallace underestimated just how desperate even his own supporters would be to keep Truman in the White House. Ultimately, the Progressive ticket failed to win any electoral votes.

Strom Thurmond's campaign would prove to be far more effective than Wallace's, but its success was substantially regionalized. On election night, Thurmond's Dixiecrats would win Alabama, Louisiana, Mississippi, and South Carolina, all states won by the Roosevelt-Truman ticket in 1944. But he too alienated many supporters by claiming that Truman's new policies and his support for civil rights reform was communist in nature, and Thurmond was far too overconfident about his appeal in the south. Governor Thurmond would even fail to carry Georgia, which was in the heart of the area he saw as winnable. Unlike his advisors, President Truman worried little about the harm Thurmond would do to his chances of winning in November. He was far more concerned about winning the farmer vote, and carrying big states like California and Ohio.

As Dewey's campaign continued, he refused to attack the President or any Democratic opponents. Four years earlier, Dewey had traveled the nation lambasting the record of the Roosevelt administration. He had been fiery and passionate. This time the Governor of New York chose the play it safe, and that decision would cost him dearly in November. The Dewey campaign in 1944 had attacked Roosevelt for a sluggish economy in the pre-war years, and America's lack of military preparedness in the aftermath of Pearl Harbor. He even accused the Roosevelt administration of being composed of Communists and Communist sympathizers, and the Hiss fiasco had proven that Dewey was at least somewhat correct. The Truman record certainly had weak points for the President's opponent to attack, but Dewey was having none of it. His advisors told the Governor that the campaign was already won, and all he had to do was not say something that might damage his substantial lead over the President. Dewey took that advice, therefore launching a dull campaign full of positive and vague messaging rather than confronting Truman's blistering attacks. His advisors had even convinced the Governor that the reason Dewey lost in 1944 was his attack oriented campaign. Thus, Dewey's inner circle became convinced that silence would be surest way to victory in November.

Although President Truman was eighteen years older than his Republican opponent, he had always looked younger than his age. Moreover, unlike Governor Dewey, Truman appeared crisp and energetic on the campaign trail. The President never felt better than when he was on the road talking to citizens across the country. Dewey, on the other hand, was cold and reserved, by no means comfortable while mingling with voters. He never appeared to be passionate or combative. Even his mustache made him look more distant and formalized.

Another point that worked in Truman's favor was that his opponent supported virtually all of his initiatives. Dewey supported the basic principles of the New Deal, aid to Europe through the Marshall Plan, the backing of Israel, a stronger national defense, and movement on civil rights. The only difference between the two candidates appeared to be their personalities. As voters began to get to know the two candidates, nearly everyone found Truman much more likeable. Dewey, so convinced that he would win, began worrying about the state in which Democrats might leave the White House when he took office, and spent little time trying to relate to everyday American voters or get them to warm to his personality.

Despite Dewey's relative silence, Republicans were still able to leak damaging reports about the Truman White House and its allies. Because the President had little patience with the FBI's dirty tactics, which Roosevelt had appeared to embrace, J. Edgar Hoover covertly supplied Dewey with reports that would embarrass the Truman campaign, as Hoover hoped to once again have an ally in the White House come next January. According to some witnesses and historians, Hoover expected a promotion with Dewey in the Oval Office, hoping for the job of Attorney General. Hoover's aides began to dig up dirt on Truman's past associations with the legendary Prendergast family in Missouri, and detailed the possible members of the administration who might have connections to Communists.

The one area in which Dewey was willing to go on the offensive was Communism. In California, the Republican Presidential candidate declared that Communism was gaining steam across the country. Dewey even accused the Truman administration of willingly encouraging a Communist revolution. But Dewey began to notice that his crowds were nowhere near as big as Truman's, and his advisors began to have second thoughts about his relatively relaxed campaign.

Truman made his way into Texas on September 26, a state many were convinced he would find little support in despite its history of being a Democratic stronghold for decades. He first traveled to meet with John Nance Garner, who had served as Franklin Roosevelt's Vice President during Roosevelt's first two terms in the White House, at his ranch in Uvalde. There they were joined by Sam Rayburn, the former Democratic Speaker of the House of Representatives, and the state's Democratic Governor, Beauford Jester. Together, the four men boarded Truman's campaign train and traveled across the country's second largest state. All three of the native Texans were very popular in Texas, and their wholehearted support of the Truman campaign reinvigorated the President's chances in the south. At one point, Lyndon Johnson, then running for a first term in the United States Senate, joined the Presidential tour.

Although most Texans supported segregationist policies just as much as voters in other southern states that supported Governor Thurmond did, Democratic officials were quite popular in the state, and the influence of Garner, Rayburn, and Jester combined was extraordinary. Truman declared that his friendship with Garner had lasted more than a decade, and would endure even if he lost the White House. Truman suggested that, much to the pleasure of the crowds that met him in Texas, he might even return for a vacation. Just as Garner had remained loyal to Truman despite their policy differences, the President asked Texans to remain loyal to the Democratic Party. They could not afford to risk having a Republican from the northeast in White House, someone who knew nothing about rural and southern values.

In San Antonio, Truman spoke to a crowd of more than two hundred thousand patrons and called himself a humble servant of the people. The President dazzled supporters with a speech that attacked the Soviet Union and the unfree world more than his opponents.

> I am the Chief Executive of the greatest nation in the world, the highest honor that can ever come to a man on earth. But I am the servant of the people of the United States. They are not my servants. I can't order you around, or send you to labor camps or have your heads cut off if you don't agree with me politically. We don't believe in that.

At a speech in Dallas on September 27, Truman attacked the Dewey campaign for disregarding the issues that Americans were confronting in their everyday lives. Dewey and his Republican supporters would only talk about unity and grand principles as a way of disguising their destructive agenda that the party would implement when Dewey took over the White House. Moreover, unity was only worth fighting for if the nation was unified on sound principles. Truman alleged that there could be no national unity that favored tax breaks for the wealthy or less support for low income housing. Unlike Dewey, Truman believed that there were principles that had to be fought for. A government that does not fight for the principles that the American people deserve is nothing more than bad government. The first civil right of any citizen is the right to be protected from greed and corruption. If the government did not fight on behalf of the little guy, Truman declared, society would be dominated by a narrow Republican elite who fought only in the interest of themselves. Without President Truman at the helm, no one would be left in Washington to fight on behalf of what he liked to call "the folks." If the American people wanted to find their champion in Washington, the President declared that they needed to look no further than Harry Truman.

Truman's campaign made a swing through Oklahoma on its way out of Texas, and over a hundred thousand people came to hear the President speak in Oklahoma City. He accused the Republicans of using the smokescreen of Communism to distract voters from the real issues of the campaign, and to try to avoid talking about the record of the eightieth Congress, which had failed to pass the laws needed by the American people. As the man behind the Truman Doctrine, the President had done more to fight Communism than any Republican. It was because of Truman that Communism had not spread to Western Europe, and under his leadership the administration's containment plan was working.

After leaving Oklahoma, Truman's campaign made quick stops in Missouri, Illinois, and Indiana before reaching Kentucky, where the President met up with his Vice Presidential candidate, Alben Barkley. Together, they barnstormed around Kentucky and went on to West Virginia, a traditional Democratic stronghold, all within three days. Many in the media painted the Truman campaign as desperate, and it was. But Harry Truman was convinced that he could win the election, and the massive crowds that greeted him around the country seemed to suggest that he had a good chance of doing so. Many reporters simply speculated that the turnout was simply due to the fact that he was the sitting President of the United States of America, but others began to sense that the momentum was moving to Truman's side.

The President returned to Washington on October 2, only fifteen days after he had departed for his whirlwind tour. He had made more than one hundred and forty stops, and intended to leave Washington only days later for another campaign trip. His re-election effort was unprecedented at the national level, as was his combative campaign style. Democratic Party aides had also been astute in ensuring copies of Truman's speeches could be translated and made available to immigrants in urban centers who had not yet mastered the English language. Nevertheless, the party was continuously hobbled in its efforts by a lack of funding support. Because nearly everyone thought that a Dewey win was inevitable, few were donating to the Democratic Party and the Truman campaign. Nonetheless, Democratic leaders even went so far as to release a short booklet to serve as the President's biography to emphasize his humble roots.

Besides meeting the Truman train in Kentucky, Senator Barkley toured across the country relentlessly, and was the first candidate to do so by air. Already in his early seventies, Barkley flew to more than two hundred and fifty destinations to make speeches, often in small towns and to intimate groups. He especially focused on reaching out to voters who were less well off, and those in rural communities. Barkley, like Truman, emphasized the benefits rural voters and those in lower classes had received on the initiative of the Roosevelt and Truman administrations, and warned them of the danger of a Republican takeover of the White House. Despite his advanced age, Senator Barkley prove to be a significant asset to the Truman campaign.

Although the Dewey campaign was the first to do make their own video, President Truman's campaign produced a ten minute short film that would be shown in movie theaters across the country. The Dewey campaign paid for an expensive filming process with professional workers, while Truman made his pitch for virtually no cost whatsoever, having his aides do all the work. Despite its hasty completion, Truman's campaign team produced a very compelling piece. Truman was portrayed as an everyday American, but the movie also highlighted the triumphs of his Presidency, such as the Marshall Plan, the Truman Doctrine, the winning of World War Two, and images of the President in the Oval Office. Reporters at the time compared the two and suggested that Dewey's was far too boring and made him look aloof, while the hastily composed Truman version was said to make quite an impression on voters, many of whom saw movies on a regular basis.

One of the biggest blunders of the Truman campaign came on October 3. Back in Washington, the President was convinced by his junior advisors to send Chief Justice Vinson to the Soviet Union to initiate peace negotiations, which they felt would play to the electorate. When Truman agreed and Vinson was summoned to the White House, he asked the Chief Justice to depart for the Soviet Union, despite the fact that the President had not even consulted his Secretary of State. Vinson protested, telling the President that such a role was improper for a member of the judicial branch, especially during an election campaign. But Vinson owed his place on the bench to the President, and he reluctantly agreed to go.

Truman decided to tell the State Department to prepare for the trip, but he had still not directly consulted General Marshall. Most in the White House believed that the President was destined for defeat unless the administration did something dramatic. A successful trip to the Soviet Union by Vinson, a man generally held in high regard, could play well with the electorate.

The President finally informed Marshall of the trip over the phone on October 5. The Secretary of State, who was then in Europe, was understandably irate that the President had made the decision unilaterally, and he furthermore argued that the entire plan would backfire to the detriment of the administration. When the President decided to call the trip off after Marshall's vehement opposition, the original plans were nonetheless leaked to the press. Truman recognized that his judgement had been very wrong, but his critics charged that he was playing politics with foreign policy, and even suggested that the idea signaled the administration's Communist sympathies. Governor Dewey was also astonished, and hoped that the President would not make any more major mistakes until he assumed the Presidency.

General Marshall returned from conferences in Europe on October 9, and immediately submitted his resignation to the President. The two men respected each other, but Marshall was already in his late sixties and exhausted from a long career in the military and public service. The General claimed that he was prepared to take the blame for Truman's actions, but the President believed that the whole scandal would have little life after a few days. Truman asked Marshall to remain as Secretary of State until his first term was completed and the election had been decided. The General readily agreed.

The day after Marshall's return, Truman boarded his Presidential train for another whistle stop tour that would span the final three weeks of the campaign. He immediately headed for Ohio, a crucial swing state that the Democratic ticket badly needed to win if Truman was to remain in the White House. Many Republicans felt that Dewey would win the state in a landslide. Ohio had a Republican Governor, and its two United States Senators were prominent leaders in the Republican Party, including Robert Taft. The vast majority of its representatives in the House were also Republicans. Dewey had even won the state in 1944, besting President Roosevelt by a narrow margin. Nonetheless, Truman was convinced that he had a chance to win the state, and toured more than a dozen small towns, making eleven speeches on October 11 alone. He relentlessly attacked the Republican "do-nothing" Congress, and fully embraced Roosevelt's New Deal, which he claimed put the interests of the average citizen above those of privilege and special interests. His speeches to Ohioans were unique at every stop, reminding voters that prosperity had not simply come on a whim, but rather because of the actions taken by Democrats in Washington. Ultimately, Truman would meet more than one hundred thousand voters across the state in a single day.

In Willard, Ohio, the President spoke of his gratitude for having received a chance to serve the American people. This election was crucial, because it would help to determine the future of freedom in the world, and the future of the economy at home. People in government should place their faith in the people, and Republicans did the opposite. Truman had tried to keep the faith with the American people, but the eightieth Congress had stood in his way. Dewey and his Republican friends in Washington did not trust the people, and that was the inherent problem with the Republican Party as a whole. Finally, unlike Governor Dewey, Americans knew where Truman stood, and, whether voters agreed with him or not, they would always know his policy priorities and his agenda that he would take to Washington.

The President then left Ohio for Indiana, another important state just west of its Buckeye neighbor. The campaign also made a swing through four towns in Illinois, including in Springfield, where Truman spoke of President Lincoln's legacy. Abraham Lincoln, the President declared, would be ashamed of where his Republican Party had been taken in the previous few decades. Lincoln's Republican Party had been a party of the people, and yet Republicans in 1948 were just the party of special interests.

Truman then departed for a handful of populous and important Midwestern states, including Wisconsin and Minnesota, where he met with Hubert Humphrey, then the mayor of Minneapolis, the state's largest city.

With three weeks left in the campaign, Newsweek magazine had already written off the Democratic Party's chances of winning on Election Day. Its writers all declared that Truman would lose to Dewey, likely in a landslide, and that the Republicans would remain firmly in control of both houses of Congress. But the Dewey campaign was beginning to worry, as was the candidate himself. When Harry Truman made a speech in Saint Paul, Minnesota, which Republicans considered to be a very winnable state, he drew a crowd of more than twenty thousand people. Days later, Dewey's crowd was less than half of that. Advisors from across the Midwestern region were warning Dewey that he was beginning to lose the farm vote. Nonetheless, the Dewey campaign continued their defensive frontrunner strategy. There was a lot within Truman's record to attack, and many of his barbs against the Republican campaign could have been similarly applied to the President's Democratic allies. In just one example, multiple members of the Truman administration came directly from firms on Wall Street, certainly not the people's party message he was trying to deliver to voters. As Dewey saw his lead dwindling, which according to Gallup had fallen to six points, he failed to take adequate action to stem the tide. Newspaper after newspaper endorsed the Republican ticket, and even those in the press were convinced that Dewey could win by keeping to his message. Evidently, they were proven to be entirely wrong.

As Truman's crowds began to grow, the President became even more confident in his chances to retake the White House on November 2. The situation in Berlin was improving, and the Vinson fiasco had been largely forgotten. On October 21, more than two hundred thousand people showed up in Miami to greet the President, and his appearance in North Carolina garnered a similar reception at a subsequent stop. In Miami, Truman took the time to try to address foreign policy, and told voters of his desire to try to eliminate some of the distrust between the Soviet Union and the United States. It was a thoughtful speech, and one of the only times the President mentioned foreign policy throughout the campaign, firm in the belief that foreign affairs should be dealt with in a bipartisan matter.

The best sign of the President's improving fortunes was the size of the crowd that greeted Truman when he arrived in Chicago. President Roosevelt, who had hailed from nearby New York, was always greeted by a sizable audience of supporters, but he had never experienced such a major swell of public support. More than half a million Americans lined up in front of Truman's parade route, and nearly twenty four thousand attended a public rally with the President. In a powerful but outrageous speech, he declared that voting for Dewey meant voting for fascism. Dewey was understandably offended, but he was once again told by his advisors to turn the other cheek and not risk his chances of victory by descending into a game of dirty politics. Truman then made his way to Boston, where two hundred and fifty thousand people greeted him with a parade and thunderous applause. Days later, after stopping in cities throughout various Eastern states, Truman made his way to New York, Dewey's home state, where he was greeted by more than a million New Yorkers in New York City on October 28. In just one day, Truman delivered five speeches across the city, and was joined by old Democratic Party stalwarts, including Harold Ickes, who had departed from Truman's Cabinet on relatively poor terms. But, friend or foe, Democrats across the country began to pull out all the stops to ensure a Truman victory.

The next day was no different. Yet again, well over a million people turned out to support the President as he continued his tour of New York City. In Harlem, Truman was met by thousands of African Americans who were supporting his cause, and he made a passionate speech on the issue of civil rights. The campaign then departed for St. Louis in the President's home state of Missouri. Truman attacked the Republican Congress, and what he regarded as a biased press, the vast majority of whom had already written the President's chances off completely. Truman declared that only the people could defeat the President, and on November 2 they would do no such thing. Unlike nearly everyone in his campaign, Truman was all but certain that he would emerge victorious. Gallup had Truman down by five points in the polls, and the New York Times even suggested that Dewey would win three hundred and fifty five electoral votes, well over the two hundred and sixty six needed for a win. The press had already even begun to speculate about what Dewey might do on his first day in office once he assumed the Presidency on January 20.

As Truman's campaign train departed from St. Louis to bring the President back to his hometown of Independence, the momentum was clearly on his side, but many still believed the President was simply too far behind. Nonetheless, Truman had given the campaign as much effort as he could have, traveling over thirty one thousand miles and making three hundred and fifty six whistle stops along the way.

Chapter Eight

A New Mandate

President Truman returned home for Halloween, and chose to remain in Independence for the last few days of the campaign. He did make one radio address to the nation on November 1, thanking the American people for the privilege of being able to serve as their Commander in Chief for the previous four years. On the morning of the election, Truman woke up especially early to get to the polls, voting with his wife Bess and daughter Margaret at his side. Truman's warm reception across the country, and his opportunity to meet millions of supporters, had convinced the President that his chances of re-election were much higher than anyone in the press predicted.

Tired of all the attention, Truman snuck out to a hotel for the afternoon of November 2, even as people began to gather in front of his home in Independence. As he listened to the radio from the hotel that evening, Truman learned that Dewey was well ahead of him in New York and Pennsylvania, but that the President was leading in the overall popular vote nationwide. The President decided to go to sleep at 9pm, and told his staff to wake him when something definitive had been declared. Back at Truman's house, hundreds of supporters and members of the press were waiting for the President to come out and greet them. But Truman had already decided to stay out of the limelight.

By 11pm central standard time, Truman was still ahead in the popular vote, and the Dewey campaign began to worry. Margaret announced to reporters that she didn't know where her father was, despite the fact that he now appeared to be almost one million votes ahead of his Republican opponent. Truman woke himself at midnight to check in on the returns. Despite the fact that the President was more than a million votes ahead of Dewey, radio correspondents were still predicting a comfortable victory for the Governor of New York. Truman's aides woke him again at four in the morning to announce that the President would be spending another four years in the White House. Truman was then ahead by two million votes, and decided to depart for Kansas City to celebrate with his supporters.

Despite trailing in important swing states such as New York and Pennsylvania, Truman was leading across the south, except for four states that had gone to Thurmond, and in California, Ohio, Illinois, and Wisconsin. The President was winning the three most crucial swing states quite narrowly, edging out Dewey by less than thirty three thousand votes in California, Ohio, and Illinois. Nonetheless, Harry Truman had proved all of the pundits wrong, and won a campaign that virtually no one had predicted would go his way. After the final results were in, the contest in the Electoral College wasn't even close. Just before 9am on November 3, it was announced that Truman had officially won Ohio. After securing that crucial swing state, the election was effectively over. Truman had won, and Dewey would be forced to concede defeat. Less than an hour later, Truman officially won California, followed by Illinois. To make matters even better, the Democrats had retaken both houses of Congress, providing the President with a legislative branch that would be ready to push his agenda forward when they returned to Washington in January. Just after 11am in New York City, Governor Dewey officially conceded the election, and Truman was greeted by elated supporters in Kansas City. The Democratic campaign was so successful that the Truman-Barkley ticket won Texas, a state many thought they would lose, by a resounding forty percentage points. The Democratic ticket had won twenty eight states, while their Republican rivals only managed to win sixteen.

People across the country were stunned by the Truman victory, as the press and Republicans had been preparing the nation for months in anticipation of a Dewey Presidency. But Truman had found support across the nation, winning easily with three hundred and three electoral votes, all gained by carrying twenty eight states. He won the support of visible minorities across the country, and held on to Democratic support out west. His ability to win over farmers across the Midwest was also essential to the President's re-election. Truman's Republican opponent was left with only one hundred and eighty nine electoral votes, and Thurmond's Dixiecrats garnered thirty nine. Henry Wallace failed to win even one state, as Truman had clearly managed to win progressive voters over to support his cause.

In the race for Congress, Democrats had retaken the House of Representatives by an overwhelming margin, beating the Republicans by nearly one hundred seats. Even in the Senate, only a third of which was up for re-election, the Democrats gained nine seats and easily retook the majority. Truman's victory had ultimately led to an even larger victory for members of his party across the country. The press had predicted Republican gains in both houses, but they were once again proven wrong. The success of Democratic candidates in the House, Senate, and in gubernatorial races helped to lift the Presidential ticket. Popular Democratic governors seeking re-election outpolled Truman in many states, but their support for the President proved to be a critical factor.

Truman beat Dewey by five percentage points in the popular vote total, and even won the state of Iowa, which was at the time considered to be the safest Republican state in the nation. The President had even come within sixty one thousand votes of winning New York, Dewey's home state. Members of the press immediately began to ponder just how wrong Dewey's decision to run a very defensive campaign had been. In the future, Dewey's relaxed and even keel style of campaigning would never again have a place in Presidential politics for a non-incumbent. Republican leaders in Congress all attributed the poor showing to Dewey's uninspiring campaign, although Senator Vandenberg did ultimately complement Truman on his well-run re-election effort. Others attributed the loss to Truman's ability to pivot the campaign away from the record of his administration, and towards a confrontation over the eightieth "do-nothing" Congress. Truman's advisors even suggested that the success in the Berlin airlift had translated into more support among voters, although voters rarely choose candidates based on foreign policy alone.

In perhaps one of the most iconic political pictures of the twentieth century, President Truman looked delighted as he posed with a copy of the Chicago Daily Tribune that was distributed on the day after the election. The paper's editor, generally recognized as a loyal Republican, had been so sure of a Dewey victory that he had the printers create a "Dewey Defeats Truman" banner on newspaper's front page, despite the fact that national results were not yet known at the time of the paper's printing. The headline is so iconic because it truly encapsulates the reaction of millions of Americans across the country who expected the prediction to hold true, and the full extent of Truman's triumphant underdog victory. Truman, smiling happily, exclaimed to enamored supporters to not "believe everything you read in the papers." The pollsters had also been proven to be very wrong, something many later reflected to be a healthy thing for a vibrant democracy.

The American people ultimately chose to send a brilliant campaigner, and a man they saw as someone who truly understood the everyday problems that faced so many citizens, back to the

White House for another four years. The 1948 election campaign was to be Truman's last, but it was also the campaign in which he worked the hardest. No one had been more active or energetic than President Truman throughout the course of the campaign, despite the fact that he was already sixty four years of age. Many attributed the win to Truman himself, and he does deserve much of the credit. Nonetheless, he was certainly helped by Dewey's lackluster performance throughout the campaign.

Sam Rayburn, who would once again become the Democratic Speaker of the House, attributed the Democratic wave in the House of Representatives and Senate as a personal triumph for the President. Moreover, after such a hard fought campaign, Truman, for the first time, would serve as a President who had been fully endorsed by the people. Four years before, the victory had been all about Franklin Roosevelt. This time it was all about Harry Truman, and his personal courage during the campaign had surpassed that of any candidate in modern American history.

Truman made his way back to Washington on November 5, and was greeted by a crowd of more than seven hundred and fifty thousand people who wanted to welcome the President back home. The Truman family rode in an open car with the Barkley clan, despite the fact that it was a rather cool day in November. On the front lawn at the White House, Truman made his way outside to thank the American people for rewarding him with another four years of public service. He also told supporters that he would do everything in his power to make sure that the following four years were a time of peace and prosperity. Ultimately, however, the next four years would prove to be very hectic for both the President and the United States as a nation.

Immediately following his re-election, Truman moved into Blair House, which was a residence normally reserved for important guests from abroad. The White House was in desperate need of repair, and officials had told Truman after his re-election that parts of the residence were in such bad shape that they could soon collapse. Truman had been hesitant to ask the government to undertake such an expense before the election, but these renewed warnings finally convinced the President to agree to the repairs. As Blair House was being prepared to become a Presidential residence, Truman and his family left for Key West in Florida for a much deserved holiday. The President was glad that the White House, one of the most recognizable buildings around the world, was finally going to be restored to pristine condition.

Truman was still allowed to use the Oval Office during construction, as much of the repairs were in the residence part of the building. Truman would have to walk across the street to go to work, something no President had done in decades. The last President to do so was Theodore Roosevelt, who had finally arranged for the West Wing to be built in 1906.

Truman's Cabinet was set to change substantially. He finally agreed to General Marshall's request to retire, leaving the position of Secretary of State vacant. James Forestall, who Truman had never been too fond of, also departed as Secretary of Defense, although the circumstances surrounding his departure would prove incredibly vexing for the President. Truman chose Dean Acheson, who had served as Marshall's Under Secretary of State, to be the General's successor, while Forestall was replaced by Louis Johnson, a Truman campaign fundraiser and former Assistant Secretary of War during the Second World War. Acheson would continue to serve with Truman for the President's entire second term, while Johnson departed only one year later.

Truman made his last State of the Union address of his first term on January 5, 1949. It was at this speech that Truman coined the phrase "Fair Deal," which was the label he placed on the litany of progressive proposals that he wanted Congress to adopt on in the coming year. Two days later, Truman officially announced Acheson's appointment to head the State Department, and requested that Congress approve a $41.9 billion budget, the nation's largest peacetime budget, with half of the spending designated for national defense and aid to nations abroad.

President Truman was sworn in for his second term on a clear winter day in Washington. January 20, 1949, was accompanied by beautiful and sunny weather, and thousands of Americans lined the parade route that was to take Truman to the Capitol for his inauguration. Vice President-elect Barkley would be sworn into office just before Truman again took the Presidential oath, and he was the first Vice President since April of 1945, when Truman had vacated the position. President Roosevelt's last inauguration had occurred during the Second World War, and Truman's 1949 inauguration was the first peacetime inauguration in nearly a decade. Presidential festivities had been suspended during the war, and this inauguration was to be the first to resume the traditional pomp and circumstance. The inaugural parade and ceremony were to be the biggest and most expensive in history, as the Republican Congress, certain of a Dewey victory months earlier, had allotted an unprecedented amount of funds for the celebratory festivities. Truman's Democratic supporters decided to spend the entire allotted fund, making the inauguration of 1949 by far the biggest and most costly ever held. More than a million people would come to hear the President's inaugural address.

President Truman decided to take the oath of office on the East Portico of the Capital building, the same place his favorite President, Andrew Jackson, had taken his oath more than a hundred years prior. Members of Truman's family and friends were flown in for the occasion, numbering a few dozen. Hollywood stars also made an appearance, including Gene Kelly, Jane Powell, Abbott and Costello, and others. More African Americans came to the Capitol than at any time in the nation's history to see their President retake the oath of office. Under Truman's direct orders, they were allowed to stay at the city's nicer hotels, a right black people had never before been afforded. Over sixty five thousand guests were invited or had paid for seats, but hundreds of thousands stood on the grounds and streets around the Capitol to catch a glimpse of the President.

Truman's inauguration was also the first to be seen on live television. President Roosevelt had never allowed himself to be seen in public in a wheelchair, therefore essentially ruling out that possibility. But Truman was thrilled to have his speech to the nation broadcast on television, with more than ten million people tuned in to watch the broadcast. More than one hundred million listened over the radio.

The morning of the inauguration, Truman attended St. John's Episcopal Church, the place of worship that numerous of the President's predecessors had attended. Bess, Margaret, some members of the Cabinet, and a few close friends of the Truman family accompanied the President to the service. After the service, Truman departed for Capitol Hill with his wife, daughter, and the Barkley family. After ceremonial prayers and Barkley's oath of office, it was well after 1pm, more than an hour after Truman's last term had expired, before the Presidential oath was administered. Truman was finally sworn in at 1:30pm by Chief Justice Fred Vinson, with Bess holding two specially chosen Bibles.

Truman's inaugural address was one for the history books, as those who watched it on the television or listened to it on the radio were part of the largest audience for such a speech in American history. His speech was emotional and powerful, perhaps the greatest moment of Truman's political career. He also took the time to directly attack Communism and praise the essence of democratic government in some important excerpts.

Truman's inaugural address was solely focused on foreign policy. His attitude was resolute, and his voice was firm and unwavering. At stake in the next four years was not just the future of the United States, but rather the future of the world as a whole. Moreover, Communism was not simply a system to deplore, one that was based on deceit and false assurances, but also a system of government that had to be contained. Truman did not make any specific proposals, but rather suggested that his administration would strive towards four major goals. America would continue to support the United Nations, administer aid programs like the Marshall Plan, pursue a new defense alliance with likeminded North Atlantic nations, and support the creation of a new government program that sought to use the benefits of science and ingenuity to help to build and strengthen third world nations. As the President readily pointed out, nations across Western Europe had realized the necessity of close security cooperation with the United States in the aftermath of the Berlin blockade, and freedom loving nations around the world would have to follow the same collaborative course.

I accept with humility the honor which the American people have conferred upon me. I accept it with a resolve to do all that I can for the welfare of this Nation and for peace in the world.

The peoples of the earth face the future with grave uncertainty, composed almost equally of great hopes and great fears. In this time of doubt, they look to the United States as never before for good will, strength, and wise leadership.

We believe that all men have a right to equal justice under law and equal opportunity to share in the common good. We believe that all men have a right to freedom of thought and expression. We believe that all men are created equal because they are created in the image of God.

Communism is based on the belief that man is so weak and inadequate that he is unable to govern himself, and therefore requires the rule of strong masters. Democracy is based on the conviction that man has the moral and intellectual capacity, as well as the inalienable right, to govern himself with reason and justice.

We will strengthen freedom-loving nations against the dangers of aggression.

Events have brought our American democracy to new influence and new responsibilities. They will test our courage, our devotion to duty, and our concept of liberty.

The latter two points of Truman's program would in fact come to fruition. North Atlantic nations came together to create the North Atlantic Treaty Organization only months after Truman's speech, a system that was meant to promote mutual defense. Truman's third world initiative was later named the Point Four Program, christened as such because it was the President's fourth major point in his address, and the scientific assistance program was approved by Congress in 1950. Unlike similar aid programs from other nations, Truman's initiative had no sympathy for profit exploitation, which was the major goal of traditional imperialism. Instead, the President sought to help more than half of the world's citizens who were living in poverty, but he wanted to do so through education and knowledge rather than money alone, which could only be of temporary benefit.

After Truman's address, he departed for his inaugural luncheon at the Capitol. Those who had served with the President in his division during the First World War joined Truman on his way to the gathering. Once the luncheon had concluded, Truman departed for the White House, and the seven mile parade that followed him from Capitol Hill lasted for three hours, after which the President finally arrived back at the Oval Office. Even once Truman had reached the confines of the Presidential residence, he remained in a glass enclosed structure to watch the rest of the parade in warmth. Vice President Barkley joined Truman, and both men sat waving to supporters for hours on end. Truman's eventual successor, General Dwight D. Eisenhower, took part in the parade, and the two men waved to each other as the latter passed in one of the parade's cars. The President then departed for the inaugural ball in his tuxedo, and did not leave the party until well after 2am.

Inauguration Day in 1949 came at a moment of national jubilation. The economy was strong, the President's speech was inspiring, and America's prestige and world power had never been stronger. Truman found that the first several months of his first full term in office were rather uneventful. Only days after Truman's inauguration, Joseph Stalin, realizing that Truman's airlift plan had been an unquestionable success, began to retreat from his hardline propaganda. The Soviets ended their Berlin blockade on May 12, and the Berlin airlift, which had lasted for fourteen months, finally came to an end. The Soviet backpedaling was a moment of triumph for Truman, the United States, and Berliners themselves. On that same day, the Americans, along with their wartime allies, created a new state out of the western occupied portion of Germany, leading to the founding of a new Federated Republic in which the German people could govern themselves. More than fifteen years after Adolf Hitler had destroyed Germany's vibrant democracy, many of the country's former citizens were finally placed back in charge of their own affairs. Nonetheless, the situation in the eastern portion of Germany, which was still occupied by the Soviet Union, remained largely unchanged.

The North Atlantic Treaty Organization's charter was officially signed on April 4, with representatives from the United States, Canada, Belgium, Denmark, France, Iceland, Italy, Luxemburg, the Netherlands, Norway, Portugal, and Great Britain signing onto the new accord. The group had been formed as a means of guaranteeing mutual security among nations in the face of Soviet expansionism. The United States had ensured that Western Europe was able to recover from the aftermath of the Second World War, but threats against the region were not purely economic. In 1947 and early 1948, Hungary, Czechoslovakia, and

Poland fell to the Communists. The Truman administration wanted to ensure that the rest of Europe remained free of Communist totalitarianism. Thus, the group's essential purpose was to guarantee the fact that an attack on one nation would be considered to be an attack on all member nations. This was a profound departure from the isolationist American foreign policy that had reigned in Washington for decades, and it was the first peacetime alliance in the nation's history.

Although the organization's creation had been opposed by conservative Republicans in Congress, Truman believed that if such an organization had existed in the 1930s, the Second World War could have been prevented. He sent the treaty to the Senate on April 12, and called on Senators to support the agreement and ratify it quickly. Despite the opposition of Senator Robert Taft of Ohio, a leading Republican isolationist, NATO legislation was approved by the United States Senate on July 21, with eighty two members voting in favor, and only thirteen members opposed. The President officially signed the treaty into law on July 25, 1949. With other nations following suit, the North Atlantic Treaty Organization was officially born on August 24.

When the NATO council first gathered on September 17, their primary concern was to work out a system under which the institution's members would be adequately protected. Rather than individual plans for specific nations, the council sought to plan an overall strategic approach. NATO's members approved of such a policy on January 6, 1950, and President Truman himself endorsed the plan on January 27. The essence of the proposal focused on the idea of having a NATO defense force that would be composed of assets contributed by all member countries. But leaders from certain nations worried about specializing their defense forces, which could prove to be fatal if its NATO allies failed to rally to the country's defense. In the United States, members of Congress wanted to make sure that the Europeans would actually do their fair share in defending NATO's members, rather than simply relying on the American military alone. The agreement was therefore designed to ensure that all nations would not be specialized to such an extent that they could not defend themselves. Nonetheless, each nation would also have to make firm commitments in helping to defend every country that had signed onto the charter. The reality of individual and specific situations would dictate the full extent of each nation's required response.

On major problem turned out to be the role of West Germany: if the Germans participated in the NATO defensive zone, Western Europe would be more easily protected. Nonetheless, allowing West Germany to participate in the organization would mean granting the Germans military sovereignty over their own territory, which had not been restored after the Second World War. France, understandably, was opposed to allowing Germany to regain some of its strength so soon after it had devastated France and so many other nations through its totalitarian brutality. Truman's new Secretary of State, Dean Acheson, proposed a compromise in which the United States military would have a greater presence in Western Europe to help defend America's allies and ensure that Germany's military might did not get too powerful. This proposal was agreed to by France, and therefore adopted by member nations.

The North Atlantic Treaty Organization's new military force would have a contingent stationed in Europe under a new Supreme Allied Commander, and the force would be integrated to include soldiers from all member countries so as to not give Germany a military force of its own. General Dwight D. Eisenhower was chosen to be the organization's first Supreme Allied Commander.

Truman's first six months after being returned to the Presidency were remarkably successful. In that time, the Berlin Airlift had achieved its objective and forced Stalin's Soviets to back down, the North Atlantic Treaty Organization was created and ratified, and the nation of West Germany was finally created. Nonetheless, President Truman's second term would soon prove to be almost as tumultuous as his first.

Chapter Nine

Trouble at Home and Crises Abroad

In Dean Acheson President Truman found his political soul mate. Despite the fact that Truman, a man who had no postsecondary education and prided himself for being a man of the people, chose to appoint a Harvard lawyer, who prided himself on his elegant attire, to be his Secretary of State, the two got along famously once Acheson took over the State Department. Acheson, as Truman would later reflect, was an exemplary Secretary of State, and Truman would come to rely on Acheson as his most important and trusted advisor on nearly every aspect of government. Moreover, Acheson showed deference and respect towards the President and treated him like a superior, something his predecessors had often failed to do. Despite his exemplary educational background, Acheson hailed from rural Connecticut, something Truman could easily relate to. Acheson would remain in government with Truman until the latter left office, and the two would remain close friends until Secretary Acheson passed away in 1971. Acheson had served as Truman's Under Secretary of State since 1945, and was the President's first choice to succeed General Marshall, who had finally been permitted to retire.

While Dean Acheson's transition into the role of Secretary of State was rather smooth, Truman had far less luck in the Defense portfolio. Knowing that he was soon to be replaced, Secretary Forrestal began to act strange and troubled in the aftermath of the 1948 Presidential election. Truman, tired of Forrestal's procrastination and waffling, had his heart set on nominating someone new to take over in the Defense Department. According to rumors, Forrestal had even been working with Dewey during the campaign, hoping to remain as Secretary of Defense under a Republican administration. The press gallery and the American people appeared to have lost faith in Forrestal's ability to serve, and so had Truman. But one of the things the President liked least about his job was the need to fire people, and he delayed taking action for several weeks. Moreover, once a member of his team was criticised in the press, Truman was always hesitant to throw him overboard.

Despite opposition from the majority of the American public, Forrestal had a decorated career in business and in the American forces during the First World War. But at Truman's inauguration, colleagues reported that Forrestal appeared to be weak and looked quite frail. He had stopped sleeping, barely ate, and had the same discussions with advisors and even the President over and over again. Forrestal, who was well aware that Truman was hoping to replace him with Louis Johnson, a widely acclaimed businessman and former member of the Roosevelt administration, met with his potential successor to brief him on important files. Johnson, after being in the same room with Forrestal for a mere few hours, concluded that the Secretary of Defense had gone mad. While President Truman would later claim that Forrestal had wanted to leave his job for months, his close association with Governor Dewey suggests otherwise.

President Truman finally asked Forrestal to step down on March 1, and urged him to take a well-deserved vacation. Louis Johnson, who Truman designated as Forrestal's successor, was confirmed by the Senate and sworn into office on March 28. Hours later, Truman awarded Forrestal with a Distinguished

Service Medal, although his former Defense Secretary failed to utter even a word at the ceremony. After Forrestal departed for a vacation in Florida, he reportedly attempted to commit suicide on multiple occasions. He even suspected that spies from other nations were following him constantly, and Truman, as a friend, agreed to ask the Secret Service to look into the matter, which they did. The President received a report by the end of March claiming that Forrestal's paranoia was baseless.

Forrestal returned to Washington in the beginning of April to be hospitalized and treated for anxiety and exhaustion problems. He was found dead in a small hospital kitchen not far from his room on May 22. Forrestal had hanged himself to escape his state of paranoia. News of his death quickly spread across Washington, as suicide had been almost unheard of in American politics. Truman was shocked and horrified, and blamed himself for not asking Forrestal to retire sooner.

Truman was joined at Forrestal's funeral by the only living former President, Herbert Hoover, and his Vice President, Alben Barkley. Many from Congress, the military, and even the Supreme Court were present to pay their respects to a man that had been valued by so many. He was buried with full military honors in Arlington National Cemetery in Washington.

The Forestall tragedy dominated the news around Washington for weeks, effectively distracting the press from the appointment of his successor. But once the hysteria subsided, members of the press and politicians from both parties in Congress expressed confidence in Johnson's ability and his reputation. He had been confirmed without any opposition in the Senate, and members on both sides of the aisle praised the President for his choice to head the Defense Department.

Despite his well-regarded reputation, Johnson quickly became a lightning rod in American politics. He immediately fired high ranking members of the Pentagon in an effort to replace them with his own allies. With the support of the President, who, because of his work on the Truman Committee, was convinced that there were billions of dollars' worth of waste spent on national defense, Johnson cut back on military spending severely. One of his first moves was to cancel the building of a new super carrier, which led to the resignation of the Secretary of the Navy. By the end of May, Johnson had slashed another $1.5 billion from the Pentagon's budget, angering many who thought the United States would fall behind the military capacity of the Soviet Union. Johnson's bullish, no holds barred attitude proved to be rather effective, but he alienated nearly everyone in Washington in the process. Forrestal, for all of his faults, had always worked quietly in the background, deferring to the judgement of the President. Johnson, who many already speculated was angling for a run for the Presidency in 1952, went around shouting at high level military staffers and lambasted any and all of his opponents.

While the President had agreed with some of Johnson's early decisions in the Defense Department, Truman, like so many other Americans, was quickly alienated by the Defense Secretary's demeanor and condescending attitude. Only weeks after the appointment, Truman began to regret his decision to nominate Johnson to serve in his Cabinet, and was anxious to find a way to replace him. Ultimately, Johnson remained in the Cabinet for only a year and a half, and Truman replaced him with General Marshall, whom the President had desperately asked to return to politics.

A major scandal broke out in Washington in mid-1949, and it revolved exclusively around Harry Vaughn, a military aide to the President who was part of the administration only because of his connections to the Truman clan in Missouri. Vaughn was disliked by senior officials around Washington and the press alike, so neither group was hesitant to pounce on the emergence of a major scandal. The controversy was over his use of his prominent position within the administration to secure his friends and cronies high profile appointments to lucrative government positions. Vaughn was also accused of helping those people secure official government contracts, off of which he would allegedly receive part of the profits. Truman was forced to remove Vaughn's friends with controversial backgrounds from government posts, severely embarrassing the President and calling his integrity into question.

Vaughn was called to testify before a Senate subcommittee to explain his actions. Led by Democratic Senator Clyde Hoey, who had previously served as Governor of North Carolina, the committee questioned Vaughn about his influence peddling. He claimed that he was simply trying to help out his friends, which many politicians did do on a regular basis. Moreover, it was not rare for powerbrokers in Washington to receive gifts from friends for their efforts, as Vaughn had. Although Vaughn had done nothing expressly illegal, his actions made the administration look unstatesmanlike and poor in judgement. Furthermore, Vaughn had hid most of those gifts from any official reports, making matters look even more suspicious.

For many around Washington, Vaughn was the epitome of governmental corruption. He represented the part of government that made Americans who believed that government should be run honorably and honestly skeptical about politicians in general. Vaughn's actions also called into question the President's judgement, as Washington insiders agreed unanimously that Vaughn would have no place in the administration had Truman not felt a special sense of loyalty to him. Moreover, when Vaughn offered to leave the administration to end the political embarrassment his actions were causing the President, Truman turned down the offer and asked Vaughn to remain in the White House. Truman's decision to allow Vaughn to stay simply allowed his opponents to continue to paint the administration, and the Democratic Party in general, as corrupt.

On July 19, 1949, Frank Murphy, who had been appointed to the Supreme Court by President Roosevelt only nine years prior, died at the age of 59. Murphy's career before he had even joined the nation's highest court was quite decorated. He had served as the Governor General of the Philippines, Governor of Michigan, and as one of Roosevelt's Attorneys General. Murphy's sudden death left a seat vacant on the Supreme Court. Truman, like Roosevelt had done nine years prior, chose to appoint his incumbent Attorney General, Tom Clark, to the Supreme Court. After Clark was swiftly confirmed by the Senate, he was sworn into office on August 19.

To replace Clark in the Justice Department, Truman nominated Senator J. Howard McGrath of Rhode Island to the post. McGrath, a loyal Democrat who had previously served as Rhode Island's sixtieth Governor, was easily confirmed by his colleagues in the Senate, and was sworn into Cabinet as Truman's third Attorney General on July 27.

While Truman was dealing with the difficult process of revamping his Cabinet, events in China were growing bleaker by the hour. The President's advisors had long suggested that China's Nationalist government would be able to withstand military and political pressure from Mao Zedong's Communist forces. Nonetheless, Chiang Kai-shek's government appeared to be collapsing, as Communist forces began to look as though they would win the brutal civil war that had begun in China in 1946. By the spring of 1949, Communist forces were in charge of nearly the entire country. While the President and his advisor had long anticipated a civil war in China, Truman himself had always been reluctant to get himself too involved in the Chinese situation, with neither side in the conflict supporting the idea of a fully democratic government. Americans were determined to assist Chiang in his fight against the Communists, but no American lawmaker dared to suggest the idea of intervening in the situation in China militarily. The nation was simply too large and too divided, and financial and technical assistance had appeared to be the only course of action. General Marshall had even been sent to China for over a year to advise Chiang's Nationalist government and encourage cooperation on both sides. Nonetheless, these forms of assistance proved to be far from sufficient in preventing the Communists from coming to power. The Nationalist cause only made things worse by pursuing a policy of confrontation rather than negotiation.

The President's critics immediately began to attack the administration for what was happening in China. Religious groups and Republicans in Congress claimed that the advance of Communism in China was an example of the perils of Truman's relatively relaxed attitude to the Communist threat abroad. But the President took the happenings in China very seriously. Truman's administration had given Chiang's Nationalist government more than $2 billion to try to stop the advance of Communist forces, but it had been to no avail. Members of the administration, including Secretary of State Dean Acheson, blamed the internal strife on Chiang's Nationalist movement. On October 1, 1949, Mao Zedong, Chairman of the Communist Party in China, officially announced the creation of the new People's Republic of China. With that, the largest nation in the world, in the eyes of the Truman administration, appeared to have fallen under Communist control.

Truman ordered the release of more than a thousand pages of government documents to inform the nation of America's foreign policy towards China since 1944. A summary of the report, dubbed the China White Paper, simply encouraged further strife over the issues. People across the country were outraged that the reports effectively signaled that the administration believed that China was already lost to the Communists, and that there was nothing America could do to change the situation. Republicans, along with other opponents of the administration, accused Truman's colleagues of simply standing by and allowing Communism to spread around the world because of their Communist sympathies. The accusation was categorically false, but memories of the Hiss fiasco and other instances when the administration had been accused of being soft on Communism were still very fresh in the minds of many.

More trouble came in September, when planes from the American Air Force flying from Japan to Alaska detected signs of radioactivity, and dozens of other American planes would soon report the same findings. The sentiment was echoed and confirmed by the Royal Air Force, whose leadership reported that the radioactive cloud had reached almost as far as the air above Great Britain. On September 20, a group of scientists and administrative officials, many of whom had worked on Project Manhattan, reported to the President that evidence suggested that the Soviets had successfully tested a nuclear bomb.

President Truman released an official statement for his press secretary to deliver to the press on September 23. The statement reported that the administration had confirmed that the Soviets had successfully tested an atomic bomb. Truman said that he believed the American people needed to be informed, and that the development of such a weapon by others was inevitable. Although the administration had forecast that it would take the Soviets another several years to construct a nuclear weapon, America's nuclear bomb monopoly ultimately proved to last for only four years. While few actually thought the Soviets would use a nuclear device to launch a quick attack on the United States mainland, it made the Soviet Union a much more powerful nation, and escalated the pressure of the Cold War atmosphere immensely.

With the Soviet Union now in control of a nuclear bomb, the Atomic Energy Agency, under Chairman David Lilienthal, initiated discussions with prominent scientists about the possibility of creating an even more powerful weapon. A hydrogen bomb would theoretically have ten times more power than a nuclear weapon, and would therefore have been more than ten times as destructive in America's bombing efforts in Hiroshima and Nagasaki. Lilienthal and others believed that if the Soviet Union was capable of building a nuclear bomb, they would now begin to pursue the creation of the hydrogen bomb. As the Chairman made clear, America would have to create a "superbomb" before the Russians did. Nonetheless, he faced staunch opposition from many scientists who had been integral in building the world's first two nuclear bombs. The military, however, believed that a hydrogen bomb was essential if only to provide the American people with a greater sense of security.

While Lilienthal himself had reservations about initiating the creation of a weapon even more deadly than a nuclear bomb, he realized that there was no other realistic course of action. On Lilienthal went to the State Department on November 1 to brief Secretary of State Acheson, who in turn discussed the details of the proposal with the President. Truman, like many other Presidents, relied heavily on the advice of his Secretary of State. Although he was far less prominent of a public figure than General Marshall had been, Dean Acheson nonetheless had the President's full confidence. In the coming years Acheson would become Truman's trusted advisor and loyal friend. Both understood each other's role, and, unlike Byrnes or Marshall, Acheson shunned the spotlight and treated Truman as a boss rather than as an equal.

The report Acheson and Truman received from the scientists at the Atomic Energy Commission recommended that the hydrogen bomb not be developed at all. Truman, however, was not entirely certain whether or not he supported the idea. Many physicists advised that Truman proceed with research on the hydrogen bomb, as did the military, while George Kennan and others at the State Department argued that escalation might thwart any possibility of an arms control deal with the Soviets. Others suggested that the only way to reach an agreement with the Russians was to arm the United States to the greatest extent that was possible. The President, after receiving conflicting advice, asked Acheson, Secretary of Defense Johnson, and Chairman Lilienthal, who had already announced his opposition to the bomb's creation, to join a National Security Commission. The three men, plus the President, would then make the final decision about whether or not to go ahead.

While George Kennan was greatly respected in the State Department for his Cold War memorandum, he was set to retire from public life, and his successor, Paul Nitze, agreed with the military that the bomb should be built. As the State Department's Director of Policy Planning, Nitze believed that because the Soviets now possessed nuclear capabilities, they would surely pursue a similar hydrogen based weapon. America, he claimed, would have to pursue a more vigorous research policy, construct the bomb, and build up the nation's defenses in every area.

Acheson revealed that he, like Nitze, was a proponent of the hydrogen bomb's construction. Although he had been hesitant at first, Acheson knew that the Soviet Union would pursue the weapon regardless of the actions taken by the American government. The United States, he believed, could not take the risk of allowing the Soviets to get ahead in an arms race, and lashed out at those in the State Department that believed otherwise. Powerful Senators on Capitol Hill were staunchly in favor of building the bomb, and they put significant pressure on the administration to give the go ahead.

When the secret three man committee met on January 31 at the State Department, Acheson announced that he was in favor of building the bomb. Johnson quickly concurred, and the two began to draft a statement for the press. Lilienthal was not so sure, and suggested that an arms race was inevitable if Truman decided to proceed, and that pursuing such a course would be inevitably dangerous. Although he was greatly respected by the President and Acheson, Lilienthal had announced his intention to retire in February, and therefore might have had less sway within the administration. Moreover, Acheson argued that not building the bomb would not stop the Russians from doing so, and that people across the country would vehemently oppose a decision by the administration to hold off on the project. Lilienthal ultimately agreed to sign the statement drawn up by Acheson, which had already been signed by Johnson, and the three men went to the White House to confer with the President. They soon learned that Truman had already decided on his own to give the go ahead, knowing full well that the Soviets were capable of building the bomb themselves. Despite Lilienthal's grave warning, the arms race was officially underway, and he reluctantly accepted that there was little chance of avoiding such a scenario.

President Truman delivered his fifth State of the Union address to a joint session of Congress on January 4, 1950. He reminded Congress of the administration's successes in 1949, including the continuation of a policy to rebuild Europe, and the creation of the Northern Atlantic Treaty Organization. Truman also listed a number of campaign promises that Congress had fulfilled on behalf of the admiration, including more support for low rent housing, and a hike in the minimum wage. He also spoke of America's new position in the world as a leader within the international system.

> Our tremendous strength has brought with it tremendous responsibilities. We have moved from the outer edge to the center of world affairs. Other nations look to us for a wise exercise of our economic and military strength, and for vigorous support of the ideals of representative government and a free society. We will not fail them.

Three days later, the President presented a budget that proposed spending more than $42 billion, which would also force the Congress to raise taxes by $1 billion. In a move that angered most Republicans and some Democrats, Truman announced that his budget would lead to a $5 billion shortfall, a very significant deficit to run during peacetime. But war debts still had to be paid, and significant aid was still being poured into the European recovery efforts. He regretted having to run a deficit, but Truman felt he had been left with little choice.

Truman's administration was again under assault from Republicans for its handling of foreign affairs. With the world's largest nation having fallen under Communist control, Republicans urged the President to fire Secretary Acheson. But the Secretary of State was Truman's closest friend and advisor in Washington, and he had no intention of doing so. Acheson's role had been called into question for his previous association with Alger Hiss, the former State Department official who had joined the Communist Party and was sentenced to five years in prison for committing perjury. The two considered each other to be personal friends, and Acheson had also worked closely with Hiss's brother, who was then employed at Acheson's law firm. Because he was under fire, the politically expedient thing for Acheson to do would have been to end any relations he had with the Hiss family, but the Secretary of State refused to turn his back on his long-time friend. He claimed that he would not do so because of his Christian compassion and the teachings of Christ, but the answer nonetheless set off a firestorm in Washington's political circles.

Senator Joseph McCarthy, who would later make himself known across the nation for his heavy drinking and ruthless attacks on those who were alleged to have been associated with Communism, lambasted Acheson on the Senate floor, asking if his compassion would also lead him to forgive any other Communists still working in the State Department. The Secretary of State immediately departed for the White House to confer with Truman, and offered to quit because of the controversy. Truman refused to accept the offer, but the episode turned out to be a political fiasco for the administration. When the President was later asked whether or not he would turn his back on Alger Hiss, as Acheson had refused to do, Truman offered no answer, further increasing the tension in Washington. Things only got worse when Senator McCarthy claimed in public that he had a list of more than two hundred Communist sympathizers in the State Department, a suggestion that was ludicrous but damning nonetheless.

Senator Joseph McCarthy, the junior member from Wisconsin representing the Republican Party, was generally regarded as a poor public servant, and had few friends on Capitol Hill. McCarthy, however, sought to make a name for himself in Washington, and decided that playing the role of the alarmist on Communist expansionism could put him in the forefront of American politics. Ultimately, he was proven to be right. His claim that he was in possession of a list of Communists within the Truman administration was baseless, and his drunken and inflammatory behavior alienated many. But the startling accusations, which, after all, were made by a United States Senator, grabbed the attention of the media and sent politicians in Washington into panic mode.

McCarthy came out swinging at the Truman administration, accusing the President of being a prisoner in a White House that was dominated by Communist sympathizers and "twisted intellectuals." McCarthy's scathing attack on Acheson for his friendship with Alger Hiss helped to attach a Communist label to the Truman administration, and forced the Secretary of State to have guarded protection around his home at all times. While some Republicans rejected McCarthy's style of politics, others rallied to support his anti-Communist crusade. Senate Democrats, convinced that McCarthy's allegations were largely nothing more than that, called for a Senate investigation into all of McCarthy's supposed findings. While they had hoped to use the investigation, through the creation of a special Senate committee, to prove McCarthy's attacks had no reality attached to them, the Senator from Wisconsin simply reveled in the attention. The whole McCarthy campaign weighed heavily on the President, who was forced to deal with outrage across the country centering on his administration's supposed support for Communist sympathizers. Truman, like virtually all Americans, hated the very essence of the

Communist system, and was certainly never a sympathizer of that system. But the verbal assaults affected him nonetheless.

As he gave the go ahead for the development of a hydrogen bomb, Truman turned his attention to the state of the American military as a whole. The Soviets had more than four times as many people in their armed forces than the United States did, and produced five times as many military planes on an annual basis. Even more troublesome was that the American government spent only six percent of the nation's gross domestic product on national defense expenditures, while the Soviets spent more than twenty five percent. President Truman had long advocated limiting defense spending in order to allocate more money to domestic programs, but even Secretary Acheson warned the President that his goal of keeping military spending under $13 billion annually was woefully insufficient. Due to Acheson's warnings, Truman reluctantly agreed to allow for a complete review of the nation's national defense policies.

As the State Department and the Defense Department worked together to complete the review process, Secretary Johnson exploded in anger towards Secretary Acheson on multiple occasions. When the Secretary of State informed the President of Johnson's behavior in March of 1950, Truman decided that his Secretary of Defense would have to be replaced in the coming months. Nonetheless, for the time being, Johnson was left in place while the review process continued.

Tired of the climate in Washington, Truman decided well before the 1950 midterm elections that he would not seek another term in office in 1952. Congress had passed an amendment to the constitution in 1947 to implement a two term limit on the number of mandates that a President could serve. Many states already had a similar law, and it appeared as though all of the states would ratify it before the next Presidential election. Although the amendment had passed under a Republican Congress, they had made an exception for the incumbent President, suggesting that

Truman would be the last President who was allowed to seek more than two terms. Unlike President Roosevelt, whose four terms helped to spark the constitutional amendment, Truman did not feel a lure to remain in the White House. The President had served in public office for nearly three decades, and, despite Roosevelt's departure from tradition, nearly every President in the nation's history had decided to keep to a two term custom that was started by President Washington himself. Only three Presidents had decided to seek a third term, and only Franklin Roosevelt received that additional mandate from the people. Although Truman felt the constitutional amendment was unnecessary, he wanted to continue the tradition of limiting a President to only two terms in office, and reinstate it personally after it had been broken by his predecessor.

By March 30, 1950, Truman was so incensed by the McCarthy anti-communist crusade that he took the time to hold a press conference to address the matter while he was on vacation in Florida. The President claimed that the greatest asset the Communists had was Senator McCarthy himself, along with other Republicans hawks in the Senate. Truman claimed that the Republicans were simply trying to find an issue that would gain traction with voters for the midterm elections in the fall. There were no Communists in his administration, and Truman made it clear that McCarthy's so called evidence was nothing more than wild speculation. Moreover, the President reiterated his previous commitment to ensure than any and all known instances of Communist subversion within the government would be fully investigated by the Federal Bureau of Investigation.

Despite the President's efforts, Senator McCarthy remained in the spotlight in Washington, continuing to whip up a Communist scare across the country. He made Truman look passive and accused him of not doing enough to rid the government of Communist supporters. It was not until June that a Republican Senator spoke out to strongly condemn McCarthy's behavior.

Senator Margaret Chase Smith of Maine, the chamber's only
female representative, warned that her colleague from Wisconsin
was taking the Republican Party towards ignorance and smear
campaigns. Unfortunately, few other Senators spoke out to echo
Smith's comments.

The full evaluation of America's national defense policies that
the President had ordered was delivered to Truman in early April.
It was composed by Paul Nitze and Secretary Acheson, along with
numerous officials from the Defense Department. The National
Security Council met on April 25, 1950 to discuss the implications
of the report. The report concluded that America's national
defense infrastructure fell short of the strength that a world
superpower should maintain. Moreover, the Truman
administration's policy of communist containment could only
work if the nation's military offered a real threat beyond nuclear
capabilities. His advisors told Truman at the meeting that defense
spending would have to at least be tripled from its current rate of
$13 billion, although the final figure could prove to be as much as
$50 billion.

The concluding paragraph of the report explained in a very
decisive manner the reasoning behind the defense spending
escalation that its authors were calling for. Moreover, it addressed
the implications of such a move, noting that doing so would signal
to the American people and those abroad that the free world was
once again at war, this time with the Soviet communists.

> The whole success hangs ultimately on recognition
> by this government, the American people and all the
> peoples that the Cold War is in fact a real war in which
> the survival of the world is at stake.

Truman did not choose to act on the report right away. He
refused to make a hasty decision without consulting outside
sources, and of course the Congress, but the memorandum's
recommendations would occupy his thoughts nonetheless.

Just a couple weeks after the President's important meeting with his top national defense advisors, Truman set off on a two week cross country tour to deliver speeches to Americans in a handful of scattered states. Truman told the American people that he fully recognized the possibility of the Cold War lasting for many years, and told the nation that they would have to get used to that reality.

Chapter Ten

Korea

On Saturday, June 24, 1950, North Korea launched an invasion of South Korea. Truman, who was enjoying a brief summer visit to Independence, Missouri, received the news on the telephone from Secretary Acheson in Washington. According to the American Ambassador in South Korea, the North Korean military had crossed the 38th parallel, which represented the border between the two hostile nations. Truman immediately decided to return to Washington to be present in the White House during a time of crisis, but Acheson told him that the situation was being handled by the State Department. He suggested that Truman wait until the following day for a more clear picture to emerge. The President reluctantly agreed, but also told Acheson that he should notify the United Nations and ask for a meeting of the Security Council.

The following morning Truman was still in Independence, and departed from his home to visit nearby Grandview with his brother Vivian, where he attempted to look as though there wasn't an urgent international crisis that the nation should panic about. Back at home by the early afternoon, Truman received word that the North Korean invasion was to be considered an all-out offensive against its southern neighbor. After once again consulting with Secretary Acheson, Truman immediately decided to leave for the airport in Kansas City to return to Washington. By just after 7pm local time, the President's plane landed in the capital, and Truman was greeted on the tarmac by his Secretaries of State and Defense, and the administration's Budget Director. The four men, along with Bess and Margaret, departed for Blair House, where the President had asked Acheson to arrange for an emergency meeting that evening to discuss the crisis in Asia.

The division of the Korean peninsula was a relatively new phenomenon. The nation of Korea had been a largely independent state until the Sino-Japanese War ended in 1895, leading to the country's fall under the yolk of Japanese imperialism. The government of Japan officially annexed Korea in 1910, and treated it as a Japanese province until the country's military forces were defeated in the Second World War. When President Roosevelt had met Chiang Kai-shek and Winston Churchill in Cairo in November of 1943, the three leaders had agreed to allow Korea to become a free and independent state after the war's end, but that its transition into a fully independent state could take decades. Stalin had also agreed that Korea should eventually gain independence, but pushed back against President Roosevelt's suggestion at Yalta that the country be place under a joint trusteeship of the United States, Soviet Union, and Nationalist China for several decades. Stalin proposed adding Great Britain to the joint trusteeship, but also insisted that Korea's independence should be much sooner than Roosevelt suggested, and most certainly within the decade.

When the Soviets declared war on Japan, Truman and Stalin had agreed to implement a demarcation line for the country's eventual occupation. The two nations agreed to use the 38th parallel as that line. Nonetheless, once the war ended, the Soviets began to treat the 38th parallel as a border, essentially disregarding the four power trusteeship that Stalin had agreed to. The Americans quickly requested that the country be unified so as to begin its recovery process, both politically and economically, but the Soviets refused. Clearly, the Soviets intended for Korea to become the basic foundation for a larger struggle between Communist and democratic forces in Asia. The Soviets chose to hold their own elections in Northern Korea in late 1946, but, as was typical for the Communists, only one slate of candidates appeared on the ballot. Without Soviet cooperation, Truman took his case to the United Nations, and an international task force oversaw free elections in the American occupied southern portion of Korea on May 10, 1948. South Korea's new National Assembly wrote a new constitution, and elected Syngman Rhee as the first President of the Republic of Korea in July.

The new Korean government had been officially recognized on August 15, replacing the American led military government that had presided over the region for three years. Once the new government had built up a substantial military contingent, American troops pulled out of South Korea in June of 1949. Soviet forces withdrew from the North as well, but they had left behind a highly skilled Communist army led by Kim Il-Sung, who had long been determined to attack the south and reunite Korea under a Communist regime. American military personnel had believed that direct aid from the United States would be enough to keep South Korea viable, but they were convinced that the South Koreans would be safe from a ground invasion. Evidently, they were very much mistaken.

Truman found himself reflecting on the 1930s on his way back to Blair House, remembering vividly the mistakes western democracies had made by not standing up for Ethiopia or Manchuria when they were invaded by Italy and Japan respectively. The President was determined not to allow the free world to make the same mistake again, especially because this time the threat came from Communist forces. Doing nothing would only embolden Communist powers in the future. Nonetheless, the coming days would be difficult. The United States had already removed all of its troops from South Korea, and no one had anticipated a full scale attack from the North Koreans. The administration had been caught flat footed, and Truman would have to decide on a course of action.

The United Nations Security Council had met on the afternoon of June 25, just a day after Truman instructed the State Department to call for an emergency meeting. The Security Council passed a resolution calling for an immediate end to any military confrontations, and for the North Koreans to respect the 38th parallel as the borderline between the two states. The vote had been unanimous, although a Soviet representative was not present for a vote that he might have otherwise vetoed.

After Truman's advisors dined with the President at Blair House, the discussion finally turned to the situation in Korea. Dean Rusk, an Asia expert from the State Department, told the President that because the United States had occupied South Korea for more than five years, the American government had a special responsibility in helping the fledging nation defend itself. Moreover, should South Korea fall to the Communists, Japan's security would come under threat, a scenario that the American government would have to try to avoid at all costs. The general consensus around the table was that Truman's containment policy essentially required that America take action in Korea to prevent Communist expansionism. There was also widespread agreement that the actions being taken by North Korea were encouraged by its ally in Moscow, and that the Soviet government was clearly testing whether or not Truman would defend his containment policy when the question of a military conflict became involved. As the President would later write, there was "complete, almost unspoken acceptance on the part of everyone that whatever had to be done to meet this aggression had to be done…this was the test of all the talk of the last five years of collective security." Truman therefore sent out an immediate directive for military supplies to be given to South Korean forces.

President Truman declared to his advisors that the line would have to be drawn in Korea: Communist expansionism could not go unchallenged. The Russians were trying to win over all of Korea in the hope that the United States would be hesitant to act. Stalin was confident that the American government would not risk intervention in the fear of provoking another war, but Truman was convinced that America would have to demonstrate that the United States was not willing to appease the Soviets and their expansionist ambitions. If the Communist forces were not stopped in Korea, there was no doubt that the Soviets would continue to make attempts to expand the reach of Communism in other areas of the world. America, Truman concluded, would have to act decisively in the face of Communist aggression.

> The attack upon Korea makes it plain beyond all doubt that Communism has passed beyond the use of subversion to conquer independent nations and will now use armed invasion and war. It has defied the orders of the Security Council of the United Nations issued to preserve international peace and security.
>
> I know that all members of the United Nations will consider carefully the consequences of this latest aggression in Korea in defiance of the Charter of the United Nations. A return to the rule of force in international affairs would have far-reaching effects. The United States will continue to uphold the rule of law.

Truman worried early on that the Russians might intervene if America chose to act. There was a real risk that a world war could be sparked, although many in the administration doubted that Stalin was prepared for that. It was quickly decided that General MacArthur, who was still actively involved in the governing of Japan, would immediately send weaponry and other supplies to the South Korean military forces. South Korean civilians close to the action were also to be evacuated with the help of the American air force. Moreover, a fleet was sent from the Philippines to the region to help prevent any possible Chinese aid to the North Korean forces, or a naval attack.

As news worsened on June 26, Truman continued to be evasive when asked about the situation by the press. Most had already concluded that the United States would fail to act, and that South Korea would likely fall to the Communists. Even General MacArthur warned Truman that the South Korean forces were so weak that they were likely to be overrun completely. As the news grew bleaker, Truman summoned his advisors to Blair House and instructed them to ensure that the South Koreans received air and naval aid from the American forces immediately, and that the United Nations be called into action. He also added that for the time being, America's goal was to enforce the 38th parallel border and not to attempt to push further north. More troops were asked to go to the Philippines, although the President had not yet approved of the use of American ground forces in the conflict.

North Korean forces had overrun Seoul, the capital of South Korea, by June 27. South Korea's government fled further south as its President claimed that the current level of American support was woefully insufficient to try to hold off North Korean aggression. On that same day, North Korea's leader, the Communist Kim Il-Sung, proclaimed that his military forces would crush the South Koreans and not stop until its neighbor was completely wiped off of the map. As leaders from Congress, the Cabinet, and the American military came to gather in the White House, Truman held a meeting with dozens of advisors and elected officials for no more than half an hour. Everyone pledged their full support for whatever course the President decided to take, including Republicans. As Truman liked to say, politics should stop at the water's edge. In this instance, it certainly had.

After Congressional leaders had departed from the White House, Truman officially announced the participation of American naval and air forces in defending South Korea from

Communist aggression. Congressional leaders had also told Truman that the President should proceed with his plans without asking for a resolution to be passed by the legislative branch, although many would later come to dispute the administration's account of that agreement. Moreover, due to the Communist threat in Korea, leaders in the House of Representatives and the Senate ensured that the draft law was extended by another year, with legislation passing in both chambers by an overwhelming majority.

A resolution was passed by the United Nations Security Council authorizing American action in South Korea. The resolution passed due to the absence of a Soviet representative yet again, who almost certainly would have vetoed the motion. Truman also found resolute support for action in Korea from the American public, with important figures such as Dwight Eisenhower, Thomas Dewey, and Franklin Roosevelt Jr. agreeing that Communist aggression would have to be confronted head on. Leaders from Canada, Australia, New Zealand, and the Netherlands offered their immediate support, indicating that they too were prepared to get involved in the conflict militarily.

Despite the President's orders for Americans to actively participate in the Korean conflict, if only in the air and at sea for the time being, Truman confidently declared that America was not at war. He continued to further that response when asked by the press on Thursday, June 29, rationalizing his declaration because the nation had not yet sent ground troops to engage in the Korean defense effort.

On the morning of June 30, Truman received yet another ominous message from General MacArthur, who told the President that the only way the South Koreans could stop the advance of North Korean troops was to have American combat forces participate on the ground. Air and naval support would not be enough to allow the South Koreans to stop the Communist advance. MacArthur therefore requested that the President send two divisions of ground troops into active combat in Korea. Despite the General's request, the nation's military forces had been allowed to dwindle since 1945, with defense spending and troop enrolment numbers cut significantly. Preparing for a conflict in Korea would require a complete reversal of the defense spending reductions that had taken place in the last five years.

The President had been up since well before 4am on June 30 agonizing over the situation. After all, the Second World War had ended less the five years earlier, and Truman was extremely reluctant to allow the nation to return to a state of war only a few years later. But the general consensus was that urgent action would have to be taken, even if there was a very slight risk of starting another world war. Truman therefore made what he would later call the most difficult decision of his Presidency, and quickly decided to approve a ground invasion of the Korean peninsula. Despite the fact that the President knew full well that he would have to act, he did worry about what the response would be not only from Moscow, but also from Beijing.

By the end of June, Truman had also decided to recall Averell Harriman from Europe to serve as his special assistant on Korean affairs, and help him to retain congressional support for the Korean initiative. Harriman told Truman that he should seek a congressional declaration of war to ensure that everyone in Washington would be held accountable for the outcome of the Korean excursion, but Secretary Acheson advised the President otherwise. Acheson and Truman both concluded that, despite the fact that Congress would surely give its approval, a war declaration would make it harder for future Presidents to act quickly in times of crisis. In the long run, Harriman's advice would turn out to have been the wisest domestic political course of action for Truman to take.

Korea is not a large nation. From the northern end of the peninsula to its southern tip, Korea is only six hundred miles long, and its east to west diameter is even less. In the two countries combined, the population was only twenty million, two thirds of which lived in the south. Nonetheless, although North Korea's population was much smaller than its southern neighbor, its economy was far more advanced, primarily based on industry, whereas South Koreans focused on agriculture. North Korea was far more prepared for a military conflict than government forces in Seoul. The 38th parallel border, while considered to be sacred by many, including the South Koreans, was a relatively new concept. For North Korea's leadership, including Kim Il-Sung, the border was largely meaningless, having only been in place for well under a decade. Moreover, the border was created to allow Japanese forces north of the 38th parallel to surrender to the Soviets, while those south of the 38th parallel surrendered to the United States. The dividing line was not expressly intended to ultimately represent a national perimeter at the time of its creation.

By the time Truman had decided to intervene in the Korean conflict, Seoul had already fallen to the Communists, and the North Korean armed forces were quickly advancing south. The distance from Seoul to the southern tip of the peninsula is only around two hundred and seventy five miles, so the North Koreans would have to be stopped quickly if there was any hope of preventing South Korea from being completely overrun. The first contingent of American forces to reach South Korea fought with what was left of the South Korean army just south of Seoul on July 5. They were quickly forced into retreat, however, heading further south, and the small American division of two hundred and fifty six men was no match for the thousands of North Koreans attacking from the north, many of whom were armed with Russian tanks. The fact that the Americans were rather poorly equipped certainly didn't help matters either.

The National Security Council met on July 6, and when military leaders were asked how many North Koreans were participating in the operation, they responded that they numbered well over ninety thousand. When Vice President Barkley asked how many

Americans and South Koreans were fighting to halt the onslaught, he was stunned to learn that, adding American and South Korean forces together, the allies were only in possession of thirty thousand soldiers. The Allied troops were furthermore not equipped with the supplies necessary to slow down the advance of the Russian made tanks, nor did they have powerful artillery.

The North Koreans were ruthless. American captives were found slaughtered with their hands tied behind their backs. Suicidal attacks from the north was also a common place reality throughout the conflict. As the retreat continued, America's armed forces were continuously embarrassed. But they were still ill equipped and did not have enough manpower to stop the onslaught. General MacArthur, now in command on the ground in Korea, insisted on a slow retreat, hoping that America and its allies would send thousands of more troops as reinforcements, thereby enabling the allies to battle to regain territory that had been lost to the North Korean forces at a later date.

On July 29, General Walton Walker of Great Britain, the United Nations tactical commander for the operation, issued a stand or die order, meaning that the policy of retreat was over. Allied forces were to stand their ground and fight with all of their strength to prevent the North Koreans from forcing them to fall back further. But asking troops to fight to the death was not only disheartening, but alienating.

General MacArthur asked Truman to send thirty thousand troops to Korea in early July. Only days later, he increased the requested total to sixty thousand. The Joint Chiefs worried that if Truman committed too many troops to the Korean conflict, it would be an opportune time for Moscow to start a conflict elsewhere. America's European allies also worried whether or not the United States would be able to defend its allies in Europe if it had already sent too many troops to South Korea. Moreover, after several years of budget cutbacks in the Defense Department,

Truman now realized that the army was too small and ill equipped to handle a wartime situation.

President Truman grew more stressed as weeks went by without a glimmer of good news. Republicans in Congress were already calling for Secretary Acheson to resign. Many Americans wanted the President to use a nuclear bomb and bring the troops home, which was unrealistic at best. Finally, on July 14, 1950, President Truman's national defense policy went under a dramatic transformation. Gone was his insistence on holding back on military spending and resources. The President and his Secretary of State both agreed that military spending would have to be greatly expanded, as would the military service. Now that the Cold War was a reality, higher spending on the military would have to be one as well.

In an address to a joint session of Congress three days later, Truman announced that America needed to send more soldiers, equipment, and expertise to Korea. America's overall military strength would have to be enhanced, and Truman asked Congress for an emergency grant of more than $10 billion for defense spending, nearly doubling the previously budgeted $13 billion. The draft would also have to be expanded.

America had a lot at stake in Korea, the President explained. North Korea's act of aggression had violated the United Nations Charter, and the United States, through the United Nations, was fighting to uphold the rule of law between nations. A set of laws within relations between states was paramount to maintaining peace in the world, and preventing another world war.

> This attack has made it clear, beyond all doubt, that the international Communist movement is willing to use armed invasion to conquer independent nations. An act of aggression such as this creates a very real danger to the security of all free nations.
>
> The attack upon Korea was an outright breach of the

peace and a violation of the Charter of the United Nations. By their actions in Korea, Communist leaders have demonstrated their contempt for the basic moral principles on which the United Nations is founded. This is a direct challenge to the efforts of the free nations to build the kind of world in which men can live in freedom and peace.

This challenge has been presented squarely. We must meet it squarely.

Truman's call to arms lasted much longer than one mere speech to Congress. Weeks later the President announced that he was doubling the size of the nation's military to three million men. The reality of the Cold War meant that America would have to be ready constantly for Communist acts of aggression. America had not been adequately prepared for Korea, and new appropriations were therefore needed. But beyond that, the United States would have to expand its military capabilities to be prepared for conflicts in the future, and to ensure that there were enough troops to keep the nation's commitment to defend its allies in Europe, Asia, and around the world. The President was able to get Congress on board with his call for greater defense spending, as lawmakers allocated nearly $50 billion for military expenditures in fiscal year 1950-1, and $60 billion in 1951-2. Those numbers represented an incredible departure from the President's own efforts to hold defense spending down to $13 billion, a policy he championed around the time of his re-election.

The crisis in Korea was worsened further by Truman's lack of faith in his Defense Secretary. Secretary Johnson acted as though he was the one in charge of every aspect of government policy, and his tumultuous demeanor had already alienated him from the rest of the Cabinet. Truman soon discovered that Johnson was calling Republican Senator Robert Taft to encourage the latter's attacks on Secretary Acheson. But Truman, who had always hated firing anyone, allowed weeks to go by before he acted on Johnson's dismissal, and by that time the administration's policies in Korea were becoming disastrous.

In addition to Truman's low regard for Secretary Johnson, he also had severe reservations about General MacArthur, who was in charge of American operations in Korea. Truman, who had always found MacArthur to be vain and arrogant, was confronted by John Foster Dulles, a prominent Republican Senator from New York and President Eisenhower's future Secretary of State, about MacArthur's role in Korea. Dulles had held meetings with MacArthur in Japan, and was convinced that he had to go. But dismissing a five star general would be a tall task, even for a President. For the time being, Truman resolved to allow MacArthur to remain in his post.

Allied forces in Korea were left defending a small beachhead at the southern tip of the Korean peninsula by the beginning of August. But they were able to hold the line there with considerable success, and had finally stopped the retreat that had gone on for hundreds of miles. As General MacArthur pondered his next move, Averell Harriman was sent to Tokyo to tell MacArthur that he had to ensure that the Chinese nationalists who had been sent into exile would not be brought into the conflict, as it might spark a greater war with Communist China. The last thing Truman wanted was a war with Mao Zedong, which could easily turn into another world war.

When Harriman returned from his brief visit to Tokyo, he immediately met with Truman to discuss General MacArthur's new plan. The General had claimed that there was virtually no chance that the Chinese or the Russians might intervene in the Korean conflict should the United States go on the offensive. But MacArthur had also briefed Harriman on his plan of attack, which was in turn relayed to the President. American forces would land on the western shore of Korea at Inchon, about two hundred miles northwest of the Allied beachhead in Pusan. The landing would be incredibly difficult because of the tide and the lack of beaches where American forces could disembark. But MacArthur claimed that such an operation had been successfully used by the Japanese decades earlier, and the General believed that such an attack would take the North Koreans by complete surprise, and therefore catch them at a vulnerable point. MacArthur's plan was scheduled to be executed on September 15, 1950.

By the middle of August, more than one hundred thousand troops were stationed in the Allied beachhead of Pusan, half of them American. The rest were either South Korean forces or small units of Allied nations participating through the United Nations.

Harriman had warned the President about how difficult it would be for MacArthur's plan to be a success, but Truman gave MacArthur his preliminary consent to go ahead as planned. By September 15, thousands of American troops had been killed defending South Korea, and the need for an offensive was very urgent. North Korean troops were especially violent, and they would often wear civilian clothing to disguise their vicious intentions. MacArthur's offensive could not come soon enough.

Tensions between the President and General MacArthur continued to mount. Truman had asked the General to maintain silence on the issue of Chinese nationalism, but he had instead released a statement on August 10 that defended Chiang Kai-shek's leadership and his important role in Asia. Truman, who was constantly worried that the Chinese might involve themselves in Korea, was furious. When the President met with Acheson, Johnson, Harriman, and the Joint Chiefs, both Acheson and Harriman expressed their outrage with MacArthur's statements, which suggested insubordination. Truman was in no mood to dismiss MacArthur, but he instructed Secretary Johnson to ensure that the General withdraw his statement. Nonetheless, by September 9, Truman officially gave MacArthur his final approval of the General's attack plan through Inchon. This was despite the fact that MacArthur was convinced that there was a very good chance that his plan would fail miserably.

On September 1, 1950, President Truman took to the television to deliver a message to the American people from the Oval Office. His intention was to clarify his Korean policy, and explain America's objectives during the mission in Korea.

> Two months ago, Communist imperialism turned from the familiar tactics of infiltration and subversion to brutal attack on the small Republic of Korea. The friendly nations of the world faced two possible courses: To limit their action to diplomatic protests while the Communist aggressors swallowed up their victim; or to meet military aggression with armed forces. The second course is the one which the free world chose. Thus, for the first time in all history, men of many nations are fighting under a single banner to uphold the rule of law in the world. This is an inspiring fact.

On September 6, 1950, Truman summoned General Marshall to the White House. Although he had retired as Secretary of State less than two years prior, the President again asked him to return to public life and succeed Louis Johnson as Secretary of Defense. Truman had decided that Johnson had to go, and believed that General Marshall would be the best replacement, especially during a time of war. On September 11, Truman met with Secretary Johnson and informed him that he must either resign or be fired. He also asked his Defense Secretary to name Marshall as his ideal replacement. Johnson pleaded with Truman to consider keeping him in his job for a little longer, and when the President had not changed his mind a day later, the Defense Secretary began to weep in front of the President of the United States. Johnson's resignation was announced on September 12, as was the President's nomination of General Marshall as his successor.

In the early morning on September 15 in Korea, which was still the afternoon of September 14 in Washington, the invasion at Inchon began. The attack took the North Koreans completely by surprise, as MacArthur had anticipated, and turned out to be a great success. Seventy thousand men had participated in the Inchon invasion, while another part of the army pushed forward out of Pusan and headed north. By September 26, Allied forces had recaptured South Korea's capital city of Seoul. By the beginning of October, North Korean forces had been pushed past the 38th parallel, meaning that all of South Korea's former territory had been recaptured, and United Nations forces remained behind to occupy the country and enforce its borders.

After three months of speculation about how long the Allied United Nations forces might last in Pusan before losing the entire country of South Korea, two weeks of a brilliant offensive now begged the question as to whether or not the soldiers should continue to push north past the 38th parallel. Republican and Democratic politicians, Truman's military advisors, public opinion, and General MacArthur all wanted to push further north, defeat the Communist forces, and unify Korea under a democratic government. Secretary Acheson also favored a new offensive, especially because the 38th parallel was nothing more than an artificial border that had been drawn up less than ten years earlier.

With nearly everyone advising Truman to give the go ahead to MacArthur to continue the offensive, the President gave his approval of further action on September 27, even before United Nations forces had officially reached the 38th parallel. Their new mission was to push north and defeat the North Korean Communist armed forces. Despite the anti-Communist push, Truman's orders clearly informed MacArthur that he could not, under any circumstances, violate the Korean border with either China or the Soviet Union.

Warnings quickly came from the Chinese government that their military would come to North Korea's aid should American led forces cross the 38th parallel, but Truman and his advisors considered the threat to be nothing more than a bluff. By early October, the United Nations Security Council approved military action to "ensure conditions of stability throughout Korea," which essentially meant that the organization fully supported a continuation of the Korean War. Because the Soviets were still refusing to partake in the Security Council, and the Communist government in China did not have a seat in the ever important institution, the initiative's sponsors had faced little opposition to further action. With the approval of the United Nations, General MacArthur led his forces on a northern offensive than began on October 9, pushing past the 38th parallel for the first time. Nonetheless, as the world was soon to find out, China's threat was not unsubstantiated. The Chinese government in Beijing decided to come to the aid of their allies in Pyongyang.

Days after the Allied incursion into North Korea had begun, President Truman left Washington to meet with General MacArthur for the first time. MacArthur had spent the last several years in Japan, and had been stationed in Asia since before Truman had even been elected as Vice President. MacArthur chose to meet the President at Wake Island, an American territory located in between Guam and Hawaii. The destination was much closer for MacArthur to travel to than for the President, but Truman did not want the General to be away from the mission on the ground for very long.

Many cynics at home suggested that Truman was only going to Wake Island for a triumphant visit with General MacArthur to help Democrats who were up for re-election in the midterm elections scheduled for the following month. Even MacArthur himself believed that Truman had requested the meeting for purely political reasons, and was rather uncomfortable with the idea. Dean Acheson had also been uneasy with the idea of Truman flying so far away to meet with the triumphant General. He thought that the visit would make the President look weak for having to travel so much further than the General for a mere campaign ploy. Truman's Secretary of State therefore chose to be excluded from the trip.

Those who traveled with the President did not believe that the meeting was a simple campaign stunt. Truman genuinely wanted to be briefed on the state of the war, and of MacArthur's plan of attack for the weeks and months ahead. The President's plane arrived on Wake Island on October 15. MacArthur had been on the island waiting for the President since the night of October 14, and made sure to greet Truman personally as the President exited the Presidential plane. Averell Harriman, one of Truman's closest advisors, had also arrived on the island before the President, and informed MacArthur that the meeting was meant to allow the two men to discuss plans for how to translate a military victory into a political one. The General was pleased that Truman wished to consult him about the political part of the conflict, and the task of rebuilding a free and democratic Korea.

As Truman and MacArthur shook hands for the first time, dozens of members of the press were there to take numerous pictures that would soon appear in newspapers across the United States. As the two men departed from the landing area to hold meetings in some nearby huts, Truman began to probe MacArthur about the possibility of a Chinese intervention. The President would later claim that MacArthur assured him that the war in Korea was essentially over, and that the Chinese were not even considering an intervention. Truman admired the General's affability and forthrightness. MacArthur was also impressed by the President's demeanor, his engaging personality, and his brilliant sense of humor.

Truman and officials that had accompanied him on the trip met with MacArthur at a roundtable conference the following morning. Members of the administration keenly recorded the frank discussions that took place in a meeting that lasted for just under two hours. The President and his advisors did not propose any new course of action, and General MacArthur also refrained from suggesting any changes that should be made in the current war effort. General MacArthur assured the President that the fighting would be over by Thanksgiving, and that the North Korean capital of Pyongyang would be captured within days. He even went so far as to suggest that most of his troops could return to Japan by Christmas, and that a unified Korea could hold new elections under United Nations supervision by early January. American troops could furthermore return to their stations in Europe by January as well, which would bring the American presence in Europe back to its previous levels.

Despite MacArthur's rosy predictions, Truman still worried about the Soviets or the Chinese coming to the defense of their North Korean allies. The General did readily admitted that a Soviet intervention would pose a real threat to those fighting to defend South Korea, but also insisted that a Chinese invasion would not be hard to turn back. MacArthur's latter prediction would soon be proven to be very wrong.

MacArthur made a point of thanking Truman and other government representatives for their wholehearted support of the General's plans throughout his mission in Korea. The discussion continued about the situation on the ground, but the General and others also began to move on and speculate about a postwar reconstruction scenario. They conversed about the future of the North Korean prisoners of war now in the possession of Allied forces, and how a viable Korean government that stood for democratic values could be installed into office. When General MacArthur was asked by Truman and others whether or not he needed more troop reinforcements from the United Nations, he simply said that the decision should be left in the hands of those in Washington. Primarily, that meant President Truman.

Truman's official roundtable meeting with General MacArthur lasted only an hour and a half, which triggered a lot of cynicism in Washington. Many claimed that Truman had traveled so far for nothing more than a brief photo op, but the President felt he had a much greater grasp on the reality of the situation on the ground in Korea after a frank face to face discussion with his top General. While an official statement was being drawn up to be released to the press, the President and MacArthur talked about politics. When Truman was asked whether or not he would seek another term in office, the President demurred, and instead questioned MacArthur about whether or not politics would be in his future. MacArthur laughed and brushed the question aside, suggesting that the only General who might challenge Truman for the Presidency would be General Eisenhower. The President replied by suggesting to MacArthur that Eisenhower knew nothing about the field of politics. As Truman would soon learn several months later, he had severely underestimated Eisenhower's political abilities.

Before the President departed on his trip back to the United States, he awarded General MacArthur with a Distinguished Service Medal, a high honor that seemed only fitting for someone who had so capably served his country for so long. On his way back to Washington, the President stopped in San Francisco to make a public address, further praising General MacArthur for having written a great new chapter in American military history. After listening to the speech over the radio, General MacArthur called Truman to thank him for his kind words, and for the support that the President had given MacArthur throughout the General's mandate in Korea.

When President Truman returned to Washington, he found overwhelming public approval for his courage in committing American troops to fight in Korea. In a period of only three months, a situation that had appeared to be an imminent calamity had turned into one of triumph and optimism. Communist aggression had been stopped in its tracks, and those who had previously questioned Truman's resolve to fight the Communists could do so no longer. The war appeared to be nearly over, and

Truman had been able to prevent another world war, which had always been his preeminent concern.

Chapter Eleven

Problems in the Pacific

While the Korean War was thought to be an unparalleled success for President Truman and General MacArthur in the middle of October, warnings of impending disaster came to the President by the beginning of November. The Central Intelligence Agency delivered reports to the President on November 1, confirming that the Chinese had officially intervened on behalf of their North Korean allies. Thousands of Chinese soldiers had been pouring into the country for days, and the joint North Korean and Chinese forces numbered as many as two hundred thousand. General MacArthur's predictions had been proven wrong, and the possibility of a quick victory in Korea appeared to be growing dimmer by the hour.

As Truman continued to be given more bad news from Korea, he was also faced with an assassination attempt on November 1, 1950. The President was taking a nap at Blair House in the early afternoon, but assailants made their way to the front lawn by 2:20pm. They were two Puerto Rican nationalists who had decided to assassinate the President to bring attention to their group's push towards Puerto Rican independence. This was despite the fact that Truman had been the first President to appoint a native born Puerto Rican as the territory's Governor, and made social security available to citizens there. But Truman was targeted, as the world would later learn, simply because he was the symbol of the American system.

The two assailants opened fire on the Secret Service guards posted outside of Blair House, killing one of them before the two would be assassins were shot themselves, with one of them dying on the scene, and the other only somewhat wounded. Two other agents had been badly hurt but managed to survive. Truman, who had been scheduled to make a speech at Arlington National Cemetery, decided to go anyway, leaving only fifteen minutes after the assailants had first approached the property. It was not until well after the speech that Truman first learned that one of his Secret Service agents had been killed in the line of duty. His name was Leslie Coffelt, and the President would later arrange for a plaque bearing his name to be displayed permanently on the front lawn of Blair House.

Despite the President's relative calm, several more agents were from then on delegated to guard Truman at all times. To the press, Truman suggested that he had never been in any real danger, and that his Secret Service agents had done a remarkable job. In private, however, Truman grieved for the dead and injured, saddened by the thought that they sacrificed themselves for the President's benefit. The one assailant who did survive, Oscar Collazo, was given the death penalty as his punishment, but Truman intervened personally to have his sentence commuted to life in prison. In a rather controversial move, Jimmy Carter granted Collazo a pardon in 1979.

Harry Truman was the last President that the Secret Service had allowed to walk about in Washington without the protection of a car. From November 1, 1950, forward, the President was confined to a bulletproof car, no longer allowed to simply walk across the road from Blair House to get to his office in the White House. Truman would later reflect that he felt more trapped than ever in the Washington bubble after the incident.

November of 1950 had gotten off to a very rough start for President Truman, and the rest of the month proved to be no different. Midterm elections were held on November 7, and the Republicans made significant gains in both the House of Representatives and the Senate, although both chambers remained in Democratic hands. Sam Rayburn's Democratic caucus suffered a net loss of twenty eight seats in the House, and Ernest McFarland and his allies in the Senate lost five as well. The defeat was far less dramatic than what Truman had suffered through four years earlier, but it was still a rebuke of the administration nonetheless. Speculation about the possibility of Communists in the State Department, and the Republican argument that the intervention in Korea had left America vulnerable elsewhere, had been rather damaging. Scott Lucas, the incumbent Democratic majority leader in the Senate, went down to defeat in Illinois, losing to Republican Representative Everett Dirksen. Senator Joseph McCarthy had pledged to do all he could to defeat Lucas, a staunch ally of the Truman administration, and it had worked. McCarthy's brand of fear based politics appeared to have made the difference in 1950.

While the Democratic losses were not so severe based on the number of seats lost in both chambers, the popular vote totals were much more alarming. Republicans won just over fifty two percent of support from voters across the country in the elections for the House of Representatives, while the Democratic candidates drew only forty two percent of the votes cast. The results in the Senate were not as lopsided, but still disheartening. The Republicans had garnered two percentage points more in the overall popular vote for the Senate than their Democratic opponents, but the Democrats lost nine percentage points compared to their showing in 1948, while the Republicans gained seven.

When many in the press, and even some of Truman's advisors, suggested that he should fire Acheson as a result of the election loss, the President adamantly refused. Acheson had been one of the major targets of Republican slander during the election, but Truman refused to even consider the idea of asking Acheson to go.

As he was dealing with his party's defeat in the midterm elections, Truman was also forced to confront a major crisis in Korea. Chinese troops were still pouring across Korea's northern border, and General MacArthur suggested that there were upwards of thirty thousand of them now in the country. MacArthur, however, still discounted the fighting ability of the Chinese troops, and was relatively unprepared for a scathing offensive that would begin days later. With Truman's approval, MacArthur ordered the air force to bomb the ends of the bridges that troops were coming across to enter Korean territory, but Truman refused to allow the General to target the Chinese end of the bridges.

Further trouble appeared to be brewing in Korea with General MacArthur's foolish decision to drive north and split his Allied forces into two contingents. The Joint Chiefs had immediately questioned the wisdom of MacArthur's plan, but his brilliant coup a few months earlier had heightened the General's credibility. MacArthur's plan was incredibly risky, but he believed that it could prove to be the one powerful strike needed to end the war completely. Many in the administration doubted the wisdom of such a decision, but no one, including Truman, Marshall, or Acheson, attempted to stop him.

MacArthur's offensive began on November 24, 1950, but the General failed to make a miracle a second time around. By November 28, news reached Washington that the Chinese had begun a powerful counter-offensive in response to General MacArthur's plan of attack, with more than two hundred and sixty thousand Chinese and North Korean soldiers participating in the operation, far more than MacArthur or his aides had suggested had entered the country. Allied forces were now severely outnumbered, and were separated into two contingencies, making matters even more unsettling. By midday on November 28, Truman called in his closest advisors to meet to discuss the emerging foreign policy crisis.

Truman and his advisors were shocked by the sudden turn of events in Korea. It had gone from a heroic success story to a full blown war in a matter of weeks. The war had been won, but MacArthur and nearly everyone in Washington had convinced Truman to push north of the 38th parallel. Once the President had given his approval, anything that happened beyond that point was his responsibility. The mission in Korea had appeared to be a major achievement and legacy for the Truman Presidency only weeks before, but it now threatened America's national security, peace in the world, and the President's record itself.

Truman placed some of the blame for China's intervention on his domestic opponents. If his Democrats hadn't lost the midterms, weighed down by Republican accusations, America's enemies would not have thought that Washington was divided enough to be taken advantage of. The drubbing of Congressional Democrats, Truman reasoned, had falsely signaled to the Soviets and the Chinese that Americans were not behind the administration's foreign policy. Moreover, the media's sensationalism was only making matters worse.

President Truman's resolve remained firm nonetheless, and he instructed his advisors to get back to work straight away. Cabinet and the Congress would have to be informed in due course, but some of the discouraging news on the Chinese front should be kept out of the press. In speaking with General MacArthur, Truman was told that the Korean War had changed dramatically. There was no longer an immediate hope of victory, with the Chinese intent on completely destroying any American presence on the Korean peninsula. MacArthur even went further, suggesting that the United States would have to bring in Nationalist Chinese troops as supporters, and bomb and blockade mainland China. His advice, Truman quickly noted, had no regard for the inevitable response from the Soviet Union to such a move. Truman's number one priority was to ensure that the Korean conflict did not instigate a third world war.

Late in the afternoon on November 28, President Truman's National Security Council met to discuss America's options in Korea going forward. The group declared unanimously that the administration would have to do everything in its power to ensure that the situation in Korea did not expand into a worldwide conflict. Vice President Barkley fumed at MacArthur's false rhetoric: the General had promised that American troops would be home before the New Year. General Marshall, who was previously the army's Chief of Staff throughout the Second World War, and was now Truman's Secretary of Defense, spoke in a very grim manner. Marshall argued that, no matter what, the United States presence had to continue as part of a United Nations mission, which would help to guard against the possibility of directly antagonizing the Soviets. Moreover, America could not afford to be pulled into a war with China. While the United States had military technology that far surpassed their Chinese counterparts, China was still the most populous nation in the world. Furthermore, going to war with the Chinese would only strengthen Stalin's hand in Moscow.

When Secretary of State Acheson began to speak, he agreed with Marshall's assessment of the situation, but reminded everyone present that America would not be able to beat the Chinese in Korea. No matter what, the Chinese would be willing to pour far more troops into the country than the United States would. He was also gravely concerned with MacArthur's plans, warning about the danger of bombing mainland China as the General had suggested, and was even more horrified by the prospect of bringing Chinese Nationalist forces into the conflict. Doing so would likely trigger a full scale war, which had to be avoided at all costs. Bombing campaigns should only take place to save Americans on the ground, and directly bombing mainland China would almost certainly lead to a Soviet intervention into the conflict. The best thing to do was for General MacArthur to find a border that his troops could hold, and hold that line until calm prevailed. Truman and the rest of the Cabinet readily agreed.

As the Chinese troops continued to pour into Korea, American troops were on the retreat, and were forced to do so in the Korean winter, which was particularly brutal that year. Temperatures were as bad as twenty five degrees below zero Celsius. The reality of the situation was that American and Allied forces in Korea would either have to retreat or be slaughtered by oncoming Chinese troops, and weather conditions would have to be disregarded.

President Truman decided to have a press conference on November 30 to address the tumultuous situation. The President had always enjoyed a rather warm relationship with those who covered him on a regular basis, and his press conferences often went quite well. This time, however, Truman made a major fumble. He began by reading a written statement, claiming that the United States and its United Nations allies had no intention of being aggressive against Chinese forces. Nonetheless, the crisis in Korea was part of an international pattern of Communist expansionism and belligerent behavior. The United States had faced difficult situations before, such as Soviet expansionism in Berlin, but the Truman administration had stood tall and withstood the pressure, and the free world had prevailed. This time it would be no different.

> The forces of the United Nations are in Korea to put down an aggression that threatens not only the whole fabric of the United Nations, but all human hopes of peace and justice. If the United Nations yields to the forces of aggression, no nation will be safe or secure. If aggression is successful in Korea, we can expect it to spread throughout Asia and Europe to

this hemisphere. We are fighting in Korea for our own national security and survival.

When the President was asked about his opinion regarding negative criticism directed at MacArthur by international observers, Truman simply suggested that anyone who finds himself in a tough situation would be critiqued. Then the President was asked if MacArthur had overstepped his authority. Truman again defended the General, saying that he had gone no further than what the President had authorized. Up to this point, the President had done remarkably well, but everything began to unravel as the press conference continued. When the subject of attacking mainland China came up, Truman quipped that he would consider all options, which likely ramped up the tension between the opposing sides dramatically. Furthermore, the President refused to rule out the possibility of using a nuclear bomb, although he had done so privately. Worse still, Truman suggested that the military would decide whether or not a nuclear weapon would be used, and whether it would target military or civilian areas. The press conference then came to an abrupt halt, and headlines in newspapers around the world suggested that the President of the United States was actively considering the use of a nuclear bomb in the Korean conflict. Moreover, Truman's suggestion that the military would decide whether or not to use a bomb was inaccurate, because only the President could make that decision, but it gave the impression that Truman was not in command of the situation, and that the trigger happy General MacArthur had the weapon at his disposal.

Europe was immediately in a state of panic, worrying about an inevitable response from the Kremlin. Prime Minister Attlee in Great Britain was so alarmed that he took off for Washington to meet with Truman immediately. The President's press secretary, Charlie Ross, immediately released a statement of clarification, but the damage had already been done. While Truman's new statement suggested that only the President could give his consent to use a nuclear bomb, and that he had not yet authorized its use, panic across the world was largely maintained.

On the following day, December 1, Truman received the first indications of a Soviet response to the nuclear threat. In a meeting with members of the Cabinet present, the Central Intelligence Agency's director, Walter Smith, explained that the Russians had just maneuvered half a million men and had consolidated their Siberian commands, all of which suggested that they were preparing for a possible military offensive.

The mission in Korea was also floundering under the leadership of General MacArthur as panic spread worldwide. Many in the press and across Europe believed that he should be replaced, questioning his military strategy and his numerous blunders. But Truman was loathe to fire a General with such stature, especially after his success in the Inchon operation. General Walker, who was the senior advisor to the Korean contingent of the Allied army, was also thought to be someone who should be replaced. Secretary Marshall, along with the vast majority of Truman's military advisors, and even Secretary Acheson, had reassured the President of MacArthur's capability to continue to manage the situation in Korea. This was despite the fact that many expert observers outside Truman's inner circle wanted MacArthur, and especially Walker, to go. But Truman relied heavily on Marshall and Acheson's advice, and no major changes were immediately made.

Matthew Ridgeway, the deputy military advisor in the administration and the man who would replace General Walker after the latter's death weeks later, demanded action at a Cabinet meeting on December 3. But everyone else in the room had no suggestions, and still nothing was done. When Ridgeway asked why the Joint Chiefs did not straightforwardly give General MacArthur simple and direct orders, he was told that the General would simply ignore his orders. Dean Rusk from the State

Department, then the Assistant Secretary of State for Far Eastern Affairs, suggested that MacArthur should be relieved of his command the following day, but again no one in the administration decided to act.

As the Truman administration failed to address the personnel problem, members of the press continued to lay the blame for the quickly deteriorating situation at the feet of General MacArthur. It was by then widely known that MacArthur was a loose cannon who often exceeded the authority given to him by the President, and the press therefore faulted Truman's role in the situation as well. The General continued to deny to the press that his military blunders had led to the Chinese invasion, despite the fact that this was the nearly universal opinion around the world.

Despite the unraveling situation, Truman was determined to push forward in Korea, and members of the administration, while skeptical of their chances of defeating the Chinese onslaught, were determined to remain in the country and secure freedom for America's allies in the southern part of the peninsula. When Prime Minister Attlee arrived from Great Britain on December 4, he suggested to Truman that America should abandon its allies in Asia to help defend the Europeans, but the President flat out refused. Attlee was displaying a level of cowardice that would never have been expected from the likes of Sir Winston Churchill. But as Truman met with his British counterpart, American forces continued to retreat in Korea, abandoning the North Korean capital of Pyongyang and heading for the 38th parallel, the old Korean border. The two leaders did agree that the war had to be contained, and that an armistice should be sought with the intention of maintaining a border along the 38th parallel. Truman, however, made it clear that giving in to Chinese pressure in the Pacific would indicate that the United Nations coalition was no longer willing to pursue the President's containment foreign policy, which was essentially the basis of NATO's intentions. Truman and Attlee later released a joint statement in which they declared that the United Nations forces in Korea were prepared to enter into peace negotiations with the Chinese in order to secure a free and independent Korea. Nonetheless, the prospects for success were far from likely.

Charlie Ross, the President's long time press secretary and a dear friend, collapsed in the White House after a press briefing, and was found dead minutes later. He died at the age of sixty five on December 5, 1950, and was at the time actually a year younger than the President. Truman was distraught, as Ross had been a close friend who also came from Independence, Missouri. When the President went to read a statement to the press, he became too emotional, and quickly returned to his office as his eyes swelled with tears. Ross had suffered from a few heart attacks in the past, but hid them from the President, determined to serve with Truman until the President left office. Ross may very well have given his life to remain in the service of the President.

Despite Ross's sudden death, Truman chose to bring Prime Minister Attlee to a concert that his daughter Margaret was singing in downtown Washington. The reviews of her performance were rather negative, and Truman would take personal offense to unflattering commentaries. In the President's eyes, Margaret had performed the best he had ever seen. A particularly scathing review in the Washington Post prompted Truman to write the author, Paul Hume, a very nasty letter, which the President decided to mail to the journalist. When Hume received the letter, he refused to comment on it publically, but the letter was leaked and appeared in the Washington News. The President was well known for his violent temper at times, but members of his administration were usually present to quell his anger. This time, however, the letter had been made public, and the impression it made on Americans across the country led them to question Truman's personality, which is never a good thing to have happen to anyone in political life, least of all the President. Many editorials questioned Truman's grip on his own emotions, and whether he was fit to remain in office. President Truman's persona as an everyday American, which had long been seen as an asset, was now coming across as a liability. The American people expected a higher level of morality from their President, and Truman had failed to live up to that standard.

President Truman met with Congressional leaders on December 13 in the White House. The purpose of the meeting was to discuss the possibility of declaring a national emergency over the situation in Korea, which would delegate more power to the President, and allow for him to make quick decisions without a specific motion of authorization from the Congress. Many Republican leaders at the meeting pushed back, questioning the President about what he would want to do with emergency powers that he was unable to do at the present. The consultation lasted for several hours, and most of the men present agreed that America's national defense infrastructure should be strengthened dramatically. President Truman promised that, should Congress agree to the national emergency declaration, he would address the American people on the subject through a television broadcast. Truman ultimately decided to speak to his fellow citizens on the evening of December 15, and notified the American people and those around the world that a national state of emergency would be declared the following morning. He ended his speech by calling for all Americans to rally on the side of freedom.

> No nation has ever had a greater responsibility than ours at this moment. We must remember that we are the leaders of the free world. We must understand that we cannot achieve peace by ourselves, but only by cooperating with other free nations and with the men and women who love freedom everywhere.

General Walker was killed in a car accident on a highway in Korea on December 23. Although the circumstances of his death were tragic, it presented Truman with an opportunity to change at least some of the military hierarchy present in Korea. General MacArthur asked Truman to send Matthew Ridgeway as his replacement, and the President approved wholeheartedly. MacArthur assigned Ridgeway the command of the Eighth Army, which had been Walker's post, and was told to act as if he was the only one in command of his contingent. Ridgeway's presence in Korea would turn out to be a positive addition to the Allied war effort, and helped to once again turn the tide of the war.

In the weeks following the Chinese entrance into the Korean War, the Eighth Army had retreated by some three hundred miles, falling below the 38th parallel. Ridgeway even decided to abandon Seoul and head further south, although a counter offensive would commence in the coming weeks. General MacArthur, meanwhile, continued to press Truman to allow the Chinese Nationalists to enter the war, and again the President refused. When MacArthur claimed that the morale of his troops was low, Truman began to lose even more faith in the General, who the President believed should be responsible for maintaining that morale, something General Marshall adamantly agreed with. Even the Joint Chiefs urged that nuclear bombs be considered to target mainland China, but the President and his civilian advisors never took the idea under serious consideration.

As 1951 began, the situation in Korea was still far from positive. Truman continued to give MacArthur his full support, although his own Cabinet members were beginning to question the General's competence. The President did, however, once again urge MacArthur to act with more prudence and caution. Truman announced a further expansion of the nation's military budget, which was by January of 1951 three times the amount it had been a year earlier. He furthermore imposed more wage and price controls, doing so through the President's heightened powers granted by his declaration of a national state of emergency. Truman also decided to appoint General Eisenhower as the new Commander of the North Atlantic Treaty Organization in

December, signaling the possibility of a widening conflict. Late December of 1950 and early January of 1951 would prove to be the darkest days of the Korean War.

On January 17, 1951, news finally came of an improvement in the situation in Korea. General Marshall told President Truman that General Ridgeway had restored morale to the Eighth Army division, and halted their retreat. He now believed that the Allied forces could hold their ground for a number of months at the minimum, directly contradicting General MacArthur's dire reports of the situation. Eight days later, Ridgeway's troops began their counter offensive.

Nearly everyone in the Truman administration, impressed by Ridgeway's success and alienated by MacArthur's false reporting, began to rely on General Ridgeway's reports and largely by-passed the Allied commander in Korea. Ridgeway's counter offensive was beginning to look like a remarkable success. Their Eighth Army retook the South Korean capital of Seoul on March 15, and continued to proceed north. The role of General Ridgeway in turning the state of the conflict around was clearly essential. Walker and MacArthur had been leading the allies into a state of low morale and forced retreat, while MacArthur had predicted an imminent disaster if the Chinese Nationalists were not brought in as reinforcements. Both had been proven wrong, and General MacArthur was by then largely seen as incompetent. In the most fundamental of contrasts, General MacArthur was in a verbal battle with the administration, while General Ridgeway was getting the job done.

General Ridgeway and his troops had once again reached the 38th parallel by the end of March, this time on the offensive. They were facing a Chinese force that had more than one hundred thousand more troops than the Eighth Army, but Ridgeway's contingent had managed to inflict huge amounts of damage on the enemy. Despite Ridgeway's success, MacArthur still appeared to be distressed and miserable, declaring that only a quick and strong offensive against the Chinese could allow Korea to be unified. He wanted to use nuclear weapons and attack mainland China. Truman again denied MacArthur's increasingly radical requests. Throughout the winter, MacArthur appeared to become jealous of Ridgeway's successes. By the end of March, Truman decided that Ridgeway's success had put America into a position from which the government could negotiate an armistice with the Chinese. But MacArthur declared that such negotiations would not occur on his watch, virtually ignoring the President's requests entirely.

President Truman and his advisors in the State Department began to draft a peace proposal without MacArthur's knowledge. The General was first informed of the proposal on March 20, 1951, and was stunned that the administration was not going to allow him to go to war with China. Despite MacArthur's objections, the administration was ready to submit a draft of the peace proposal the following day to other members of the United Nations coalition partnership in Korea. To help stymie the peace proposal, MacArthur issued a statement to the Chinese lambasting them for their lack of industry, and threatened to expand the Korean conflict into a larger war by attacking the Chinese mainland. Truman's peace proposal efforts had been killed by one short statement released by the General, and he had not even been informed that MacArthur was planning to release a statement, let alone its contents.

After the President's top general in Korea had issued a statement intended to inflame the situation, Truman was no longer able to send a conciliatory statement to the Chinese, which would have threatened his credibility entirely. MacArthur appeared to think as though he was not accountable to anyone in Washington, least of all the President. Truman believed adamantly that major military decisions had to be made by elected officials, something MacArthur continually demonstrated he did not understand. Acheson, Marshall, and virtually all of Truman's advisors were calling for MacArthur's immediate dismissal. But the President managed to convince others in the administration that firing the General would be incredibly unpopular with the American people, who still revered MacArthur. As he pondered what to do with the personnel situation in Korea, Truman's popularity had plunged to its lowest point since the President had entered office.

Another bombshell broke on Capitol Hill on April 5. Former Republican Speaker of the House of Representatives Joe Martin rose to reveal to the chamber that he was in possession of a letter from General MacArthur. Martin had been calling for Truman to allow Chiang Kai-shek and his Chinese Nationalist followers to join the Korean conflict. The President, of course, feared that doing so would lead to a wider conflict. But General MacArthur had written a letter to Martin agreeing with the former Speaker about bringing the Nationalists into the war. In the General's eyes, the war against Communism began in Asia, which was why he was so eager to attack the Chinese directly. MacArthur declared that losing to the Communists in Asia would mean that losing Europe would become inevitable as well. While MacArthur was certainly within his rights to present his personal opinion to the President, he was most definitely wrong to share an opinion that clashed with Truman's policies to anyone outside of the administration, least of all his Republican opponents in Congress. Truman, once he had heard about the existence of Martin's letter from General MacArthur, failed to register a significant reaction at the outset. But in the coming hours the President became convinced that something would have to be done, and he called in his closest advisors for a meeting in the White House the following day.

General Marshall, Secretary Acheson, Averell Harriman, and Omar Bradley, the Chairman of the Joint Chiefs, were all summoned to the Oval Office to discuss the future of General MacArthur, and the situation in Korea as a whole. Both Marshall and Acheson knew that MacArthur would have to go, but they also warned Truman to exercise caution. Firing the General would mean admitting that the present situation in Korea was not where it should be, and asking a decorated wartime leader to step aside would not be an easy task. But MacArthur had already caused Truman so much trouble that everyone present in the meeting advised the President to replace his top General in Korea. Truman still chose to think the matter over for several days, calling on Vice President Barkley for his advice, which turned out to be the same guidance the President had received from his top military and foreign policy advisors: fire MacArthur.

While General Marshall knew MacArthur would have to be replaced, he worried about the effect the firing might have on his own reputation, which would likely be called into question for advising the dismissal of a former close colleague. Marshall, Truman, and their advisors were still no closer to a decision on April 7 than they had been a day earlier. By Monday, however, the Joint Chiefs had unanimously told Truman that, from a military and strategic standpoint, MacArthur would have to be relieved of his command. When Marshall, Acheson, Harriman, and Bradley once again joined Truman to discuss the matter that morning, they finally reached a verdict. On April 9, 1951, President Truman decided to fire General Douglas MacArthur.

News first broke of MacArthur's dismissal on Capitol Hill, where an unnamed source revealed to the Washington Post that Truman had finally decided to replace his General in the Far East. Despite the reports in the press, General MacArthur was not yet aware of his firing, and he told reporters in Tokyo that he was still on the job. Truman refused to answer questions on the issue as well. Nonetheless, at just after 3pm on April 9, President Truman officially signed the executive order that was to relieve MacArthur of his command. He quickly dispatched military aides to inform ambassadors from every country participating in the United Nations mission of the firing. A cable was also sent to MacArthur in Tokyo that he was to be replaced, and notified General Ridgeway that he was to be that replacement.

A letter from President Truman announced to the American people and others around the world at a press conference held in the middle of the night on April 11 that he had asked General MacArthur to step aside. The General would later claim that he would have simply retired if Truman had informed him of his intentions, but the President was adamant that he wanted MacArthur to be fired before he had a chance to quit. MacArthur, by then on the verge of deliriousness, suggested that Truman must have had a chemical imbalance in his brain that caused mental instability, and that the President would drop dead within six months. As it turned out, Truman would live for another twenty one years. In Truman's statement to the press, he was careful to emphasize the necessity of MacArthur's dismissal.

> With deep regret, I have concluded that General of the Army Douglas MacArthur is unable to give his wholehearted support to the policies of the United States Government and of the United Nations in matters pertaining to his official duties. In view of the specific responsibilities imposed upon me by the Constitution of the United States and the added responsibility which has been entrusted to me by the United Nations, I have decided that I must make a change in the Far East.

Hysteria broke out in regions across the United States. Truman had anticipated a negative reaction from the general public, but it was worse than anyone could have expected. Republicans on Capitol Hill spoke of impeaching the President for his decision, with prominent leaders such as Senator Taft of Ohio supporting the idea. Joseph Martin, the Republican Minority leader in the House, announced that General MacArthur would be invited to testify before Congress as part of a process that would fully examine the President's military policies. Senator Richard Nixon of California, the future President of the United States, also urged Truman to immediately reinstate MacArthur to his post. But Democrats were also outspoken in defending their President. Many pointed out that, by supporting General MacArthur over Truman, the Republicans were essentially calling for an all-out war with China. Even some moderate Republicans, such as Senator Henry Cabot Lodge Jr. from Massachusetts, supported Truman's decision.

As chaos took over Washington, riots broke out across the country. Thousands of people walked away from their jobs in protest, while others flew their flags at half-mast. Tens of thousands of Americans from every region of the nation signed various petitions demanding MacArthur's reinstatement. State legislatures in Florida, Illinois, California, and Michigan passed resolutions condemning Truman for the firing. Thousands of the telegrams from across the country that flowed to representatives in Congress overwhelmingly called for Truman's removal from office immediately. The President's most staunch liberal allies, however, held firm. Eleanor Roosevelt, Justice William Douglas, and others all announced their support for Truman's decision to replace the fear mongering, trigger happy General. Truman had always been adamant that citizens, and not those who were in the military, should remain in charge of the nation's foreign policy. MacArthur had repeatedly overstepped his bounds, and the President's only choice was to uphold that principle.

Reaction in Europe was nearly polar opposite to the reaction across North America. Europeans were ecstatic that MacArthur had finally been removed from command in Korea. Politicians across the continent had feared that MacArthur would instigate a larger war through his provocational threats directed at China, which would directly endanger the states that were so close to the Soviet Union, whose leadership would surely come to China's aid.

Although Republicans in Congress and many Americans across the country were angered by Truman's decision, thereby largely discounting MacArthur's insubordination, most editorials in the nation's major newspapers lauded Truman for the General's dismissal. They praised Truman for his strong character, and for being willing to endure the negative political fallout of his unpopular but wise decision. Many Presidents in a similar scenario would have avoided firing MacArthur in the fear of angering American voters.

Truman decided to make a short televised statement to the nation on April 11 to discuss General MacArthur's dismissal. The General had spent his career serving America with distinction and valor, but he had been standing in the way of peace in Korea. Moreover, America's mission in Korea was the same mission that had instigated the creation of the Marshall Plan and the Berlin Airlift: to contain Communism expansionism.

> If history has taught us anything, it is that aggression anywhere in the world is a threat to peace everywhere in the world. When that aggression is supported by the cruel and selfish rulers of a powerful nation who are bent on conquest, it becomes a clear and present danger to the security and independence of every free nation.
>
> The question we have had to face is whether the communist plan of conquest can be stopped without general war. Our Government and other countries associated with us in the United Nations believe that the best chance of stopping it without general war is to meet the attack in Korea and defeat it there.
>
> So far, we have prevented World War III.
>
> I believe that we must try to limit the war to Korea for these vital reasons: to make sure that the precious lives of our fighting men are not wasted; to see that the security of our country and the free world is not needlessly jeopardized; and to prevent a third world war. A number of events have made it evident that General MacArthur did not agree with that policy. I have therefore considered it essential to relieve General

MacArthur so that there would be no doubt or confusion as to the real purpose and aim of our policy.

It was with the deepest personal regret that I found myself compelled to take this action. General MacArthur is one of our greatest military commanders. But the cause of world peace is more important than any individual.

Just when life in Washington appeared to be returning to a state of relative calm, General MacArthur's arrival back in United States heightened tensions dramatically. Most Americans, already questioning why their country was fighting in a conflict in Asia anyway, were eager to side with a military man of such distinction rather than a President who was leading the nation through an unpopular war. Truman's talk of a limited war angered those who believed that the United States should decisively win any military conflict it entered into, while the ten thousand troops that had already sacrificed their lives appeared to be doing so for nothing more than a stalemate. Harry Truman, famous for campaigning for office as an everyday American, had fired America's most distinguished general in a generation.

When General MacArthur landed in San Francisco on April 17, 1951, it was his first time back to the United States mainland in more the fourteen years. Thousands of Americans came out to greet the General at the airport, and his arrival in Washington was no different. Truman refused to discuss the MacArthur matter before the press the following day, which was the day before the General was scheduled to testify before Congress. He believed adamantly that the right decision had been made, and Truman was convinced he would be vindicated by history. In the decades following the end of the Korean War, the President was proven to be largely right.

Opinion polls showed that the vast majority of Americans disapproved of the possibility of going to war with China, which was essentially the plan of action that MacArthur had proposed. The General had also led the United Nations coalition forces through one of the most ill-advised military blunders in American history in his November of 1950 offensive. But MacArthur carried with him a sense of authority and charisma that Truman never could. Truman, therefore largely abandoned the Washington limelight, preferring to allow MacArthur to testify before Congress without commenting on the matter. He did decide to throw out an opening pitch to kick-start the 1951 baseball season for the Washington Senators at Griffith Stadium, a tradition that every President since William Howard Taft had honored. Rather than a standing ovation, as most Presidents might expect to receive, Truman was booed by the crowd until he had walked back into the dugout. Only Herbert Hoover had experienced a similar humiliation, but even that had been in the midst of the Great Depression.

Back on Capitol Hill, MacArthur arrived to appear before Congress with much fanfare. Truman had insisted on being quite cordial, sending General Marshall and the Joint Chiefs to greet MacArthur upon his return to the nation's capital. But MacArthur would later largely decline to extend the President a similar curtesy.

General MacArthur entered the House of Representatives to make an official address to a joint session of Congress on the afternoon of April 19. Only Vice President Barkley was present to observe the speech as a member of the administration, with everyone else in Truman's Cabinet having decided to skip the event. As he began his speech, MacArthur declared that the President's decision to intervene in Korea had been the right one to make. But the General alleged that when he had requested more troops, the President had refused to accommodate his request.

Unlike Truman, MacArthur noted that he had wanted permission to allow Chinese Nationalists to participate in the conflict, and to bomb Chinese mainland targets in order for the United States to win the war decisively. The President appeared to want peace without victory, something that was unwise and naïve. MacArthur even alleged that Truman was prepared to appease "Red China," although he pointedly failed to mention that he had secretly proposed to the President that nuclear weapons be used in the conflict. He also claimed that the Joint Chiefs secretly supported his point of view, but that the President had not permitted them to disclose their own personal opinions. Moreover, failing to decisively beat the Chinese in Asia could lead to the endangerment of Europe, although once again MacArthur failed to mention that this was the primary reason for his own dismissal, as Truman had feared the General's aggression could lead to a world war if left unchecked. Nonetheless, MacArthur finished his speech with a standing ovation, which more than thirty million Americans would see live on television. One positive thing for President Truman, however, was that MacArthur insinuated at the end of his address that it would be the final time he spoke before the nation. MacArthur had delivered quite a performance, but at least it would be his final act.

Chapter Twelve

Controversy and Corruption

In the spring of 1951, Senate committees held an investigation into General MacArthur's involuntary departure from Korea. The central inquiry was chaired by Richard Russell, a Democratic Senator and former Governor of Georgia who had served alongside President Truman in the Senate for a decade. While Russell had ruled that the committee's hearings would be held in private, transcripts of the accounts given by witnesses were released to the public. President Truman felt that the hearings would only further embolden Communist forces in Asia, who would take note of the deep divisions within the American government.

The Russell Committee's first official witness was General MacArthur himself, who argued that his controversial strategy that would include an offensive against China was the best way to win the war. He argued that the Truman administration was pursuing a policy of indecisiveness and did not have the will to win the conflict, which was why the President and MacArthur had clashed. Refusing to take any blame for the disastrous situation he had left behind in Korea, the General spent hours trying to heap his own praise. MacArthur blamed the Central Intelligence Agency for not foreseeing the Chinese intervention into the conflict, despite the fact that he personally had guaranteed the President that such an intervention would not occur. When Senators further questioned MacArthur about the feasibility of his plan to take the offensive into China, the General predicted that the Soviets would never join such a war, notwithstanding the fact that every indication suggested otherwise. If the Soviets did join the war, MacArthur claimed that even if the idea to attack China was his idea, a Soviet intervention would not be of his doing. More than anything else, MacArthur's testimony on Capitol Hill seemed to vindicate the President's reputation by demonstrating just how poor the General's judgement had become.

MacArthur's case took a further beating when Secretary Marshall came to Capitol Hill to testify at the hearings. Contrary to what General MacArthur had claimed, Marshall declared that he had never supported the General's plan to launch an offensive against China, which he emphasized would probably lead to another world war. A decisive win in Korea would in fact likely lead to more conflict in the future. The Joint Chiefs also came to the committee to echo Marshall's comments, suggesting that no one in Truman's inner circle supported MacArthur's ludicrous plans, contrary to what the General had kept emphasizing. They also made it clear that Truman had not fired MacArthur on a whim, but rather he had waited to do so until there was a sense of unanimity among his military advisors for him to take such an action.

Despite General MacArthur's reputation, much of the testimony from General Marshall and others seemed to help justify Truman's actions. As Marshall himself claimed, while he had great respect for the General and his wartime record, he felt compelled to come before the committee and directly contradict nearly everything MacArthur had said. In effect, Marshall was willing to put his own reputation on the line to help discredit his former colleague, something President Truman would never forget. Korea was a limited war, and had to remain so in order to uphold peace in the world. General Ridgeway understood that reality, something General MacArthur had never been able to do.

When General Bradley took the stand, he echoed much of what General Marshall had said, but he also further attacked MacArthur for his planned offensive against Communist China. MacArthur, he claimed, would involve the United States "in the wrong war, at the wrong place, at the wrong time, and with the wrong enemy." Along with the Joint Chiefs, Bradley again emphasized that no one had supported MacArthur's ill-advised plan for a strategic offensive against the Chinese, which they all agreed would likely have provoked the Soviet Union. Bradley also told the Senators that MacArthur's dismissal was an essential element of victory in Korea, and the decision made by the President was in the best interest of the United States.

With General Marshall, General Bradley, Secretary Acheson, and virtually all of the nation's military officials testifying against MacArthur at the committee, the Republicans appeared to be out of ammunition. As Truman had hoped, the commotion would largely wind down by the end of the spring. In a matter of weeks, MacArthur had gone from the status of a national hero to that of an absentminded official whose time to retire was long overdue.

While MacArthur's reputation had finally taken a beating, Truman's was hurt as well. The entire firing process had been one debacle after another, and skepticism about the war in Korea among American voters was spreading quickly. Despite the fact that Truman had made the right decision, he declined to make his case to the nation, having hidden from the limelight since his television address in early April. While the vast majority of Americans were beginning to recognize that Truman had been right to fire MacArthur, the President had still failed to convince voters that American troops should be involved in the conflict at all. Whether he was too tired from seven years in the White House or no longer worried about having to fight another election, Truman largely abandoned the bully pulpit and made few attempts to rationalize his decision to Americans across the country. This would prove to be a major blunder on the part of the President.

Truman would later admit in his memoirs and interviews that the biggest regret of his presidency was not firing General MacArthur months earlier than he did. Although his initial hesitation was understandable given the inevitable backlash that would sweep the nation, Truman regretted not having made the decision earlier, and the fact that public opinion had made such a major impact on that timeline. But his decision to fire MacArthur, despite the General's support from voters across the country, was courageous, and it would turn out to be one of the most important decisions of Truman's political career. In firing MacArthur, President Truman initiated the process that began to improve the American position in the Korean conflict, and enabled his successor to be in a position to end the conflict altogether. He also restrained a military menace who believed that he should be able to act fully independent of the President's authority. Most importantly, Truman's rebuke of General MacArthur also pointed to his steadfast determination in preventing the Korean War from becoming another world war, which would ultimately prove to be achieved because of the administration's restraint. His decisions may not have been popular at the time, but Truman clearly charted the right course.

Truman was convinced that victory in Korea would have to be avoided at all costs, if only to ensure that the world remained in a general state of peace. While it may sound like an incredible statement, a decisive victory in Korea, along the lines of what General MacArthur had wanted, would have meant risking further escalation and therefore the possibility of a world war, which was far less desirable than a stalemate in the Korean conflict. Moreover, sending more troops to Asia for a large scale war would mean leaving Europe defenseless against Soviet aggression, which was likely the outcome that the Russians had been hoping for all along.

On June 25, 1951, President Truman officially announced that he wanted to find a peaceful end to the war in Korea through a ceasefire at the 38th parallel. When officials in Russia appeared to be willing to encourage a Korean armistice, Truman gladly welcomed his Chinese and North Korean opponents to the bargaining table. The President would seek a political solution that would leave South Korea with an independent and democratic government, and a military solution that would guarantee the integrity of the nations' 38th parallel border. Speaking in Tennessee, Truman declared that the Soviets were ultimately responsible for the conflict in East Asia: "the Kremlin is still trying to divide the free nations. The thing that the Kremlin fears most is the unity of the free world."

Although American representatives began holding meetings with North Korean and Chinese representatives at peace negotiations in the summer of 1951, talks which were supervised by the United Nations, the fighting in Korea waged onward, with thousands of Americans still putting their lives on the line to defend America's allies in the southern portion of the Korean peninsula. Republicans in Congress, now less eager to defend General MacArthur, still attacked Secretaries Marshall and Acheson relentlessly, further damaging the administration's rapport with their Republican opponents. Worse still, by the end of August, the number American soldiers killed in Korea had passed thirteen thousand, with more than eighty thousand wounded. Truman's relations with Congress took yet another blow when his old friend Arthur Vandenberg, who had been the President's closest Republican ally in the Senate, passed away at the age of sixty seven after a short battle with cancer. The long-time Senator from Michigan died while still in office.

As the MacArthur crisis died down, and the Korean conflict wore on, speculation began to build in the summer of 1951 that Truman was preparing for another run for the White House. As the last President who would not be impacted by the twenty second amendment to the constitution, Truman was certainly eligible for another four years in the White House. In 1952 the President would be sixty eight years old, but he continued to appear young, vibrant, and active for his age. Truman showed no signs of slowing down, continued to exercise daily, and never appeared tired on the job. He told reporters that he felt better than ever, which many took as a sign that the President would attempt to follow his predecessor in seeking a third term. Truman was still unwilling to commit himself one way or the other in public.

Senator Joseph McCarthy of Wisconsin, who had badgered the administration over its supposed sympathy for Communism throughout Truman's stay in the White House, once again stepped up his attacks on the Truman administration in the latter half of 1951. He attacked Marshall and Acheson for being part of what he called to be a Communist conspiracy that would bring down the nation. Rather than MacArthur, McCarthy blamed Marshall for the crisis in Korea and America's poor relations with China, despite the fact that Marshall had not even been Secretary of Defense when the war first began more than a year prior. With no evidence to back up his still baseless allegations, the vast majority of his Senate colleagues began to walk out on McCarthy's speeches, including almost all of the chamber's Republican members. Truman, finally at the breaking point, summoned top Democratic Senators to Blair House to discuss the McCarthy situation. McCarthy was ripping the nation apart, and Truman was determined to find a way to oppose him. Nonetheless, despite the fact that Senate Democrats had an abundance of damaging details of McCarthy's personal life that could discredit the Wisconsin Republican Senator forever, Truman refused to play dirty politics in the manner that McCarthy so thoroughly enjoyed.

McCarthy's attacks would finally take their toll when General Marshall submitted a letter of resignation to the President in September of 1951. He had served as Secretary of Defense for only one year, but had only agreed to do so as a temporary favor to Truman in a time of crisis. The now seventy year old war hero was ready for a permanent retirement, and Truman reluctantly agreed to Marshall's request. While Marshall claimed that McCarthy's attacks had nothing to do with his departure, they certainly may have helped push him towards making a final decision. In praising his retiring Secretary of Defense, Truman declared publically that Marshall had been one of the greatest public servants the United States had ever seen.

As the fall of 1951 approached, evidence of corruption within the Truman administration continued to surface. President Truman had continued Franklin Roosevelt's practice of rewarding Democratic fundraisers and supporters with posts in government, but could never quite come to grips with the possibility of some of his appointees acting in an unethical or illegal manner. News came from a report delivered by a Senate committee investigating favoritism and influence in the Reconstruction Finance Corporation, which was tasked with providing low interest loans to business. High ranking members of the Democratic Party, and even an aide in the Truman administration, were accused of favoring Democratic friendly corporations. These riveting charges suggested a line of corruption that came all the way from the Truman White House, and the President appeared to be unable to control unethical conduct within his administration and the Democratic Party. Those at the center of the conspiracy included William Boyle, the Chairman of the Democratic Party, Donald Dawson, an administrative assistant to the President, and E. Merl Young, whose wife worked at the White House, all of whom came from Missouri, helping to further implicate the President in the eyes of the general public. They were all friends of Truman or his close aides, and the President's opponents suggested that America's government was once again headed back to the type of corruption in the White House that had not been seen since the Harding administration.

Truman, angered by many who suggested that he was a party to government corruption, denounced the Senate report, which only pushed Senate Republicans to launch public hearings. While Truman's allies were accused of using their influence to further loans for friends of the Democratic Party, the President astutely found copies of letters from his opponents in Congress, many of whom had criticised his conduct, who had also written to him asking for similar help for their own friends in the business community. Nonetheless, Democratic Senators came to visit Truman in the White House, and told him that some of his friends had not been loyal to him and were clearly partaking in corrupt practices. Truman reluctantly admitted that it appeared to be the case, and inferred that action would have to be taken.

As a first step in restoring public confidence in the Reconstruction Finance Corporation, Truman nominated Stuart Symington, a former Secretary of the Air Force and future Senator from Missouri, to end the rampant corruption within the organization. Symington, a well-respected public official who had played an instrumental role in the Berlin airlift, immediately returned a sense of credibility to the controversial organization. But when Doyle, Dawson, Young, and others were called to testify before the Senate's public hearings investigating government corruption, political mud was thrown on both sides, further damaging the already shaky reputation of the Washington establishment. It was furthermore becoming clear that corporations that had been on the road to bankruptcy were rescued by the government through loans simply because of their political connections.

Along with the collusion in the Reconstruction Finance Corporation, more evidence of corruption was found in the tax department. Then news broke that William Boyle, the Democratic Party Chairman, had received $8,000 for arranging a loan for a St. Louis printing firm through his influence in the Truman administration, and that the payment had been received after his nomination to lead the Democratic Party. It was Truman who had secured several job opportunities for Boyle, who he had known since he was a young boy in rural Missouri. But Truman's advisors recognized Boyle for what he was: an alcoholic, an influence peddler, and a crook. They urged the President to fire the corrupt members of his administration and the Democratic Party, but Truman refused to admit that any of his associates had conducted themselves in a grossly illegal manner. He did, however, allow for an investigation into possible administrative corruption to be conducted by his legal counselor, Charles Murphy. Murphy found no evidence of Boyle acting in an improper manner, and Truman chose to stand by his friend, although he once again emphasized to the press that no party official should ever take fees or bribes for any decisions made by the administration. Nonetheless, Boyle felt compelled to resign, and he did so before the end of the year.

Truman was greatly relieved when news broke in the fall of 1951 that the Republican Party's leadership had been allowing for rampant corruption within their own organization. Guy Gabrielson, the Chairman of the Republican National Committee, freely admitted when testifying before a Senate hearing that he had been paid $25,000 for helping to ensure the Reconstruction Finance Corporation offered to help with loans to a corporation in Texas. Nevertheless, just as the heat was beginning to be taken off of the Democratic National Committee and most of its officials had been cleared of any wrongdoing, a scandal in the tax department exploded into a full blown crisis.

In April of 1951, before the tax crisis reached its climax, St. Louis's tax collector, James Finnegan, resigned from his post, despite having been cleared of all criminal charges by a grand jury. By the beginning of the summer, two more tax collectors in major cities had to be fired: Denis Delaney in Boston and James Smyth in San Francisco. Months later, Brooklyn's tax collector, Joseph Marcelle, was also forced from his post. Despite the fact that the corruption found appeared to be isolated in a handful of cities, all four of the men who were forced from office, or in Finnegan's case by resignation, had been appointed to their posts by Bob Hannegan when he was the head of the Internal Revenue Service under President Roosevelt. Hannegan and the men he hired also happened to be active members of the Democratic Party, and at least three of them were found to have participated in corrupt practices: Delaney for taking bribes, Smyth for fixing false tax claims, and Marcelle for cheating on his own tax returns. As this corruption was revealed, Truman's head of the Internal Revenue Service, George Shoeneman, resigned, as did his assistant and the bureau's top lawyer. Hannegan could not be called on to defend his own reputation because of his sudden death in 1949. Nevertheless, the fact that he was a former Chairman of the Democratic National Committee and devoted Truman ally from Missouri allowed for the administration's critics to draw causal links between Hannegan and his corrupt appointees.

While the scandals surrounding the tax department continued, Truman and his officials were quick to point out that all of those that had been found guilty of corruption up until that point had been Roosevelt appointees. But by the fall of 1951, Truman was forced to fire General Lamar Caudle, a man that he had appointed to the tax division in the Justice Department, for gross criminal negligence. As 1951 came to a close, President Truman had fired one hundred and thirteen officials in the Internal Revenue Service, including regional collectors from states across the country. As more corruption continued to be revealed, Truman pledged to the nation that no more partisan patronage appointments would be made Internal Revenue Service, instead allowing for civil servants to oversee the organization. The President was determined to end the rampant corruption that appeared to be plaguing his administration, which was already seeming to be a major stain on his Presidential reputation.

On June 29, 1951, President Truman issued a directive to General Ridgeway in Korea to reach out to the Communist commander to propose a new round of cooperative settlement talks. Two days later, Ridgeway received a reply indicating that the Communists were prepared to meet United Nations forces at the bargaining table. Officers from both sides initiated discussions on July 7. Nonetheless, despite agreeing to the meeting, the Communist representatives did all they could to stall any chance of an agreement. President Truman informed his delegates that in the event negotiations failed, he wanted to ensure that the blame for the lack of cooperation was placed squarely on the shoulders of North Korean and Chinese Communist forces.

Despite Truman's best intentions, negotiations became more complicated when South Korea's President, Syngman Rhee, declared that he would accept no other outcome than the unification of Korea. Further issues about the exchange of prisoners of war complicated the situation. On January 1, 1952, President Truman proposed that any troops captured by either side be returned to their respective countries. He was determined to bring every American captive home, especially because of the reports of the extreme brutality the prisoners were forced to endure in the hands of the Communists. Nevertheless, the President was also adamant about allowing Chinese and North Korean prisoners of war who did not want to return to their native countries be allowed to remain in a free and democratic South Korea, something Communist negotiators were steadfastly against. As Truman himself proclaimed, America would "not buy an armistice by turning over human beings for slaughter or slavery."

Communist negotiators agreed to an exchange of all prisoners of war in early 1952, but would not accept Truman's ultimatum of not returning those prisoners of war who sought to remain in the free world. Truman asked General Ridgeway to leave Korea in May of 1952 in order to succeed General Eisenhower as the Supreme Allied Commander in Europe. Eisenhower had stepped down to prepare his campaign for the Presidency later that year.

General Mark Clark was chosen as Ridgeway's replacement in Korea.

Chapter Thirteen

The Search for a Successor

While President Truman had decided in the spring of 1950 that he did not want to seek another term as President, by late 1951 several members of his administration wanted to see their leader fight one more election. The most prominent concern, of course, was who would replace Truman as the Democratic Party's standard bearer. If the President did not run in 1952, many questioned whether or not there was someone who could keep the Democrats in the White House. In many cases, when an incumbent President retires, his Vice President seeks to succeed him. But Alben Barkley would be seventy four by the time of the election, effectively ruling him out entirely. Truman desperately wanted to escape the confines of the White House, but his determination to prevent a Republican from gaining the Presidency had the potential to convince him otherwise.

There were many signs, however, that, should President Truman choose to seek a third term, he would have just as hard of a battle in 1952 as he did in 1948. The Korean War raged on, and, despite the faint glimmer of peace on the horizon, American soldiers continued to die on the battlefield. One of the major roadblocks towards peace was the question of what to do with such a large number of prisoners of war that were being held in

United Nations custody: some one hundred and thirty two thousand Chinese and North Koreans. While the United States had suggested at the beginning of the negotiations that the American military would support an exchange of prisoners of war, nearly half of the Chinese and North Korean troops did not want to return home and face the wrath of a brutal dictator in Mao Zedong or Kim Il-sung. Truman, remembering the tens of thousands of Soviet troops that were executed by Stalin's regime in the aftermath of the Second World War, wanted to give the Chinese and North Korean troops a choice as to whether or not they wanted to be repatriated. The President was unwilling to send thousands of troops back to China and North Korea in a move that would likely condemn them to a life of abuse and slavery.

In the aftermath of the summer of 1951, the number of American casualties in Korea continued to decline by the month, but the nation's politics and its citizens had been polarized by the Korean experience, heightening tensions across Capitol Hill and the nation as a whole. More than fifty percent of Americans now claimed that they favored General MacArthur's idea of using a nuclear bomb to end the conflict, and, as Truman refused to step up the war effort, his favourability among the public continued to plunge. To many Americans, Truman seemed willing to risk the lives of their sons, brothers, husbands, and fathers to avoid a much larger conflict in Asia, a faraway place that found little empathy among the American public. In reality, Truman wanted the war to end just as badly as the rest of his fellow citizens, but he also had a duty to try to uphold world peace and prevent yet another world war. Once again, the President was willing to pursue an unpopular policy for the long term good of the nation.

With war raging in the Pacific, Republicans began to look to the 1952 Presidential election just as anxiously as they had awaited the same contest in 1948. But Republican leaders had learned their lesson from the previous campaign, and were itching to take on the Democrats in what promised to be a much more aggressive electoral effort. Moreover, both parties were hoping to recruit Dwight Eisenhower to run on their Presidential ticket, with Republicans believing that victory would be assured, and Democrats convinced that the former General would allow them to hold onto the White House. Truman's popularity had dropped to only twenty three percent by the end of 1951, and the likelihood of another run for the White House appeared to be declining by the hour.

Although Americans and many political pundits were still unsure as to whether or not Truman would run in 1952, the President had already told his staff that he intended to retire. In November of 1951, Truman officially announced to his close aides during a trip to Florida that he would not seek another term. The President had actually written the statement that he would release to the public in the spring of 1950, and there was nothing anyone accompanying him on the trip could do to convince him otherwise. Truman planned to release his statement in April of 1952, and asked all of his close friends not to share the information with anyone in order to keep the news away from the press. On August 2, 1927, President Coolidge had stunned the nation by declaring "I do not choose to run for President in 1928." Truman's letter would be far more eloquent, and the move would be far less surprising.

President Truman entered the final year of his Presidency with a visit from Sir Winston Churchill, who just months earlier had surprised the world by being elected as Prime Minister of Great Britain at the age of seventy seven. Truman and Churchill had always had great respect for one another, and Truman was thrilled by the Prime Minister's visit. Churchill landed in Washington on January 5, 1952, and was greeted at the airport by the President himself. Both Truman and Secretary Acheson were extremely fond of the Prime Minister, and each had come to believe that he was perhaps the greatest statesman of the twentieth century. The two leaders discussed Soviet expansionism and the United Nations effort in Korea, which Churchill fully supported. He praised Truman for his steadfast leadership in the face of Communist aggression. In what was possibly the greatest compliment Truman would ever be paid in his political career, Prime Minister Churchill told Truman that he, "more than any other man, ha[d] saved Western civilization."

After three years of renovations, the White House was finally able to welcome public visitors in April of 1952. Truman and his family had been forced to vacate the residence three years prior, and had only recently moved back to Pennsylvania Avenue. The President had taken great pride in playing a very prominent role in deciding on the final renovations and many of the smaller details. Truman welcomed Walter Cronkite of CBS, Frank Bourgholtzer of NBC, and Bryson Rash of ABC to join him on a televised tour of the White House on May 3. No script had been planned, and the President was as charming and affable as ever. Truman was always at his finest when he was able to speak on a whim. More than thirty million Americans across the country sat down to watch the broadcast, and President Truman was able to impress the nation with the wide breadth of knowledge he had learned about the building's history.

Although he did not want to serve in the White House for another four years, President Truman was very concerned about ensuring that the next occupant of the Oval Office would be a man to his liking. Truman was rather sure that the Republicans would nominate Senator Robert Taft of Ohio as their candidate, one of the President's least favorite politicians in all of Washington. Truman had at first thought of Chief Justice Vinson as the ideal candidate to lead the Democratic ticket, but Vinson was convinced that he did not want to return to the political arena. The President then considered Dwight Eisenhower, the man he had wanted to lead the Democratic Party in 1948. Truman had even offered to stand aside and essentially hand the General the

Presidency four years earlier, but Eisenhower was reluctant to commit himself to a specific political cause.

Eisenhower came to visit Truman at the White House in late 1951, and the President sought one final time to convince Eisenhower to lead the Democratic ticket in 1952. The New York Times would later break a story that suggested that Eisenhower refused to allow Truman to help him pursue the Democratic Party's nomination, instead declaring that he was a Republican and could not simply switch his party affiliation to run for office. Truman had immediately denied the story, but two Justices from the Supreme Court would later reveal that Truman had recounted his conversation with the General to them directly, and that they had been the New York Times' secret source. Eisenhower denied the conversation had happened as adamantly as Truman did, but the President, disappointed by Eisenhower's decision, called on Justice Vinson one final time to visit him in Florida. Truman essentially promised to hand him the nomination, but Vinson declined because of his ill health: the Chief Justice would drop dead less than two years later at the age of sixty three.

Dwight Eisenhower received a letter from President Truman in December of 1951 urging him to do what was best for the country, therefore implying that the General should think hard about running for President in 1952. At the time, Truman was still convinced that Eisenhower could be persuaded to run as a Democrat. Eisenhower, unlike many Republicans, such as Senator Taft, was an ardent internationalist who rejected the temptation of isolationism. On January 1, 1952, Eisenhower wrote to the President suggesting that he had ruled out a run for the Presidency entirely. He did, however, note that circumstances might change, and that a sense of duty to the nation may alter his retirement plans.

On January 6, 1952, Republican Senator Henry Cabot Lodge Jr. of Massachusetts announced that he was forming a recruitment campaign for General Eisenhower to run for President. Lodge, a moderate Republican who also recognized the importance of internationalism, was one of President Truman's favorite Republicans, but he was still a Republican nonetheless. Only one day after Lodge had announced the formation of his committee, General Eisenhower, still in Paris as the Supreme Allied Commander in Europe, declared that he would be open to accepting the Republican nomination for President. Truman, disappointed that Eisenhower would run as a Republican, still praised the General publically, but he privately lamented the almost near certainty that the twenty year Democratic reign in the White House was about to end.

General Eisenhower's candidacy found widespread support across the nation, and President Truman was desperate to find a Democratic candidate who could pose a significant threat to the General's hope of easily securing the Presidency. After Chief Justice Vinson had turned Truman down, and Eisenhower had come out as a Republican, the President turned to Governor Adlai Stevenson, who was still in his first term as the Governor of Illinois. Stevenson was a darling of the liberal establishment, and Truman saw him as someone who could successfully carry forward the Roosevelt New Deal legacy. Truman had momentarily considered the possibility of Vice President Barkley as his replacement, but the former Senator from Kentucky was far too old, and the President speculated that he would be dead within months of taking the job. Ultimately, Barkley did eventually pass away within the next Presidential term.

Governor Stevenson was a young politician with youthful vigor. At fifty one, he was ten years younger than General Eisenhower, and he would present a new generation of the Democratic Party to an electorate that was growing tired of having the same party in the White House for so long. Stevenson had also won his first election handily in a swing state, and Truman was impressed by how easily the Governor connected with voters. Stevenson, the President believed, would be the Democratic

Party's best candidate to oppose the formidable Dwight Eisenhower. This was despite the fact that the Illinois Governor was largely unknown across the country, and had, unlike Truman, an extensive educational background and came from a wealthy family. In many ways, Stevenson represented a class of society that Truman had never felt comfortable with, and the President had only met the Governor on a handful of occasions. Nonetheless, Truman was convinced that Stevenson would be the Democratic Party's best shot at keeping the Presidency, and he planned to do everything he could to secure Stevenson the party's Presidential nomination.

President Truman summoned Governor Stevenson to Washington for a meeting at Blair House. They met on January 22 for well over an hour, and Truman officially informed the Governor that he would not seek the Presidency again in the election that November. Truman essentially offered Stevenson the Democratic nomination without a contest, as the incumbent President's support would essentially win over the convention.

Stevenson was shocked by the President's offer. He had not expected Truman to ask him to be the party's candidate, especially because he was a relative newcomer to politics, having served as Governor of Illinois for only three years. The President turned to history to convince Stevenson that his offer would essentially mean a path towards the Democratic nomination: Washington had picked Adams, and many Presidents had done the same in recent years. Truman also told Stevenson that he could have him nominated as the candidate even if the Governor had no desire to accept it. Despite the President's generous offer, and his desperation to find a strong candidate to oppose Eisenhower, Stevenson turned Truman down on January 22, but that would not be the last time that the two men would converse on the subject.

Although Truman was quite fond of General Eisenhower, the President believed that, because he was a newcomer to politics,

Eisenhower would be subject to undue influence from other strong figures in the Republican Party, such as Senator Taft. Thus, despite Eisenhower's own personal convictions, Truman believed that others in the Republican Party would push the General to return to an era of American isolationism. According to Governor Stevenson, Truman was bent on saving America from an Eisenhower Presidency.

Stevenson, unlike Truman, was not convinced that electing a Republican to the White House would be such a bad thing. The Democratic Party had been in power for so long, and it was perhaps time for the party to rejuvenate. Beyond that, Stevenson wanted to remain as the Governor of Illinois and seek a second term, something a run for the Presidency might prevent. He was furthermore concerned that a Truman endorsement of his candidacy would have more negative implications than positive ones. The President was still deeply unpopular across the country, and running for the Presidency as Truman's preferred candidate might doom his chances of success altogether. Stevenson also believed that if Dwight Eisenhower won the Republican nomination, no man could stop him from securing the Presidency.

Governor Stevenson returned to Washington on March 4, and again visited the President at Blair House. According to Truman, Stevenson informed him that he had fully intended to run for another term as Governor, and would be letting the people of Illinois down if he did not follow through with those intentions. Moreover, Stevenson had made his re-election announcement publically, making it even harder to back out of another gubernatorial run.

By the end of March, Truman's advisors began to worry that if Stevenson did not run for President, he would choose to seek a third term. But President Truman was very unpopular across the country, and would be putting his entire legacy on the line to enter a contest that they were sure he would lose. A number of

Truman's supporters wrote to Governor Stevenson urging him to reconsider his decision.

Despite the fact that Truman regretted having to retire without a strong candidate to lead the Democratic Party in his place, the President announced on March 29 at a party fundraiser that he would not seek another term. He spoke of all of the achievements of his administration, and the numerous times when congressional Republicans had stood in his way, trying to block the programs that Americans wanted and desperately needed. Besides declaring that he would not run again for the Democratic nomination, Truman furthermore declared that he would not accept that nomination should he be awarded it by delegates at the Democratic Party Convention in July. Supporters were flabbergasted, and they too worried about who might take Truman's place. But, as President Truman had written in a letter to himself years earlier, "eight years as President is enough and sometimes too much for any man to serve in that capacity. There is a lure in power. It can get into a man's blood just as gambling and lust for money."

Interestingly enough, Truman had long toyed with the idea of running for his old seat in the Senate after vacating the Presidency. He likely would have gone through with it if his wife Bess had not been so adamant that she wanted their family to leave Washington for good.

After Truman's announcement, Governor Stevenson sent the President a letter in which he expressed his surprise about the President's decision. Stevenson may have hoped that, because Truman had not found an ideal candidate that would replace him, he would have no choice but to seek a third term. But with Truman taking himself out of the race, Stevenson implied that he would reconsider his decision. Truman was thrilled, and wrote back to Stevenson that America need a President who would continue the Roosevelt-Truman legacy on foreign policy. Moreover, the American people deserved to have someone in the

White House who understood the essential role government had to play in the lives of the people, and not someone who would only be concerned with pleasing members of the upper classes and those with special interests, as a Republican President surely would.

As March turned into April, President Truman's attention was forced back towards crises in Washington. His Attorney General, J. Howard McGrath, the former Governor and Senator from Rhode Island who had served in Truman's Cabinet for not yet three years, was implicated for obstructing Justice Department investigations into corruption within the Internal Revenue Service. On April 3 Truman finally decided to fire McGrath, who he had initially hoped would lead the effort to clean up corruption within government. Truman once again lamented the reality that many of the corrupt officials within the administration were his friends and former colleagues, and that those who he had placed his faith in had clearly let him down. The fact that McGrath was the former Chairman of the Democratic National Committee certainly did not help the situation, and he had been accused for months of obstructing the investigation to protect his allies in the Democratic Party.

Truman was, as usual, reluctant to fire one of his own appointees. He liked McGrath as a person, but the former Senator had clearly not gotten the job done. The public relations messaging of the situation could not have been worse. Howard McGrath, the man Truman had brought in to clean up corruption within the government, had himself proven to be less than trustworthy and rather incompetent. Truman's credibility as an effective manager of the executive branch was once again being called into question.

In the spring of 1952, Truman was faced with another series of strikes that threatened to be as crippling as the postwar strikes of 1946. The telephone and telegraph workers had gone on strike, and the steel workers were once again threatening to do the same. By this time the President had become thoroughly exhausted, and it appeared as though seven trying years at the helm of the American government was finally taking its toll.

As the steel workers declared on April 7, 1952, that they would go on strike the following day, President Truman again decided to take a firm line against the workers and their unions that had chosen to walk off the job, as well as the management that had failed to negotiate a new agreement with its workers. The United States, Truman declared to the nation in a televised address on April 8, could not afford to endure a steel strike in the middle of a war abroad, even if he agreed with most of the new benefits striking workers were hoping to obtain. A strike would hurt the nation's ability to equip troops in Korea and build up the North Atlantic Treaty Organization's troop presence in Europe. The economy would furthermore by thrown into tumult. Weary of the dangerous consequences of a strike, the President decided to have the government seize the steel mills.

Truman did recognize that the steel workers were right in their demand for increased wages. The steel industry was booming, but workers had not received a wage increase for two years. In the previous November, steel workers and their unions had asked for a thirty five cent raise on an hourly basis. But management refused to even negotiate. With a strike all but inevitable, Truman had utilized the Wage Stabilization Board to delay the strike by a few months. But the unions told the President early on that they would walk off the job on April 8 if no new agreement was in place. The Wage Stabilization Board had recommended a wage increase of twenty six cents an hour, which was agreed to by the unions, but management again refused to negotiate. With no deal, steel workers walked off the job on April 8, 1952.

The President had been given the authority by Congress to send workers back to work for an eighty day term. But they had already held off their job action since November, and Truman could see no reason why they should simply wait another eighty days to achieve the same result. He had always sided with labor over business throughout his political career, as Truman always had an inherent distrust of management in big companies, but America could not afford a strike. The steel companies wanted to increase the price of steel, which would cause inflation and make the monetary cost of the war in Korea that much higher. The President therefore decided to seize steel mills across the country as a temporary, albeit extreme, measure. To rationalize his actions, Truman took chose to address the nation on the evening of April 8.

> My fellow Americans, tonight our country faces a grave danger.
>
> A prolonged shutdown would bring defense production to a halt and throw our domestic economy into chaos.
>
> Our national security and our chances for peace depend on our defense production. Our defense production depends on steel.

On April 9 steel workers returned to work, but they were now reporting to Charles Sawyer, Truman's Secretary of Commerce, in Washington. Steel production continued, but the President's actions were met with outrage across the country. Truman was accused of being an autocrat in the tradition of fascists in Europe. He had directly intervened in a private industry, and effectively had the army take control of an entire sector of the economy. While Truman did send a message to Congress on April 9 to try to convince its members that his actions were a temporary measure of last resort, many on Capitol Hill avowed that the President should be impeached for his power grab that had flouted the role of the legislative branch.

Editorials in newspapers across the country condemned the President for his unprecedented action, which many predicted would prove to be the greatest stain on his Presidency. Many further speculated about what else Truman would be willing to do if he had already taken such drastic measures. When reporters lightheartedly questioned Truman about whether or not he would be willing to seize the press, the President responded that he would do what was in the best interest of the country. To many, this signaled that Truman was willing to go much further, but the President likely did not recognize how much his statement would be misinterpreted.

As was expected, the steel industry immediately sued President Truman and the American government to reacquire its property. After a federal district judge ruled Truman's actions as illegal, the Supreme Court announced that they would hear the case on an expedited basis. The President publically announced that he would abide by the Supreme Court's decision, and had no wish to become an autocratic dictator, but rather to see that the interests of the United States of America were protected.

Truman's legal representative at the Supreme Court's hearing was Philip Perlman, a distinguished lawyer who served as the President's Solicitor General, and also happened to be the first Jewish man to hold that position. The steel industry's legal representative was John W. Davis, a former Democratic member of the House of Representatives and the Democratic Party's Presidential candidate in 1924, when he lost to the incumbent, Calvin Coolidge, by twenty three states. Davis was also a long-time lawyer, and was very experienced in representing clients before the Supreme Court.

When the Supreme Court delivered its verdict on June 2, 1952, the President's actions were deemed unconstitutional by two thirds of the presiding justices. The six who voted against Truman were Hugo Black, a former Democratic Senator and Roosevelt appointee, Robert Jackson, Roosevelt's former Attorney General who had been appointed to the court in 1941, Felix Frankfurter, another Roosevelt appointee, William Douglas, the man who Truman had wanted to be his Vice President, Tom Clark, a Truman appointee and his former Attorney General, and Harold

Hitz Burton, a former Democratic Senator and Truman appointee. All of the dissenting members worried about the precedent Truman's actions might have set for Presidents in the future. Voting in favor of the President were Chief Justice Fred Vinson, a Truman appointee who had served both in the President's Cabinet and as a member of Congress, Stanley Forman Reed, a Roosevelt appointee who had also served as his Solicitor General, and Sherman Minton, a former Democratic Senator who had served alongside Truman and was appointed to the Court in 1949. They argued that the President ought to have the authority to exercise temporary measures to keep the nation from endangering its future. Nonetheless, all three agreed that any action would have eventually required support from Congress.

The Supreme Court ruling was perhaps the most humiliating moment of Truman's Presidency. Every member of the Supreme Court had been appointed by either Roosevelt or Truman himself, making the decision all the more painful for the President. With Truman's seizure of coal plants having been declared unconstitutional, a widespread strike among steel workers began that night, and continued for almost two months, proving to be one of the most costly strikes in American history, something the President had tried desperately to avoid. Two million steel workers and workers related to the industry walked off the job for seven weeks, costing the nation more than twenty one tons of steel production. When the strike finally came to a close, the agreement resembled the one that Truman had promoted weeks earlier, a deal which could have avoided the strike entirely. The final deal was actually orchestrated by the President himself, who called the leaders of the two sides to the White House on July 24 to demand an agreement. That very day, the two men finally found a bargain that they were both willing to agree to after so many weeks of a strike that cost both sides dearly. But the strike hurt the nation's economy dearly, and severely restricted the nation's wartime equipment production.

The Republican National Convention began on July 7, 1952. Heading into a final vote for the party's Presidential nomination, Senator Taft had the most delegated committed to his cause. He ferociously attacked Republicans from the northeast who he saw as far too centrist, such as Thomas Dewey, who was still the Governor of New York. This time Dewey and his supporters had thrown their weight behind Dwight Eisenhower, and, despite being behind in committed delegates, the momentum was on the General's side. Notwithstanding the predictions and nasty infighting, Eisenhower won a commanding victory on the first ballot, and was quickly awarded with the Republican Presidential nomination. To be his running mate, Republicans chose to hand Richard Nixon, a young forty one year old Senator known for his hardline stance on Communism, the post. The Eisenhower – Nixon ticket would prove to be a very formidable opponent for any Democratic candidates that ran on the ticket to oppose them.

As President Truman departed from Washington to Chicago on July 24, the Democratic National Convention had already begun, and no one was certain about who the party would nominate as its Presidential candidate. Averell Harriman, a long time Truman advisor, declared his candidacy, championing Truman's "Fair Deal" policies. But Harriman had never held elected office, and many Democrats saw this as an inherent handicap.

As the Democratic Convention began, Estes Kefauver, a freshman Senator from Tennessee, led all the other candidates in committed delegates. President Truman, however, disliked Kefauver, and was resolved to find nearly anyone else to nominate in his place. Moreover, although Kefauver led significantly in the delegate count, it was well known throughout the party that any candidate Truman chose to endorse would effectively win the nomination. Thus, Kefauver's path towards the Presidential nomination would be very difficult, if not outright impossible.

Early on in the Convention, support for Vice President Barkley to lead the Democratic ticket swelled, but many labor activists declined to support a Barkley candidacy, citing his age as the primary factor. Barkley therefore informed Truman that he intended to withdraw his name from consideration. On the day before Truman departed for Chicago, he received a phone call from Governor Stevenson, who asked the President about whether or not he would approve of his intent on seeking the nomination. Truman, thrilled, reminded Stevenson that he had been trying to get the Governor to commit to running for months, and that, with his help, Stevenson would be able to win the nomination handily.

When Stevenson arrived at the Democratic National Convention, his opening speech thrilled delegates from across the nation, and the momentum quickly turned to the Governor's side. On July 25, after the first two ballots had been cast, Stevenson was running a close second behind Senator Kefauver, so President Truman departed to a hotel to meet with senior Democratic Party stalwarts, including Speaker Rayburn and the party's Chairman, Frank McKinney. The three agreed that the party should nominate Stevenson, and the President quickly notified various Governors and important delegates of their choice. Harriman had already decided to remove himself from the race and support Governor Stevenson. On the third ballot, having received the support of Harriman's delegates, Stevenson took a commanding lead, but did not officially win the nomination until well after midnight.

Stevenson's victory speech was thoughtful and elegant, in which he declared that the American people were too intelligent to allow a Republican administration to retake the White House. Truman also declared that he would do everything in his power to put Stevenson into the Oval Office, graciously putting himself at the behest of the Governor. The Democratic Party, however, had not yet chosen Stevenson's running mate. Stevenson and others proposed Senator Kefauver, but Truman's severe dislike of his colleague from Tennessee convinced other senior party members to choose someone else. After a lengthy discussion, they finally settled on Senator John Sparkman of Alabama, a young politician from a southern state, which Truman and others hoped would help maintain Democratic support in the south.

In a move that would anger President Truman in the coming months, Governor Stevenson took every available opportunity to distance himself from the Truman administration, despite the fact that the President had essentially secured the Democratic Party's Presidential nomination for him. He made no effort to consult Truman on his plans for the campaign, nor did Stevenson seek any advice from the President about communicating with voters, which Truman had proven to be masterful at four years earlier. Stevenson further offended the President by replacing his handpicked party chairman, and moving the Democratic Party's national headquarters out of Washington D.C. and into Springfield, Illinois. When Stevenson released a letter claiming that he was intent on cleaning up the mess in Washington, Republicans used the Governor's words to demonstrate that even Democrats thought that work had to be done to clean up the mess President Truman would be leaving behind. Needless to say, the letter further alienated Truman from Governor Stevenson. The President would later write that Stevenson had turned the Democratic campaign into a circus.

In one of the worst confrontations between Truman and Stevenson in the midst of the 1952 election campaign, the Governor sent his new party chairman, Stephen Mitchell, to recommend that the President ask Secretary Acheson to announce that he planned to retire after the election, something Stevenson thought would aid the Democratic campaign. Truman, stunned, refused to entertain the idea, and later revealed that the Stevenson campaign only further saddened him about the dire state of the Democratic Party. The relationship was patched up slightly after Stevenson accepted Truman's invitation to meet with his Cabinet in the White House on August 12. The Governor of Illinois allegedly told the President at the meeting that Truman appeared to want him to win more than Stevenson wanted to win himself. President Truman, however, once again promised Stevenson that he was prepared to do anything he could to keep the Presidency in Democratic hands.

Truman dove headfirst into the election campaign by September, certain that the choice Americans made in electing their next President would be a referendum on his legacy. Stevenson traveled across the country by plane, while Truman traveled separately, and the two men never appeared at a campaign event together. Truman attacked the Republican Party in general, but, because of Dwight Eisenhower's popularity, chose instead to paint the General as in over his head. He furthermore declared that an Eisenhower administration would be controlled by the radical Republicans in Congress, a similar charge Truman had issued towards Dewey four years earlier.

The Republicans had no intention of allowing Truman to attack their candidate without a hard line response, as failing to fight back had been their biggest mistake in 1948. Eisenhower campaigned on the need for change in Washington, and attacked Truman's record in foreign policy. The General attacked the corruption that plagued the Truman administration, and Richard Nixon campaigned against the Democratic record on Korea, Communism, and corruption. Moreover, Stevenson was nowhere near as effective as Truman in connecting with voters by exemplifying an everyday American persona. Unlike Truman, voters did not see Stevenson as someone who represented traditional America, but rather as a member of the nation's limited political elite. Eisenhower, the General who had helped win the Second World War, was seen as much more down to earth and relatable than Stevenson, although the latter was very good at making impassioned speeches to large crowds. Nonetheless, in a contest between Stevenson and Eisenhower, the Republican candidate, in contrast with the campaign in 1948, was clearly the more likeable and affable choice.

As they had in 1948, the vast majority of America's newspapers supported the Republican ticket, and the Eisenhower campaign outspent the Democrats by more than two to one.

For President Truman the most angering moment of the campaign came in October, when General Eisenhower refused to repudiate Senator McCarthy and his tactics while visiting Wisconsin, despite the fact that he wished to do so privately. Eisenhower furthermore charged that the nation's supposed tolerance for Communism had lasted two decades, clearly insinuating that Communism in America had been on the rise throughout the twenty years of Democratic administrations. The loss of China, Soviet expansionism in Europe, and the war in Korea were all caused by Communism sympathizers in Washington. Moreover, Eisenhower did not voice his support for General Marshall in public, who had been accused of being a Communist sympathizer by McCarthy, despite the fact that his aides had told the press that the Republican candidate would do so. This caused a firestorm across the country, and angered many Republicans who were tired of Senator McCarthy's wild accusations and hard hitting politics. In the mind of President Truman, through failing to defend General Marshall, Eisenhower had put morality aside for the sake of ugly politics. It was a move that Truman would never forgive, and ruined whatever warmth that was left in the relationship between the two former friends. Truman alleged publicly that candidate Eisenhower was not the honorable man that he had once been associated with, but rather a candidate who had sold his soul for political gain.

Not only had Dwight Eisenhower served with George Marshall during World War Two, but the former Secretary of Defense had also been his boss. Eisenhower's career and his triumphs during the war were largely due to General Marshall's faith in his ability. President Roosevelt had given Eisenhower a number of promotions during the war, all due to Marshall's recommendations. Marshall had put his trust in Eisenhower during the war, and now Eisenhower was refusing to honor his friend during election season. As Truman continued to hammer Eisenhower for his lack of respect for General Marshall, the Republican candidate was angry at him for his aggressive attacks, claiming what Truman was doing was beneath the dignity of the Presidency.

Riding a wave of personal popularity, nearly every public opinion poll suggested that Dwight Eisenhower was on his way to the White House. For many Americans the central issue in the campaign was the war in Korea, and General Eisenhower, with his own impressive military track record, was seen as the candidate who could win the war and finally bring the American troops home. Eisenhower promised to end the war, and moreover pledged to go to Korea and survey the situation on the ground personally, a trip that President Truman had never indicated he was willing to make.

Despite a tremendous effort on the part of President Truman, and a strong campaign run by Governor Stevenson, the Eisenhower – Nixon ticket won in a landslide. Eisenhower's promise to end the war in Korea had been his central campaign commitment, and Americans had responded to that pledge overwhelmingly. The Republican ticket beat out the Democrats in the popular vote by more than ten points, and Eisenhower won thirty more states than Stevenson did. General Eisenhower even managed to beat Governor Stevenson in his home state of Illinois, winning four hundred thousand more votes than his opponent across the state, the man who was the incumbent Governor. The loss of Illinois was a major humiliation for Governor Stevenson, who had only managed to muster eighty nine electoral votes. Truman was also stunned to learn that the General had managed to win his state of Missouri by a margin of thirty thousand votes, a state that almost never went Republican.

Democrats were also stunned to learn that they had lost their tight grip on Congress. The House of Representatives would once again by controlled by Speaker Joseph Martin's Republicans, who had gained twenty two seats in the chamber. Helped by the popularity of General Eisenhower, Republican Senators were also able to retake ownership of the Senate, with Robert Taft finally able to serve as the party's majority leader. The majority in the Senate, however, was much smaller than the victory in the House: Republicans were only able to lay claim to one seat more than their Democratic colleagues. Nonetheless, in the event of a tie vote, Vice President Richard Nixon would be able to ensure that Republicans were able to maintain a firm control over the chamber.

After twenty years of Roosevelt and Truman Democratic administrations, Americans had decided that it was time for a change in Washington. The need for change, combined with Eisenhower's personal popularity, had almost guaranteed that the Republican ticket would retake the White House. Eisenhower would become the first Republican President since Herbert Hoover had been forced out of office twenty years prior during the depths of the Great Depression. Two decades later, America was prosperous, united, and free. The Roosevelt and Truman administrations would leave behind a very colored legacy, and, unlike what Truman and others had feared, much of their liberal welfare programs remained largely intact.

Truman sent Eisenhower a congratulatory message following the General's victory, and offered him the use of his Presidential aircraft if Eisenhower still had a "desire to go to Korea," a nasty jab that Truman's successor would not soon forget. Despite the fact that Truman had thought Eisenhower's promise to go to Korea was made only for the purpose of the election, the General did in fact depart for Korea at the end of November on a military plane, although the trip was kept as a secret from nearly everyone. Eisenhower, Truman quickly realized, might prove to more of a formidable President than he had long expected the General to be, despite the fact that he had never before experienced life in the political arena. Truman even expressed worry privately for the safety of the next President of the United States in advance of Eisenhower's trip.

Chapter Fourteen

President Eisenhower

Despite all of the animosity that had built up between President Truman and his successor, he graciously extended Eisenhower an invitation to join him in the White House to discuss the administrative transition. Truman's invitation, one that is in the present day recognized as standard procedure, was the first of its kind in American history. No President had ever contacted his successor, especially one from another party, to work out a smooth transition from one administration to the next. But Truman was genuinely concerned with ensuring that the change in government that would happen in January of 1953 proceeded in an exemplary fashion, and wanted to provide Eisenhower with the guidance Truman had never received before taking the Presidential oath almost eight years earlier.

President-elect Eisenhower joined Truman at the White House on November 18, 1952. The President and his Cabinet then provided Eisenhower with a full briefing on all of the government's most important files. Nonetheless, despite the fact that Truman had been so cordial in inviting Eisenhower to the White House, the latter remained distant and uncomfortable throughout the entire meeting. The President also believed that General Eisenhower was not prepared for the responsibility he was soon to accept, and that his transition into the Presidency would not be as smooth as Truman had first hoped.

Harry Truman penned a State of the Union speech one final time, which he had delivered to the Congress on January 7, 1953. In stark contrast with his previous seven addresses, Truman decided to send a letter to members of Congress rather than deliver it in person. His address was nonetheless a powerful one. As the President announced with great satisfaction, seven million more Americans were going to work the following day than they had on the day he took office. The economy was thriving, household income was up, and businesses were doing remarkably well. In terms of the American economy, the state of the union had never been stronger.

Truman had also created the Defense Department, the Central Intelligence Agency, and the National Security Council, desegregated the military, left civilians in charge of controlling nuclear arms, and reduced the national debt. He lamented the fact that he was unable to substantially improve education, public housing, and the health insurance industry. But the Truman administration had also saved Greece and Turkey from Communism, rebuilt Europe in historic fashion through the Marshall Plan, and continued to act to contain Communism from expansion around the world. He also announced that the Hydrogen Bomb had been successfully developed.

The most central theme in Truman's address, besides summing up the failures and successes of his administration, was that of an orderly transition of power. Truman also spoke of the unfortunate circumstances under which the transfer of power took place eight years before, and gladly reminded Congress and the American people that a peaceful chance in government on January 20, 1953, was a time to celebrate democracy in action.

In just two weeks, General Eisenhower will be inaugurated as President of the United States and I will resume, most gladly, my place as a private citizen of this Republic. The Presidency last changed hands eight years ago this coming April. That was a tragic time: a time of grieving for President Roosevelt, the great and gallant human being who had been taken from us; a time of unrelieved anxiety to his successor, thrust so suddenly into the complexities and burdens of the Presidential office.

Not so this time. This time we see the normal transition under our democratic system. One President, at the conclusion of his term, steps back to private life; his successor, chosen by the people, begins his tenure of the office. And the Presidency of the United States continues to function without a moment's break.

As Truman looked back on his record in the White House, he gradually began to take pride in all of his accomplishments as President. He might have been set to leave office with an approval rating well below fifty percent, but Truman's Presidency would be vindicated by history. The President chose to write his own farewell address rather than have an aide write one for him, and reviewed all of the most important decisions of his Presidency. Truman also took the time to try to explain the rationale for American involvement in Korea to the nation one more time. The Korean War, like many of Truman's decisions, may have been unpopular in his own era, but would later come to be regarded as a necessary measure to further support his containment policy, a strategic approach that Presidents would continue to abide by for decades.

Truman wrote final letters to members of his Cabinet and the administration, and his note to Secretary Acheson was particularly affectionate. Calling his Secretary of State nothing less than his right hand man, Truman told Acheson that he believed his

Secretary of State would rank among the greatest officials to ever hold that office.

For all the abuse Truman had taken in the press and during the election campaign, and all of the mistakes the President had made along the way, Harry Truman led the United States through eight of the most tumultuous years in American history, which were also eight years of great importance in the history of the world. Truman was forced to make many tough decisions. To this date, he is the only world leader in history who ever consented to the use of a nuclear weapon. He also chose to lead the United States to war only five years after a devastating world war had ended, and engineered America's foreign policy for the next several decades. Harry Truman was never one to give up, nor did he ever shy away from taking controversial, but decisive, action. Ultimately, a farmer from Missouri, one who had never attended a college or been successful in business, would prove to be one of the most masterful world leaders of the twentieth century. Always underestimated, President Truman never failed to over perform.

On January 15, 1953, President Truman delivered his farewell address to the nation on radio and television. Truman spoke of the great changes that the world had undergone in the last eight years, and delivered very accurate predictions of where the Cold War might be headed in the future. He also spoke of how unexpected his ascension to the White House had been, even though he had known early on that Roosevelt's health was on the decline. Most of all, Truman was proud that democracy was on the march, and emphasized the need to defend American and democratic values around the world. He again called for a continuation of his internationalist foreign policy, which had helped to lead to the creation of the United Nations. Truman reminded Americans that, although he had befriended world leaders, made decisions about nuclear bombs, led the nation to war, and forced Germany and Japan to surrender, he was still

Harry Truman from Missouri, an everyday American in the White House.

In retrospect, so many of the tough decisions Truman would have to make occurred during his first four months in office, and it is easy to lose sight of the remarkable job the President did in his first months on the job. In that time, Germany had officially surrendered, the nuclear bomb was first built, a meeting was held with Stalin and Churchill at Potsdam, and a nuclear weapon was used for the first time on the nation of Japan. In all of these events, Truman had been a crucial and central player. Without President Truman leading the United States through those momentous eight years, the world very well may have become a much more dangerous place. In his farewell address, Truman did a remarkable job of recounting his time and record as President in the White House.

Next Tuesday, General Eisenhower will be inaugurated as President of the United States. A short time after the new President takes his oath of office, I will be on the train going back home to Independence, Missouri. I will once again be a plain, private citizen of this great Republic.

That is as it should be. Inauguration Day will be a great demonstration of our democratic process. I am glad to be a part of it, glad to wish General Eisenhower all possible success, as he begins his term, glad the whole world will have a chance to see how simply and how peacefully our American system transfers the vast power of the Presidency from my hands to his. It is a good object lesson in democracy. I am very proud of it. And I know you are, too.

The greatest part of the President's job is to make decisions--big ones and small ones, dozens of them almost every day. The papers may circulate around the Government for a while but they finally reach this desk. And then, there's no place else for them to go. The

President, whoever he is, has to decide. He can't pass the buck to anybody. No one else can do the deciding for him. That's his job.

I suppose that history will remember my term in office as the years when the "cold war" began to overshadow our lives. I have had hardly a day in office that has not been dominated by this all-embracing struggle; this conflict between those who love freedom and those who would lead the world back into slavery and darkness. And always in the background there has been the atomic bomb.

But when history says that my term of office saw the beginning of the cold war, it will also say that in those eight years we have set the course that can win it. We have succeeded in carving out a new set of policies to attain peace -- positive policies, policies of world leadership, policies that express faith in other free people. We have averted World War Three up to now, and we may already have succeeded in establishing conditions which can keep that war from happening as far ahead as man can see.

President Truman was unequivocal in declaring that his decision to go to war in Korea was the most important of his Presidency. Free nations had failed to stop undemocratic aggressors in the 1930s, and America had a duty to ensure that the Soviet Union and its Communist allies were not given the same opportunity. Truman also emphasized the fact that, although he had led the nation to war to stand up to undemocratic aggressors, his administration's policies were also successful in limiting the war to a regional, rather than global, military battle. Moreover, Truman offered an ambitious prediction that foresaw a victory for freedom in the Cold War.

As the free world grows stronger, more united, more attractive to men on both sides of the Iron Curtain, and as the Soviet hopes for easy expansion are blocked, then there will have to come a time of change in the Soviet world. Nobody can say for sure when that is going to be, or exactly how it will come about, whether by revolution, or trouble in the satellite states, or by a change inside the Kremlin.

Whether the Communist rulers shift their policies of their own free will--or whether the change comes about in some other way - I have not a doubt in the world that a change will occur.

I have a deep and abiding faith in the destiny of free men. With patience and courage, we shall some day move on into a new era -- a wonderful golden age – an age when we can use the peaceful tools that science has forged for us to do away with poverty and human misery everywhere on earth.

Many believed that Truman's farewell speech was the best of his career. Five days later, President Truman awoke early in the morning on January 20, 1953, to see his successor be sworn into office. Truman said a final goodbye to his staff in the White House, who had come to adore the Truman family and their warm treatment of the staff posted in the residence, something that was often missing in the Roosevelt era.

As the time to depart for the inauguration neared, General Eisenhower decided against coming into the White House to have an early lunch with the President and his wife Bess, as was the Presidential tradition. In fact, Eisenhower even insisted on waiting outside, hesitant to enter the Oval Office until he had taken his Presidential oath. The Eisenhowers waited in the car for the Trumans rather than join them for a cup of coffee, a move that struck Truman and those in the press as a grave insult.

President-elect Eisenhower finally showed his thanks to President Truman after learning that his son John, a Major in the army, had been ordered home for the inauguration, a specific request made by the President himself. Eisenhower was surprised by Truman's warm and personal gesture, but he would later send a letter thanking the President for all of the courtesies that President and Mrs. Truman had extended to himself and his wife Mamie. Eisenhower was all the more gratified upon learning that John was not even made aware that the President had put in a personal request for the Major to return home, as Truman preferred not to try to take credit on such an important day for President-elect Eisenhower.

After President Eisenhower was officially inaugurated just after noon, the Truman family made their way to the home of Dean Acheson, where a farewell luncheon had been planned for the departing President, who was thrilled to be returning to Independence. As Truman proudly declared before his close colleagues and friends, after years of service in public office, he was once again Harry Truman, private citizen. When the President, Bess, and Margaret finally did depart for the train station, thousands of supporters flooded the area to see Truman off.

President Eisenhower had arranged for the Trumans to be allowed to use the Presidential train car that Truman had used so often as President, most importantly in his re-election campaign. In front of the media, Secretary Acheson declared that Harry Truman was his best friend and a dear colleague, and dozens of Democratic Party officials and members of Congress came to see the President one final time before he departed for Missouri. For the entire ride home, Truman was greeted at every station by hundreds of cheering supporters until he finally reached Missouri the following morning.

The Truman Administration

Vice President	1945-9: None	1949-53: Alben Barkley		
Secretary of State	1945: Edward Stettinius Jr.	1945-7: James Byrnes	1947-9: George Marshall	1949-53: Dean Acheson
Secretary of the Treasury	1945: Henry Morgenthau Jr.	1945-6: Fred Vinson	1946-53: John Snyder	
Secretary of War	1945: Henry Stimson	1945-7: Robert Patterson	1947: Kenneth Royall	
Secretary of Defense	1947-9: James Forrestal	1949-50: Louis Johnson	1950-1: George Marshall	1951-3: Robert Lovett
Attorney General	1945: Francis Biddle	1945-9: Tom Clark	1949-52: J. Howard McGrath	1952-3: James McGranery
Postmaster General	1945: Frank Walker	1945-7: Frank Hannegan	1947-53: Jesse Monroe Donaldson	
Secretary of the Navy	1945-7: James Forrestal			
Secretary of the Interior	1945-6: Harold Ickes	1946-9: Julius Krug	1949-53: Oscar Littleton Chapman	

Secretary of Agriculture	1945: Claude Raymond Wickard	1945-8: Clinton Anderson	1948-53: Charles Brannan
Secretary of Commerce	1945-6: Henry Wallace	1946-8: W. Averell Harriman	1948-53: Charles Sawyer
Secretary of Labor	1945: Frances Perkins	1945-8: Louis Schwellenbach	1948-53: Maurice Tobin

Index

Harriman, W. Averell, 17, 18, 46, 66, 171, 176, 177, 181, 201, 235, 236, 252
Hartley, Fred, 74
Hillenkoetter, Roscoe, 82
Himmler, Heinrich, 21
Hirohito, Emperor 46
Hiss, Alger, 114, 122, 154, 158, 159
Hitler, Adolph, 10, 23, 36, 37, 143
Hitz, Harold 234
Hoover, J. Edgar, 16, 123
Hoover, Herbert, 20, 25, 57, 149, 207, 241
Hume, Paul, 195
Humphrey, Hubert, 104, 109, 130

I

Ickes, Harold, 56, 132, 251

J

Jackson, Andrew, 91, 139
Jackson, Robert, 29, 223, 233
Jacobson, Edward, 8, 90, 91, 93
Jester, Beauford, 124
Johnson, Alvanley, 63
Johnson, Louis, 138, 148, 149, 150, 156, 160, 175, 176, 177, 178, 251
Johnson, Lyndon, 104, 124

K

Kefauver, Estes, 235, 236, 237
Kelly, Gene, 139
Kennan, George, 60, 83, 155, 156
Keynes, John Maynard, 55
Kim Il-Sung, 166, 169, 172
King, Ernest 13
King George VI, 44
King, W.L. Mackenzie, 71
Krug, Julius, 57, 251

L

Leahy, William, 13
Lilienthal, David E., 71, 72, 73, 111, 112, 154, 155, 156
Lincoln, Abraham, 82, 130
Lodge, Henry Cabot Jr., 203, 225
Lovett, Robert, 94, 251

M

MacArthur, Douglas, 27, 47, 48, 168, 169, 170, 173, 176, 177, 179, 180, 181, 182, 183, 185, 188, 189, 190, 192, 193, 194, 197, 198, 199, 200, 201, 202, 203, 204, 205, 206, 207,

Lists of Works Cited

"American Experience: Truman Transcript." *PBS*. PBS, n.d.

Web. 31 Aug. 2014.

<http://www.pbs.org/wgbh/americanexperience/feat

ures/transcript/truman-transcript>.

"American President: Harry S. Truman." *Miller Center*. N.p., n.d.

Web. 31 Aug. 2014.

<http://millercenter.org/president/truman>.

"Audio Collection." *Truman Library*. N.p., n.d. Web. 31 Aug.

2014.

<http://www.trumanlibrary.org/audio/audio.htm>.

Harry Truman Acceptance Speech. C-SPAN. 14 July 1948.

Television.

McCullough, David G. *Truman*. New York: Simon and Shuster,

1992. Print.

"Presidential Audio/Video Archive - Harry S. Truman." *The

American Presidency Project*. N.p., n.d. Web. 31 Aug. 2014.

<http://www.presidency.ucsb.edu/medialist.php?presi

d=33>.

"The American Presidency Project." *The American Presidency*

Project. N.p., n.d. Web. 31 Aug. 2014.

<http://www.presidency.ucsb.edu/index.php>.

"Truman Library: News and Special Features." *Truman Library.*

N.p., n.d. Web. 31 Aug. 2014.

<http://www.trumanlibrary.org/news/features.htm>.

Truman, Harry S. *Year of Decisions.* Garden City: Doubleday,

1955. Print.

Truman, Harry S. *Years of Trial and Hope.* Garden City:

Doubleday, 1956. Print.

About the Author:

Jonah Goldberg is an undergraduate political science and history student, as well as a Dean's List Scholar, at the University of Toronto. *Truman* is his sixth book and first on American history. He lives in Toronto, Canada with his family.

The cover photo of Harry Truman's Presidential portrait is taken from the public domain. It was painted by Greta Kempton.

28627618R00155

Printed in Great Britain
by Amazon

Rom

WN

Also by this author under the name of Patricia King:

Puppy Training

The Cat Puzzler

The Dog Puzzler

TRUST ME

Patricia H. Squire

authorHOUSE®

AuthorHouse™
1663 Liberty Drive
Bloomington, IN 47403
www.authorhouse.com
Phone: 1-800-839-8640

Published by AuthorHouse   05/22/2012

ISBN: 978-1-4685-0475-0 (sc)
ISBN: 978-1-4685-0476-7 (e)

CONTENTS

For David whose unfailing support has made
so many things possible

CHAPTER ONE

Anita shifted on the plastic seat in a vain attempt to find some ease. You had to admire their creators, she thought, to find that fine edge between enough comfort to be better than standing or sitting on the floor, and that unrelenting hardness was a real achievement. She sighed as Luke again paced away from her over to the glass wall separating the departure lounge from the main concourse of the airport and peered through it. She wished they would get a move on and call the flight. They could get on the plane and Luke could be strapped into his seat. That should keep him still, she smirked inwardly. Then within a few short hours they would be in Spain, and could begin their holiday in Salou.

She looked up as Luke approached her again. "Sit down, for God's sake. You're tiring me out. I never would have pegged you for a nervous flier."

Luke sank down beside her. "I'm not nervous," but his eyes, darting round the other passengers and along with his absent tone, appeared to refute his words.

Anita grimaced. "Talk to me then. We are supposed to be going on holiday together. Taking our relationship a step forward—remember?"

"I know," he smiled at her briefly. God, things were unravelling so quickly. He had expected to have more time. What he had not expected was for his feelings for Anita to develop the way they had. To begin with, it had been her straight, shoulder-length, light brown hair, even features

1

and average height that appealed to him. She epitomised normality. She was the perfect cover. If they both had some fun, with no strings, where was the harm in that? He rolled his eyes inwardly. Who would have expected him to find her energy and quirkiness so captivating? The range of expressions that danced across her face ensured she would never be a good poker player, but they mesmerized him. In no time at all, it seemed to him, she had filled his thoughts—whether they were together or not. She must have laid a spell on him, as now instead of seeing her primarily as part of a disguise to conceal himself, he had to admit he was at the very least infatuated with her. He only hoped that was all it was, the last thing he needed at the moment was to find himself irrevocably in love. It could not be a worse time. To pull this whole escapade off, he was going to need all his wits about him.

"Everything will be all right once we get to Spain," he said to her, looking away, not sure if he was trying to convince her or himself. God, he shouldn't have involved her, and would not have if he had had any premonition of the mess into which the whole thing was turning. He groaned, wishing he could turn the clock back.

They sat in silence. Anita could not help but notice how Luke was sweating, yet the airport was quite cool. If he really was not nervous, then he must be on drugs or something. She should have known he was too good to be true. Still she'd never have believed he could behave this way. Her mind slid back over the last couple of months. The Luke then bore no resemblance to the Luke of today. Then he'd been the super cool salesman who, ever since his arrival in the office of Crown Industries Ltd a couple of months ago, had been a magnet for male and female staff with his cool, big city sophistication. She looked at him sitting beside her. She also had been drawn to him even though she normally went for the dark brooding type. And there were times when he'd raised her hopes with a special smile or a quick wink. But then she would catch him making similar gestures to other girls in the office, particularly Isabel, who was personal assistant to Mr Franks the branch manager. Isabel saw herself as a cut above the rest of the girls and there was no doubt she had intended to claim Luke as her own. Anita sometimes wondered about her. No one in the office appeared to like her, even those she deigned to socialise with, the ones who could help her claw her way upwards through the company. Isabel was already at Crowns when Anita started, and she had made one or two overtures at the beginning, but it was soon clear that Isabel didn't see her as a possible asset and after that Anita only approached her when her work necessitated it. She didn't like her, but could not help feeling a bit sorry for her. Still, it seemed to be how she wanted it. It was no loss to Anita, she had made friends with several of the others in the office, in particular Maggie who had become a great friend out of the office as well as in it.

Anita was a realist and aware she was not a raving beauty: usually men like Luke wanted to be friends with her—the kiss of death to romance. In fact she'd been sure he and Isabel would get together. Particularly as Isabel was obviously attracted to him, often calling him over to her office. Anita smiled. Her "office" was a bit of a misnomer, it was more an alcove to one side of Mr Franks' office. Nevertheless, Luke was often to be seen chatting with her in her alcove or the small kitchen area where they made their drinks. At the same time he had appeared to flirt generally without taking matters any further with anyone, including Isabel. Not, that is, until he had asked her, Anita, out that Friday evening. Along with several others from the office, they had wandered over to the pub across the road for a social drink to celebrate the end of the week. They often did this. It was noisy and fun, a letting off of steam before the freedom of the coming weekend. On this particular Friday, Anita found herself next to Luke as they began to disperse.

"How do you feel about going on somewhere else, just us? We could find a bite to eat while we get to know each other better," he had asked her.

Stunned, she had stared at him until one of his eyebrows slowly elevated. This had broken the spell and she'd managed some sort of stammered acceptance. What her exact words had been, she had no idea, but apparently it had been sufficient as he had smiled and taken her arm before weaving their way to the exit. Anita had glanced back at the others and, seeing her friends' wide-eyed stares, had laughed and waved her free arm. Maggie had mouthed some words that she had correctly interpreted as a warning she would be expected to tell all on the Monday morning. She'd nodded, still laughing until she had caught Isabel's face, twisted in disbelief, That had given her a second's pause, but with Luke tugging her after him she had soon forgotten about it and had determined she was going to enjoy herself.

They'd enjoyed a spicy meal at a Mexican restaurant furnished with the requisite sombreros and cacti. Anita had soon recovered from her initial confusion, reverting to her usual high spirits and they had enjoyed a lively conversation. She found herself telling him about her childhood. How her family always seemed to just get settled before her father would announce their next move where she would have to settle into a new school and make new friends all over again. Luke's constant attention focused on her was intoxicating. It was only now, in retrospect, she realised she had done most of the talking.

She snorted slightly. Well, as an exercise in "getting to know each other better", as he had said, it had obviously been a failure. If she didn't know better, she would have thought the Luke sitting next to her almost vibrating with the tension gripping him was a different person to the Luke she had spent all her free time with over the last two weeks. She frowned, thinking, now that she thought about it, in terms of actual hours together, there hadn't been that many, he had been out of town on the road a lot of the time, and of course in the office they each had their own work although it was no secret they were seeing each other. Perhaps she did not know him as well as she thought. She certainly would never have imagined him getting into such an agitated state before flying off on holiday. Would it really magically be all right once they got to Spain? She was beginning to have serious doubts.

Suddenly, nasal tones announced their flight boarding at Gate Nine. Anita started to gather her bags when Luke abruptly stood up and strode off without his carry-on. She stood, staring after him. Well, that took the biscuit, she certainly was not going to carry his stuff and where had he gone now?

Almost immediately he returned, almost at a run. "Look, Anita, I can't explain right now. Just get in the queue for boarding. I've got to check something quickly but I'll be with you before you reach the desk. If, for any reason, I'm not, then fall out and wait for me here, even if it means missing the plane." He picked up his bag and the next moment he was several yards away, disappearing behind the sea of people, some of which were preparing to join the boarding queue while others rushed to claim their vacated seats.

Anita slowly shut her mouth that had been about to question Luke. Who did he think he was? She was not his servant or minion, or whatever he seemed to think. He was certainly going to have to do a lot of explaining!

As she shuffled forward obediently in the queue, her temper grew. By the time she faced the boarding gate, she had built up a good head of steam. She was not going to sit down meekly and wait for him. At the rate things were going they would miss their flight and, quite frankly, she had had enough of waiting in airports with Luke. It was too exhausting. She showed her boarding pass to the official and stomped into the tunnel that would lead to the plane. If necessary, she would spend the holiday on her own. Just because he seemed to have gone mad that was no reason why she needed to miss out.

Her anger carried her onto the plane and into her seat. She stowed her bags before sitting and pulling the seat belt across her lap. She looked out of the window on to the dark tarmac. A little self-pity crept in. She had been so looking forward to this. Going away with Luke. She remembered her friends' envy and Maggie's demand to hear 'every detail' on her return. They certainly would not envy her now.

Feeling someone sink into the seat beside her, Anita's head whipped round. Luke had made it! But no, a stranger sat there. He looked back at her and smiled, "Are you on your own?"

Controlling her disappointment, Anita said, "No, I'm expecting my boyfriend and that's his seat."

Regretfully he shook his head. "I don't think so. I was on stand-by and this seat was issued to me."

Looking at him, Anita began to feel uneasy. Something was wrong. It was more than just Luke behaving oddly, this man unnerved her somehow. She stood up, "Would you let me by, please. I'm getting off."

As she was pulling her bags out into the aisle, a stewardess offered her help. "Let me put them away for you."

"No, I'm getting off. I've changed my mind about travelling." By now, Anita was experiencing a cocktail of emotions with a strong feeling she should disembark overriding the rest.

"I'm afraid that's impossible," the stewardess said as she firmly pushed the bags back into the storage compartment. "There is no time. We would have to find and remove your baggage from the hold and then we'd miss our take-off slot. Please get into your seat."

"But my boyfriend isn't on board. We're supposed to be going on holiday together."

"I'm sorry," the stewardess was adamant. "I'm sure he'll take another plane and join you out there. In any case, we are about to take off and you must sit down for safety."

Anita succumbed to the inevitable and returned to her seat to stare glumly out of the window as the engines revved and the plane began its journey to the take-off runway. She was stuck here now. She should have controlled her temper and done as Luke said and not got on.

Once aloft, a combination of her reluctance to pursue any more conversation with Mr NextSeat leading her to stare out at the endless blue with sporadic clouds through the porthole, along with the soporific droning of the engines, resulted in her dozing off. When she woke the plane was beginning its descent. The nap, however fitful, had refreshed her sufficiently that her natural optimism reasserted itself.

Once stationary on the ground in Barcelona, Anita collected her hand baggage and joined the shuffling line of people leaving the plane. Mr NextSeat was ahead of her, but somehow on reaching the terminal he was behind her. There was something about him that raised the hair on the nape of her neck. She was sure she felt his eyes on her the whole time, but managed to stop herself turning to check. She'd be glad when they finished with officialdom and she need never see him again.

When she entered the arrivals hall, after passport control and collecting her baggage from the carousel, she noticed a bank of drivers holding up the names of their previously booked passengers. As she was about to move away to find what coaches were available for the last lap of her journey, her brain caught up with her eyes as she recognised Luke's name. Her spirits perked up. This was more like it. She approached the sign holder and identified herself.

"But whhhere ees Señor South?" he asked while looking behind her.

"He missed the plane and will come on later."

"I supposed to collect Señor South. No one say nothing about you".

Anita firmed her lips, she'd had more than enough of her wishes being ignored. "Nevertheless, here I am and here he is not. I'm sure he will be very annoyed if you do not take me to our hotel."

The driver, whose name was found to be Esteban, stood his ground valiantly all the way out to his car. But ultimately Anita, bolstered by the emotional buffeting she had endured throughout the day, prevailed. Triumphantly she got in the car as Esteban stuffed the luggage in the boot.

Esteban was still muttering as he slid behind the wheel and set off, driving with one hand and apparently ignoring all other traffic despite discordant horns and flashing lights. The car's efficient air conditioner was a relief after the dry heat outside, even though it was night. Spain was certainly a change from England's cool May weather. Soon the traffic thinned and the car picked up speed. Suddenly a ring tone drew Anita's attention from the darkness outside. Esteban answered it and soon was gabbling indecipherably. It didn't sound like Spanish. At least not like her GCSE Spanish. Probably a dialect, she decided.

With nothing to see outside and Esteban's voice rabbiting on, crowning her day of mega-stress, Anita let herself zone out.

When she came to, a couple of hours later according to her watch, the car was still travelling through the pitch of the night and Esteban was still on the phone. Surely he had not been on for the whole time? Ingrained manners initially held her back from interrupting, but eventually, with no way of knowing how long the call was going to take, the need to have some questions answered won out and she tapped on the glass partition which was only half drawn across. His eyes met hers in the mirror. He appeared annoyed as he lifted his hand off the steering wheel to gesture towards the phone in his other hand at his ear. With no warning the car slewed towards the middle of the road. Anita screamed. Esteban's hand was quickly back on the wheel as he readjusted the car's direction with no discernible disruption to his phone conversation, although it might not have been quite as heated as before. Anita slumped back in her seat, defeated.

Finally, Esteban finished his conversation and slid the phone onto the dashboard before turning up the radio with the obvious intention of discouraging conversation. Undeterred, Anita leant forward and raised her voice. "How much further?"

Her only response was a Latin shrug of his shoulders. Not sure if this meant he did not know the distance or did not understand the question, Anita gave up and flopped back in her seat. There was not much she could do anyway.

The journey continued until eventually the car slowed and turned off the main road onto a rough, unmade track. There didn't appear to be any lights or buildings. Where the hell were they? Anita sat upright and tasted the metallic flavour of fear flood her system. This was not Salou, with its promised bright lights from numerous bars and clubs.

The car drew to a halt in front of a small building. It was not possible to see much in the dark, although some light could be discerned behind badly drawn curtains at a window. Esteban turned in his seat. "We arrive," he announced unnecessarily.

"But where? This is not Salou," Anita said.

"No," he agreed. "Not Salou. This is where I bring Señor South. You say you want to go without him, I bring you here." Twisting back, he opened his door and got out. At that moment, the front door of the building opened, framing a man in crumpled trousers and a dirty vest. Scruffy and the driver exchanged a few remarks and then Esteban opened her door. "Come."

Anita obstinately remained sitting, "Please, where are we? There has been a mistake. I want to go to Salou."

"No Salou," Esteban began to show a bit of irritation. "Señor South to come here. You here in his place. Come." He took her arm and pulled her towards him. Anita scrambled out to avoid being unceremoniously dragged. Once on her feet, she shook off his arm and, straightening her shoulders, turned to face the unknown. She would explain the mix-up to this new person as, however disreputable his appearance, he appeared to be in charge of the driver and insist that she be taken on to the holiday resort. Or even back to the airport, if they preferred. This whole trip had been a disaster from their arrival at Gatwick, starting when Luke had seemed to undergo a personality change.

She was guided inside the house to a room whose décor left much to be desired. Uncomfortable, her heartbeat was so fast she felt in danger of collapse. Scruffy made no effort to talk, just silently stared at her. Vaguely she wondered if she should try to initiate a conversation to find out more about why she had been brought here. But just as she felt the silence start to overwhelm her, footsteps and voices sounded in the hall and she turned to the door at the same time as she heard a car starting up and crunching away. Great, now the transport was gone, she was truly stuck here.

The car's departure seemed to galvanise Scruffy. "Where is Señor South?"

"He missed the plane. Who are you? Why was I brought here?"

"Señor South, he is in England still?"

"I don't know. He may be. Or he may have caught another flight," she shrugged with pseudo indifference.

"Which flight he catches?"

"I don't know. I don't even know if he has caught another flight?"

"When you expect to meet with him?"

"I've told you. I DO NOT KNOW."

After staring at her intently during a further silence, Scruffy suddenly left the room. Anita sat down. Could things get much worse? She was heavens knows where in a strange country where it was being assumed she had information wanted by a couple of unsavoury—to say the least—characters. When would someone eventually listen and take in that she had no idea where Luke was now or where he was intending to be in the future? On her own, her thoughts went to her family. Her childhood had been spent in various bubbling hotspots both in South America and the Middle East, wherever her father's work had taken him. She had even received basic specialist training in case they were attacked, held hostage or kidnapped. She remembered the main watch word had been to keep calm, do as told and wait for an opportunity to escape.

She drew a shaky breath. Who would have thought after no problems in those seething cauldrons that she would have to draw on that advice after planning to go on a holiday to Spain with her boyfriend. The irony briefly amused her, which had the effect of centring her, enabling her to draw on a mantle of calm.

A noise at the door made her look up. Scruffy came back in followed by another man. She stared. She couldn't help it. Even her panic took a back seat. He was the type of Hispanic that would be quite at home adorning the front covers of romance novels. Tall, with aquiline features hinting of his hidalgo ancestry, accentuated by his thick, swept back, midnight hair that was just that bit too long, but exactly the right length to invite fingers to run through it. His jeans and T-shirt were worn but clean and he exuded an unmistakeable air of control. Anita mentally pulled herself together. She needed to concentrate.

The Hispanic smiled, "I am Manuel." His accent was a surprise. Strongly American with only a hint of Spanish. "We need to know where Luke South is."

Brought back to earth, Anita sighed. "Like I told your friend," indicating Scruffy. "He missed the plane."

"You told Esteban he would be on the next flight."

"Oh, that was just to pacify him so he would take me to my hotel in Salou. I wish now that I'd just got on the next plane back to England." She could feel herself unravelling again as the onset of panic reasserted itself, and took a deep breath. Now was not the time for hysterics.

Manuel sat down opposite her. "What is your relationship with him?" His calm tone reflected patience and unconsciously Anita relaxed.

What relationship? As she had recognised before, they hadn't really spent all that much time together and, as she had earlier realised, while Luke knew practically everything about her life, she in turn knew relatively little about him. They hadn't even progressed beyond a few gentle kisses.

"This is our getting-to-know-you phase," he had said. "Once we're in Spain, free from work and obligations here, we can explore each other to our heart's content." He had produced his seductive smile as he added, "I can't wait!"

She huffed inwardly, once she was back home and safe, there was no way after today she was having any more to do with him. Apart, of course, from telling him exactly what she thought of his behaviour. Of course this presupposed she did see him again, at the moment nothing seemed sure.

"We work together, been out a few times . . ."

Sudden energy speared into Manuel. "You work together?"

Anita nodded.

Manuel turned, speaking to Scruffy. Unfortunately too rapidly in Spanish for her to understand what was said.

Manuel left the room, leaving her with Scruffy. On his return the two of them talked briefly. It sounded like instructions for Scruffy, before Manuel turned to Anita with a charming smile. "We are to leave immediately. I am sorry that it is more travelling for you, but Señor Bolaño is expecting us.

"This Señor Bolaño, no chance, I suppose, he's in Salou?"

Manuel regretfully shook his head. "We will talk with him and no doubt clear up the problem of South."

Anita considered. She could make a fuss, but to what end? She certainly didn't want to be stranded here with Scruffy. On the other hand, she could find herself leaping from the frying pan into the fire. Deciding on the fatalistic approach, she stood up. "Fine."

CHAPTER TWO

He led her outside and round the side of the house where a sleek black BMW waited. Scruffy morosely loaded her luggage into the boot while Manuel helped her into the front before settling himself into the driver's seat and setting the car in motion. With the darkness outside and the radio playing soft classical music the atmosphere inside was intimate. Anita relaxed in the luxurious seat, feeling the ambience eroding her stress. Then, as she realised this, she stiffened, they were not on a date for heaven's sake! She felt a need to break the silence.

"How far it is?"

"Not too far, about another 25 minutes."

After a few minutes of more silence, Anita asked, "Who is Señor Bolaño?"

Manuel gave her a sharp glance. "You don't know?"

"I've never heard of him."

He seemed to hesitate a moment, then, "He is a business man. A very successful one." A further pause before he continued, "He made a business arrangement with South and he is not pleased he is not here to honour it."

Anita considered this. "I know nothing about it. I'm not going to be able to help him."

Manuel nodded. "Do not worry about it. As I said, he's a business man, not a monster."

Settling back into her seat and closing her eyes, Anita muttered, "I hope you're right!"

As they cruised through the night, Anita considered her position. When had she stopped being frightened? She had been kidnapped, even if she'd unknowingly colluded at the airport. She felt uncomfortable, annoyed and irritated but not terrified. The whole day appeared unreal. These sorts of events did not happen to people like her. She huffed inwardly. No doubt everyone who found themselves in some sort of mire like this thought exactly the same thing. It was always other people who got kidnapped or shot or drowned or whatever. Still the question remained, why was she not scared to death?

She glanced at Manuel in the dim light from the dashboard. Sensing her regard, he gave her a quick look and smiled. There was no doubt about it, she thought, he really looked as if he had been conjured from a romantic fantasy. As for his voice, that slight accent sent ripples of awareness through her.

She frowned as a thought occurred to her. How could she be so attracted to him? It was less than a day since she had been excited about extending her relationship with Luke. What did this say about her character? Was she that shallow? Shrugging philosophically, she let that problem slide for the time being. It was hardly her most pressing concern at the moment.

Manuel drove the car automatically, his hands expertly guiding it in the direction he wanted. Meanwhile, he considered his passenger. He was starting to incline towards the belief that she really was an innocent caught up in events out of her control. He pondered on how exactly South had intended to use her. Had he meant her only for camouflage, or would he have given her some role to play, even if unwittingly on her part? Of course, he could be wrong and she was actually a very clever actress.

Sensing her eyes on him, he glanced over and smiled. Poor little thing, whatever the truth of the matter, she must be exhausted from the roller coaster of experiences she had been on today. Musing further, he realised why he favoured the view of her not being involved in this affair. She was easy to read. Take now, for example, she was thinking so hard he could hear it. And, he thought with satisfaction, at the moment she was thinking about him. He was not really surprised. He felt such a strong attraction to her, that it would be incredible if she did not reciprocate to some degree. It was a pity they hadn't met in more conducive circumstances but, he shrugged philosophically, desire was either felt or not whatever other events may be taking place at the time.

Shortly afterwards, as the first signs of dawn appeared on the horizon, the car slowed as they entered the outskirts of a town and soon they turned into a gravelled drive that wound in a wide circle leading to a large pink villa with dark brown shutters lying open. In the soft light Anita could just discern the trellis supporting a profusion of bougainvillea scrambling over the villa's walls.

Manuel came round to open her door. As they approached, the front doors were opened by a small sleepy man who greeted Manuel in a friendly manner. Obviously, Anita realised, he was not a stranger here. Whether that was a good or bad thing was uncertain, she ruefully acknowledged.

After speaking briefly to the little man, Manuel turned to Anita. "Paco, here, will take you to your room. It is still very early and I would suggest you go to bed and get some rest. You could do with it, no?" he smiled.

Anita automatically smiled back as she nodded. Manuel turned to go outside again and suddenly she felt as if he were abandoning her.

"Wait," she reached for his arm. "Where are you going?"

He rested his hand over hers. "I am just going to park the car and bring in our bags. Do not worry, I will see you later when you are refreshed."

Anita felt her cheeks warm as she ducked her head, embarrassed, and turned to follow Paco. What must he think? For that matter, what was she doing? He might be a dream in the looks department, but she had to remember he was a member of her kidnapping group.

Paco led her into a room, bowed and silently departed. Anita took stock of her surroundings. The whitewashed walls, wooden dresser, cupboard and small dressing table. The bed, with a woven mat lying beside it, was covered with an intricately crocheted yellow throw. It looked very Spanish and very peaceful.

She slipped off her shoes and dress, deciding to lie down. She would never sleep, there was too much churning through her mind and she must try to think of a way out of this mess. She started to lie down to at least allow her body to relax and was asleep before her head fully connected with the pillow.

* * * * *

Anita woke four hours later when a maid entered with a tray, which she placed on the bedside table. "*Su desayuno*, Señorita," she pointed.

On the tray were a tall goblet of freshly squeezed orange juice and a glass mug of milky coffee. A basket of halved rolls and some sweet cupcakes, that she thought she remembered were called Magdelenas, looked inviting, while a bowl of pureed tomatoes less so. She drank the juice as the maid brought in her luggage, opened it and began to unpack.

Anita felt hungry and was prepared to eat the rolls dry if necessary, but decided to ask if something could be provided. With her few words of Spanish and much gesticulating, the maid eventually comprehended.

"Ah, *si*," she said and pointed to the tomatoes that Anita had been avoiding. The maid spread some thickly on a roll, adding a few drops of olive oil before offering it to Anita. Tentatively, she bit into it and was surprised as the flavour flooded her mouth. It was delicious.

Finally, as she finished her breakfast with a sweet Magdelena, the maid, having finished unpacking, approached Anita and spoke slowly. Grasping the name of Señor Bolaño and from the maid's gestures at the clock and raised fingers, she understood she was expected to be ready at ten o'clock to meet her host. Brought back to reality, Anita nodded to show her understanding and started to get up.

Once dressed and ready, she realised she didn't know where to go. However, on leaving the bedroom, as if on cue, Paco appeared and gestured for her to follow him. He took her to a formal study with a dark stained wooden floor and matching heavy furniture. It was west facing, so the shutters were open to admit a modicum of natural light. A man rose from behind the desk and stepped towards her.

"Ah, Señorita, how nice to meet you." He took one of her hands between both of his and for a moment or two looked intently into her face. Then smiling and giving her hand a small pat before releasing it, he turned her towards the door. "Let us go and sit outside. This dark room is not for one such as you."

She was not sure exactly how she had pictured him, but possibly *The Godfather* film had influenced her. However, Señor Bolaño did not conform to this stereotype. He was small both in stature and physique and very precisely dressed. Yet his overwhelming feature was his teeth. Very white and showcased by his smile. They were riveting to such an extent that Anita almost missed the blackness of his eyes. They did not reflect his smile.

Suppressing a small shiver, she allowed herself to be escorted to the veranda. There they sat in green rattan chairs around a matching table. The Señor poured them both some coffee and indicated she was to help herself to cream, sugar and a selection of sugar-dusted biscuits. Without the problems she seemed to have inherited from Luke, this could be a delightful place, with its warmth and luxury. She closed her eyes to better inhale the mixture of rich soil recently watered and the aromas filling the air from the exotic, loudly coloured bushes and plants making up the garden.

"So," he said following his first sip of coffee. "Where is your friend, Luke South?"

"Please believe me," she leant forward in emphasis. "I wish I knew. The last time I saw him was at the airport in England."

Señor Bolaño appeared a little bewildered, "But surely he must have told you his plans?" As she started to shake her head, he held up a palm to forestall her. "Even if only when he plans to meet with you?"

Anita sighed, "No such plans because he did not intend me to come to Spain without him." She ran through her explanation, almost by rote now, but with little hope of it being believed. She was not disappointed, Señor Bolaño proceeded to put questions to her, most of which she couldn't answer. She noted with rising anxiety that his charm was becoming a little forced and his white teeth were no longer so conspicuous as his smile appeared less frequently.

Relief washed over her when Manuel strolled out of the house and approached them. "*Buenos dias* Anita, Señor," he nodded at each of them. Before she could respond, the Señor engaged him in a brief, very fast discourse.

Anita sipped her coffee, looking sightlessly across the garden. It was hard to believe, considering Manuel was obviously 'one of them', that his presence immediately reassured her. Obviously on some level she trusted him to take care of her. But a small niggle caused her to frown. She hoped her intuition was correct as it was just dawning on her that no effort had been made to conceal identities or places from her. Wasn't that a bad sign?

Manuel interrupted her ruminations. "Come for a walk with me round the garden," he invited. "We need to talk a little."

Anita rose with alacrity. The Señor's white teeth were now not in evidence at all and she was glad to escape. They walked for a few minutes in silence before Manuel spoke. "You really should tell us anything you know."

She suddenly felt close to tears. "Don't you think I would, if I knew anything? I'm not stupid, I know I'm in a lot of trouble. But I can't tell you what I don't know!"

"*Calme*, calm down," he took her hand. "Let me think, yes?"

For a time he racked his brains while she hoped for some sort of miracle, like waking up and finding it all a dream. He muttered as if to himself, "The problem is what must we do with you?" There were obvious reasons why she could not just be let go. She knew about them, of course. But the main reason for holding on to her was to ensure she could not contact Luke. He was reasonably sure she was an innocent but . . . he could be mistaken. Perhaps he was letting his attraction to her outweigh his sense?

"Come," he said, and led her back to the veranda where the Señor still waited. The two men talked, again too quickly for Anita, although she did catch Manuel's "*Ella sabe nada*." She knows nothing.

Señor Bolaño abruptly rose, nodded at Anita, "Señorita," he murmured, then looked hard at Manuel before disappearing within the house.

Manuel turned to her and smiled. "You will stay here as a guest. There is a pool at the back and the servants will be pleased to help you." His smile dimmed, "The only restriction is you cannot leave the grounds." As she started to speak, he continued rapidly. "It will not be for long. There are many people now looking for South, and soon he will be found."

She considered this while looking at him. "And you will be here?"

He shook his head regretfully. "No, I wish I could be, but I must leave tomorrow—pressure of work."

Snorting inwardly, she let her eyes drop. "Doesn't look as if I have much choice."

"I am sorry, really. But it will not be for long. Of that I am sure."

She nodded and turned towards the house. "I'll see you later, then?"

"Yes, of course," he sounded relieved. "At lunch."

"Okay," Anita went indoors. She could not stay here without Manuel. She did not trust the Señor at all. Thinking hard, her priority, she decided, must be to contact Luke. She had his mobile number. Obviously he was not answering when the Spanish contingent tried to phone, but he might answer her call. If not, she could leave a message about when she would ring again. He certainly had a lot of questions to answer!

Ten minutes later she had to accept that her mobile battery was flat, and she had no charger. Great, what else could go wrong? Tossing her hair back, she realised she would have to find a telephone in the house and use that, hopefully without being discovered. They would never believe she knew nothing if they found her talking with Luke.

After a lunch full of silences, broken intermittently by unsuccessful efforts at conversation mainly between the two men, Señor Bolaño had his driver bring a car to the front and soon disappeared down the drive. Manuel explained, "I must do some work—I am expecting an important call. Why do you not rest and later we can swim together?"

Anita's heart leapt, now if only he did not use the study, perhaps she could. "Good idea," she replied coolly.

Manuel watched her walking away. She seemed to have accepted the idea of staying here very well. He scratched his head. Too well, perhaps? Well, that must wait, he had business to deal with.

A quarter of an hour later Anita slipped into the study and crossed to the desk, on which stood a telephone. Consulting her scrap of paper with Luke's number, she began dialling.

Manuel strode down the hall. He had forgotten some papers left in the study. He pushed the door open and was confronted with sweetly-accepting-her-fate Anita dialling out. Quickly and silently he crossed the room and depressed the telephone button. Anita jumped, a little startled, before raising her defiant eyes to his.

"Okay, you caught me. I can't just sit here twiddling my thumbs until you, or someone else, decide I can go. Or even *if* I can go." She shrugged, but Manuel could see she was near the end of her tether. "I need to know what's happening. I've been brought here, told I must stay, questioned by everyone and anyone. All of whom, I have to say, appear to know much more than me!"

Manuel sighed, removed the receiver from her hand and replaced it. Indicating she should sit, he leant against the desk. "Yes, you do seem to know nothing. I will try to explain."

"About time," she muttered.

"The company you work for, Crown Industries, have developed a breakthrough in external data storage. No more disks, CDs or memory sticks. They have developed a prototype using nanotechnology. You knew this?" Manuel cocked a brow at her.

"No, but I wouldn't unless it was available for sale."

"This was top secret in your Research and Development Department, but it is almost impossible to keep anything really secret." He smiled slightly and continued, "Maybe someone in the Department tells a friend . . . or maybe someone in the companies that Crown Industries had approached talk about it. Who knows how the information gets out? Anyway South agreed to sell the prototype to Señor Bolaño. He was given a down payment. But now he intends to sell it to the highest bidder. We know this because the Señor is a representative of one of several parties that wish to obtain this prototype."

"My God," Anita considered this. "Why include the Señor if he was double-crossing him?"

"Good question," Manuel acknowledged. "Either he is very clever or very stupid. What do you think?"

Slowly she answered, "Well, I don't think he's stupid."

"No," he agreed. "But perhaps you now understand our interest in you. After all, you are not only his friend, but work at the same company."

"But I've got nothing to do with Research and Development. I work in Sales—processing orders and filing. For heaven's sake, I didn't even know about this prototype you're after."

Manuel nodded and glanced at his watch. "I must return to my room. The call I am expecting is due very soon." He collected some papers from a cabinet before indicating the door. "You must leave this room, I cannot allow you to talk with South, you understand?"

She nodded reluctantly and trudged out. Manuel followed, closing and locking the door. He looked at her despondent face and capitulated. "Go, wait for me on the veranda. I will not be long and then we talk."

She nodded agreement and wandered off to sit and gaze at the garden while her mind raced with all sorts of possibilities. Should she try to escape from here? If she did, where would she go? Where exactly was she now anyway? Who could be trusted? The Señor was probably considered a pillar of society here. If she stayed here . . . well who knew what might happen! Not to mention she would go crazy just waiting passively for whatever they had planned for her—possibly her death? Could she beg Manuel not to leave her, but take her with him?

Finally he joined her. "We have some news, South was seen on a plane coming to Spain."

The initial relief was huge. "Thank God. Now there's no need to keep me, is there?"

He smiled wryly, "Do you really believe that?"

She subsided, "I can't sit here until something happens."

"Yes, I know. I have been thinking about that. If I take you somewhere else, can I trust you to do as I tell you?"

"Oh yes, I just want to get away from here and the Señor."

He looked at her pensively for a moment. He was sure she meant what she said. He was also sure that if left on her own, her fertile imagination and impetuosity would get her into all sorts of trouble. If he took responsibility for her, he would have to keep an eye on her—he smiled inwardly, not that that would be such a hardship!

He checked the time. "Collect your belongings then meet me out here in half an hour."

"Fine," she jumped to her feet. "It won't take me that long, I've not got that much to pack."

"Well, I need the time. I have got some arrangements to make, but I will be as fast as I can. It might be better if we are gone before the Señor returns."

"God, yes." Anita rushed off to her bedroom. She was elated, he was taking her with him. Not only was she getting away from this dangerous place, but she would be spending more time with him. A frisson of excitement sparked through her.

CHAPTER THREE

The heat of the day was beginning to wane as Manuel steered his car down an unevenly cobbled street that wound its way through a small fishing village. Anita looked at the colour washed walls of the houses that propped each other up, their fronts flush to the road. Some had long trestle tables along their fronts on which wares for sale were displayed.

"It's beautiful," she said. "Like something from another time."

"Yes, just now it looks its best. But," he glanced her way, "it is difficult to make a living here. These are people who work very hard."

"I realise that." She felt reprimanded before indignantly recollecting that of the two of them, she was the law abiding one with a legitimate job, while his work could hardly be called 'legal'.

There was silence until they drew up in front of a small house with dusty pink walls. "Here we are," he said unnecessarily. Then he leant back, "I am sorry if I offended you. It is just . . . just I was raised here and can remember when tourists came to the village, usually by chance. They would say how pretty is the village and the fishermen so quaint. Like we were not real but a show for them."

She was immediately assailed by guilt. "I never thought of the people like that—just the houses, the street, the colours . . ."

He patted her knee. "I know. I am too sensitive, I think."

Relieved, she smiled in response. "It's understandable."

"Come," he opened his door. "We will go in."

The house was dark inside and, thanks to the stone walls and drawn shutters, cool. It did not take long to show her the parlour, bathroom, two bedrooms and kitchen. He left her to settle in while he went out, only to return soon with a matronly woman.

"This is Marta. She looks after my house while I am away. I rang her before we left and she has agreed to cook a meal for us this evening."

"*Buenos dias*, Marta." But Anita's smile soon gave way to confusion as she understood nothing of the response.

Manuel laughed. "*Muy, muy despacio*," he advised Marta, who nodded in understanding before speaking again to Anita much more slowly. She left soon afterwards, following a brief rapid exchange with Manuel.

"She will return soon with our supper," he explained.

Later, after a delicious paella followed by fresh fruit, they decided to go for a walk. It was now much cooler outside and both felt the need to stretch their legs after a tiring but sedentary day. Manuel guided her to the beach where they removed their shoes and ambled across the sands. There was a medley of salt, ozone, hot dust and traces of cooked fish in the air, while seabirds dived for food and stridently called to each other. At intervals they passed overturned boats, some with fishermen sitting on them, their gnarled hands mending and sorting nets or else smoking as they gossiped desultorily before heading to their respective homes for their evening meals or perhaps to one of the three bars in the village for a drink.

For awhile they walked in companionable silence, each busy with their own thoughts. It was so peaceful and picturesque. A companion like Manuel was a fantasy come to life, and she determined to pretend they were on holiday together and to put aside all thoughts of stolen prototypes and Crown Industries, menacing men and fears for her future, at least for the time being. They did not belong in this world. She spied a large, pink, spiral shell with iridescent colours glistening inside and picked it up. "Look at this," she showed it to him.

He admired it while wondering who she really was. There was this Anita, the child absorbed by an interesting shell; Anita the accomplice—although he was pretty sure she was an innocent in the game of corporate espionage and theft; which led to Anita the victim or pawn. She did not seem to be fully aware of the precariousness of her situation. He felt it was up to him to make sure she was safe and out of this whole situation as soon as possible. He resolved to see Señor Bolaño and persuade him that he, Manuel, could look after her—especially as it looked as if he would have to leave Spain shortly. He would take her with him and keep her close under both his protection and his control.

They meandered back to the house, keeping the conversation well away from the problems besetting them. He unlatched the door and she walked into his small house, turning as he spoke.

"Go and get some sleep. I will be leaving early in the morning but will come back as soon as I can."

Her face mirrored her returning concern. Sighing, he stepped forward and took her face into his hands. "Believe me, I promise to look after you." His head slowly lowered until their lips met. Automatically her mouth opened immediately, welcoming him without hesitation. What he had intended to be a kiss of reassurance ignited into the most electrifying kiss of his life. Breaking it off was one of the hardest things he had done.

He stared into her eyes until reason finally began to return. "Go on, Anita, get some rest. I have to go and see Marta, to let her know what's happening." Turning abruptly, he left the cottage.

* * * * *

The following morning, with the day to herself until Manuel's return, Anita enjoyed a leisurely breakfast before deciding on a stroll round the village. She had hoped it would give her a chance to try to sort things out in her head, but last night's kiss continued to dominate her thoughts.

Although the day was hot it was tempered by a stiff breeze coming off the sea. She was obviously of interest to the locals, but felt it was benign, judging by the smiles and murmured greetings. Deciding to have a break and enjoy a cup of coffee, she headed towards the bar-come-café they had passed the previous night. Suddenly, she was jolted out of her complacency as she caught sight of a familiar form. It was Mr NextSeat from the plane. He was sitting outside the café, talking with voice and hands to a waiter.

With pounding heart she turned tail and walked as naturally as she could before she came to a side street that she could slip into. She leaned against the wall and concentrated on breathing slowly to ease her frantic heartbeat. This could not be a coincidence. She needed help. She would ring Manuel. Oh God, her mobile was still flat. A brainwave hit: the post office. She had passed it earlier and remembered that nestling inside were some public telephones.

Peering around the corner she confirmed Mr NextSeat was still involved with the waiter before slipping out and heading off in the opposite direction. In the post office, after a little difficulty overcome with the help of a postal worker,

Anita dialled Manuel's number. He had given it to her for emergencies only. Surely, she thought, this qualified as a real emergency.

Although she let the number ring for some time there was no reply. Feeling jittery in case Mr NextSeat came passed and saw her, she thought only briefly before trying Luke's mobile number. While here, she might as well try, she could do with more light shed on the situation, not to mention her role in it. However, there was no reply from him either. Disconnecting, she dialled again, this time to her friend Maggie at the office. At last she got an answer.

"Good morning, Crown Industries, Sales, how may I help you?" Maggie's familiar voice came over clearly.

"Maggie, it's me, Anita." As she heard a startled indrawn breath, she hastened to add, "Try not to let anyone know it's me you're talking to."

"Where are you?"

"Spain, of course. Look there's a lot going on, but I wondered if you'd seen Luke?"

"Luke?" Maggie's puzzled voice was low. "Isn't he with you?"

Anita tried to resist the urge to roll her eyes. "No, he missed the plane. Look, I haven't got time to go into everything now. I'll explain when I see you."

"Wait, don't hang up. Whatever you're up to, is it anything to do with work?"

"Why?"

"I don't know, but you're being very secretive and since you left for your romantic holiday there have been some odd goings on. We have several strange people wandering in the corridors and a sudden flurry of confidential managerial meetings. No one seems to know what's happening, but everyone is jumpy."

This did not sound good, Anita thought. "I don't know much myself, but I promise to tell you whatever I do know when I see you. In the meantime, keep your head down and please keep quiet about this call. I've got to go now." She replaced the receiver firmly.

She would have to wait for Manuel's return. But where? The house may not be safe, any number of people could direct Mr NextSeat there. Carefully, keeping a look out, she made her way to Marta's house. Manuel had pointed it out in case she needed her. As it turned out, she did, and big time! Luckily, Marta was in and communicating with her threadbare Spanish, backed up with increasingly adept hand gestures, Anita was soon made comfortable within the security of Marta's protection.

After a tasty lunch with Marta of a bean soup followed by a shellfish casserole, Anita helped in the clear up before going to sit under a faded umbrella in her small but picturesque courtyard. She was not cut out for this. All she wanted was to go home. Have her life back to normal. As if none of the past few days had happened. But then she thought of Manuel—perhaps not all, she realised with a small shiver of excitement.

The day was starting to lose its white heat when Anita heard Manuel talking to Marta. It was only then she realised how tense she had been since seeing Mr NextSeat. Just the sound of his voice was enough for her to feel the tension begin to leave her. She watched as he emerged from the cool darkness of the house. The memory of their kiss sparked through her. With fleeting regret she wished she had met him normally, like on a real holiday, without all this danger and intrigue surrounding them.

"Are you all right? Marta said you had a big scare this morning." He pulled a chair close to her and took one of her hands, enclosing it in both his.

"It was such a shock, especially as I was enjoying my walk round the village. I felt safe, I suppose."

"Who did you see?"

"On the plane coming to Spain a man had the seat next to me. Then when I saw him today I panicked and could only think of getting away before he saw me."

"What did he do on the plane?"

"Nothing really," she laughed uncomfortably. "It's probably just me, my imagination. We only said a few words, and then later I just felt uneasy—like when someone stares at you, or you think they are. You know what I mean?" Manuel nodded.

"I feel a bit stupid now, making such a big thing out of seeing him. It's probably just a coincidence and nothing to do with me at all!"

"No, I do not like coincidences, especially in circumstances such as this." He frowned as he patted her hand absently. "I must think," he added slowly.

Anita looked at him, keeping still so as not to distract him. Why did she trust him so much? It was illogical, she had met him only because he was part of some conspiracy involved in stealing from the company she worked for—hardly a ringing endorsement. All right, he was wickedly good looking and his accent alone was enough to make her toes curl, but Luke was just as attractive although in a different way. Of course, Luke appeared to be less than honest as well . . . although now that she thought about it, she only had this from Bolaño and his men. Why couldn't everything be simple? She could hardly believe that only a couple of weeks earlier she had complained to Maggie about the lack of excitement in her life. It just went to show the old adage on being careful for what you wish was right on the mark.

Now that Manuel was back with her, rightly or wrongly, she felt safe. As she relaxed she became aware of the smell of cooking food wafting through the small courtyard. Her stomach rumbled. She clapped a hand over it, embarrassed, while Manuel laughed.

"Come, your body is getting loud in its demand for food."

Anita smiled ruefully. "It's the wonderful aromas coming from the kitchen. Marta is such a good cook."

"You must tell her, she will be pleased."

They entered the kitchen to find Marta in the process of laying the table. Anita stepped forward to take over, leaving her free to serve the supper. Shortly the three of them were seated and starting their meal of *habas con jamon*, which consisted of serano ham with broad beans.

Remembering Manuel's suggestion, Anita looked at Marta then pointed at her food. "*Muy bueno.*"

Marta grinned and nodded while she burbled a response, too fast for Anita to understand. At the end Manual translated, "She says thank you."

Anita looked at him in disbelief. "She speaks, fast, for about a minute and all she said was thank you?"

"Well, that was her meaning." He shrugged. For a while there was just a background chink of cutlery on crockery as they enjoyed their meal.

Anita took a sip of wine. "Please explain to Marta for me how grateful I am for her help today. I was in a real panic when I appeared here, she must have thought me mad. But she was so kind and accepting, even though I'm sure she didn't fully understand what I was telling her."

Manuel turned to Marta, "*Ella está agradecida por lo que usted hizo para ella hoy.*"

"*Era todo que ella digo, ella habló mucho más,*" Marta replied.

Manuel burst out laughing. "*Es solo lo que ella digo.*" Marta laughed as he looked at Anita, "Like you, she complained that you said much more than I translated."

The merriment relaxed them all and the rest of the meal continued with Manuel doing his best to keep lines of understanding open between the two women. After helping Marta clear the table, Manuel drew Anita to one side.

"I am going out to see what I can discover about your travelling companion." As she opened her mouth to speak, he continued quickly. "I realise it may be a coincidence. But, like you, it seems to me to be not so likely. Stay here with Marta and I will return soon to collect you."

Anita looked indeterminate. "I could come with you, point him out if he's still here."

"No, it is possible that he does not know you are here, not for sure anyway, and I do not want to give him that surety. You will be safe here with Marta, and I will not be long." He paused, watching the parade of thoughts clearly crossing her face framed between his two hands. "You will wait here, yes?"

Anita gave in ungraciously, "Okay, but you'd better not be too long."

He smiled with relief and kissed her quickly. "Thank you." Then, turning, he left the house. Anita watched his departure with one finger on her lips. Then, shrugging ruefully, she returned to the kitchen and Marta.

* * * * *

34

Manuel entered the cantina and made his way to the bar. Once he had ordered, he turned and leant against the bar as he looked around. The stranger was sitting at a table near the back of the room. He collected his beer and approached him.

"You have been asking about an English girl who came to Spain yesterday, yes?"

The stranger looked up at him. "Do you know if she is in this village?"

"First to make sure we talk about the same person."

The stranger nodded once, "I'm looking for Anita Wright. Twenty-three years old, straight brown hair, around five feet five."

Manuel dropped into the chair opposite. "I know where she was," he took a mouthful of beer.

"Was? You don't know where she is now?"

Manuel assessed the man. He did not appear stupid, nor even drunk. He would have to tread warily and act as the Englishman would expect.

"What is she to you? How much is my information worth?"

The English man's lips twisted in distaste. "To me, personally, nothing. But a friend asked me to track her down. They had a fight. My friend wants to tell her he's sorry."

"You came all the way to Spain to find your friend's girlfriend?"

"No, I was coming here anyway, on business, and my friend asked for my help."

Shaking his head slightly, Manuel observed, "You must be very good friends to go to this trouble for him."

The stranger shrugged, took a drink then leant forward. "Do you know where she is?"

"I know only where she was," Manuel paused indicating his empty glass. "My drink is finished, I need to get another."

Taking the hint, the stranger motioned for a waitress. "Let me take care of this."

Manuel thanked him and looked round the cantina. As usual there were no females except for the two waitresses who were very busy keeping glasses filled. Once their new drinks were in front of them, the stranger leant forward again.

"If your information is good, I'll make sure you're rewarded. So what can you tell me about Anita Wright?"

Manuel spread his hands, "Not much, alas. But I know she was in Zaragoza this morning. Whether she is still there . . ."

"How do you know this?"

"I was at Zaragoza airport when I met a friend, he drives a taxi. He spoke about his fare, Señorita Wright—she is the one you look for?"

"Yes, yes. Go on."

"My friend had brought her to the airport. He thought it was strange. I think she did not catch a plane, she had no luggage, but did not act like she was meeting someone."

The stranger rested back in his chair as he digested this information. So she really was not hiding out somewhere in this back-of-beyond. Manuel finished his beer and wiped his mouth. "My news was good, no? You will pay now?"

CHAPTER FOUR

On his way back to Marta's house, Manuel considered the situation. The village was not safe on a long term basis, both Bolaño and the Englishman now knew about it. And earlier today, Bolaño had not been disposed to abandon all interest in Anita. He saw her as a potential tool against South, added to which he was volatile and could be dangerously unpredictable. Nor did he trust the Englishman he had just left in the cantina. Hopefully, he would believe him and leave, but you could never be quite sure. He might hear something and decide to search here further and Anita could not be kept hidden all the time. The other thing that worried him was that the Englishman was very obviously connected to Luke, but in what way? For or against him? Whichever way he looked at it, he needed to get Anita away from here for her own safety. He could send her back to England, but how safe would that be? One or other of the players in this game may decide she knew too much, or possibly the authorities would think she was involved. Either way it was too risky. The only answer seemed to be to keep her with him where he could look after her. Suppressing a small voice of conscience accusing him of keeping her with him for reasons totally unconnected to this situation, he quickened his pace.

At Marta's house he and Anita thanked her for both her hospitality and help. There was another swift exchange between Marta and Manuel but, judging from Marta's knowing looks and Manuel's amusement, Anita decided not to press for a translation.

As soon as they were on the street Anita asked, "What did you find out this evening?"

"A little only. Wait until we get in and I will tell you."

Once inside he asked her if she would like a coffee, which he prepared efficiently while she sat at the kitchen table and tried to exercise patience. Obviously he was not going to tell her anything until he was good and ready.

Finally he sat down next to her and stirred some sugar into his drink. He took a sip and smiled at her expression as he relented.

"First, I do not think anyone told him about you being in the village. There are some advantages to growing up in such a tight-knit community, we may fight among ourselves but unite against outsiders."

"Lucky for me that I'm with you!"

Manuel dipped his head in acknowledgement and continued. "He has a connection with South, but what exactly I do not know." He went on to relate their conversation.

After a short silence spent in consideration, Anita spoke. "He turned up here very quickly. I mean, I don't see how Luke could have asked him to come. He was on the same plane as me."

"Yes, I too thought of that. The only answer is if he had been at the airport with South. You said South went off suddenly."

"But if he was following me, how did he lose me? I mean, I wasn't being secretive or trying to lose anyone trailing me."

"When you came through airport controls, how long before you left with Esteban?"

"Not long," her voice quickened. "Not long at all. I saw him with Luke's name and was so relieved that I wouldn't have to find a bus going to Salou or have to pay for a taxi, that I may have been a little assertive and we left immediately." Sotto voce she added, "Unfortunately."

Manuel laughed knowingly. "That is what happened then. You and Esteban left too quickly for him to keep up, and once you were gone he could not follow." He ruminated for a while. Anita was getting used to his periods of reflection, rather an endearing mannerism really, she thought.

"The question is, how did he track you here? A bit too clever for him on his own. He must have help, but I still do not understand how it is possible, no one knew I was bringing you here."

Anita shivered. "What are we going to do now?"

Manuel took one of her hands in both his, "You will continue to let me keep you safe, yes?"

She nodded solemnly.

"Good. Early tomorrow we leave here. I must go to Portugal and you will come with me." As she opened her mouth to speak, he continued quickly, "It is the only way I can look after you, it is not safe here and I do not want to leave you in a strange place on your own. Also, I do not know how long I need to be in Portugal. Even if I send you back to England, you know too much, and could be in danger there."

"Yes, I was afraid of that." Anita considered her options, not that there were many. She could hardly stay here on her own, even if there were no danger. So the alternative to going with Manuel was to make her way home alone and take her chances both in eluding Señor Bolaño and Mr NextSeat, as well as with the English authorities. She wrinkled her nose, none of those scenarios, as well as being on her own, appealed to her. That left Manuel. Was he to be trusted? Yes, she was sure he was. After all, if he had intended to harm her he already had had plenty of opportunities. And then, she grinned in remembrance, there was that kiss!

She looked at Manuel, "I'll come with you."

With fascination, Manuel had watched her thought processes as they travelled over her face. At her words, he smiled and, covering her hand with his, said, "Good, it is the best decision, and I thank you for your belief in me."

Anita nodded before sipping some coffee. They talked about the travel plans to Portugal until Manuel noticed her trying to suppress a yawn.

"You are tired and we must leave early tomorrow. It is time for bed."

She agreed, rose and rinsed their mugs out. With Latin courtesy he accompanied her to her bedroom door. She opened it and, just before going in, looked up at him. He groaned, unable to resist, and drew her against him as his mouth covered hers. Immediately her arms rose around his neck as she responded, her body softening against his hard masculine frame. His hand rose to support her head while his other arm kept her close. Leaving her mouth he nipped and kissed his way over her face then down her neck, interspersed with soft words in his own language. Anita fleetingly thought Spanish was full of the most romantic sounds she had ever heard. She heard small moans before belatedly realising that it was she who was making them. Her whole body had become ultra-sensitive, ultra-responsive while her mind was empty of everything but absorbing the feelings and emotions he was stirring up with his sure and knowledgeable caresses.

Then both his hands gripped her head as he raised his face. "We must stop," he gritted.

"No," she tried to reach his mouth.

"If we do not stop now, it will be too late for me," he warned.

"I don't want you to stop. I've never felt like this," she almost pleaded.

Manuel stared into her face, her eyes, trying to read the truth behind her siren words. Then, with a sibilant expulsion of air between his teeth, he buried his face in her neck as he lifted her off the floor and carried her into the bedroom. He released her long enough to pull her top over her head and reach for the fastening on her skirt. In moments he had her lying on the bed, where he allowed himself to drink in the sight of her naked and highly aroused body. Oddly, she felt no embarrassment, it seemed natural as she revelled in the lust apparent in his eyes.

Stretching sinuously, she smiled, "Are you going to join me?"

Her words broke his stillness and he moved quickly towards the bed.

"Don't you think you're a bit overdressed?" Her words stopped him. He smiled sinfully as he threw off his clothes before joining her on the bed. Instead of immediately taking up where he had left off, his hand smoothed her cheek as he stared in her eyes.

"I had not planned this," he growled.

"No, I know. But it's right," she ran one hand through his luxuriant hair as she returned his serious gaze.

"It is right," he agreed. "Maybe too soon, but . . ." He kissed her deeply. Then lifting his head again, "You need not worry, I will look after you."

"I know," she managed before he took command of her body and she was unable to do more than feel and respond.

Then, just when she thought she would expire in a ball of desire if he did not enter her soon, he drew back. His face, a combination of frustration and self-disgust. "No protection," he gasped.

Anita pulled at his shoulders. "Doesn't matter." At his resistance, she added, "I'm on the pill."

He kissed her hard in relief before gripping her hips, holding them steady, as he finally eased his way into her body. Not that she had vast experience for comparison, but he was taking her far into new waters as she struggled with the feelings, both emotional and physical, in which he was immersing her. All the fears and frustrations of the last couple of days were obliterated as she gave up all pretence of self control under his love making until finally her release overtook her, causing her body and soul to shiver under its impact.

Later, pleasantly exhausted, she lay spooned within his curved body and, as she drifted into sleep, her only thought was of feeling protected and completely safe for the first time since her arrival in Spain.

CHAPTER FIVE

When Anita awoke she had a moment of disorientation before recollections of the previous night made her stretch luxuriously. It was early morning, judging from the pale light skidding across the floor, and she was alone.

It was so quiet she felt she was probably alone in the whole house. Briefly she felt disappointment, but then relief. She wanted time to remember the passion of the night before and was a little shy about facing Manuel. He was so unlike anyone else she knew. He had an old world charm that was captivating. And, of course, he made her feel secure. He had got her away from Bolaño who had frightened her. He had brought her to his house here and searched out Mr NextSeat for information on her behalf and was taking her with him so he could continue to look after her. She frowned slightly. Of course, she must remember that he was clearly in league with Bolaño but, her face lightened, he was obviously putting her ahead of Bolaño's wishes. Her face smoothed out as she admonished herself for trying to over think things. She had made her decision to cast her lot in with Manuel and now she needed to let all this second guessing go. He would look after her—hopefully, she grinned, both regarding her safety and in making love to her. As she stretched again she felt twinges in muscles well-used the previous night.

After showering and dressing, Anita straightened the bed before packing away the few things she had out. Finally, she went in search of Manuel. She followed the cooking aromas and found him frying bacon, platna, eggs and potato slices. He looked up with a grin.

"Good morning, you are feeling refreshed?"

"Quite," she smiled. "And I'm starving." Everything was so natural, she completely forgot to feel self-conscious.

Scooping the food onto warmed plates, he placed them on the table where already there were hot rolls and cold butter, as well as steaming mugs of coffee. They sat down.

"I am sorry you woke alone, but you were sleeping so peacefully I did not want to disturb you. I had to go out to make some arrangements for us and I bought our breakfast on my way back."

"You were right," she reassured him. "The last couple of days have been stressful to say the least. And anyway for food like this I forgive you!"

"But now you are more relaxed, no?"

She looked up sharply, caught his eye and blushed. "Yes," she replied primly.

He burst into laughter and after a moment she joined in. The rest of their breakfast was eaten in harmony. Afterwards, as they cleared away, Manuel explained his immediate plans.

"I'm already packed," she told him.

"Good, the earlier we can leave the better."

"I would like to see Marta. Just to thank her and say goodbye."

"No, we should leave immediately," he finished wiping down the last surface.

"It needn't take long and it would be rude not to," Anita hung up the tea towel.

"She will not think so," he saw her face turn mutinous and quickly continued. "I will leave a note for her and include your thanks." He watched as she turned away, making a small hurrumph noise, and smiled. She was very different from other women he had known, but *ella creció en tu*—she grew on you.

Shortly afterwards, Manuel was driving out of the village. No one, apart from some fishermen he knew, was about. As he accelerated up the hill, he relaxed and glanced at his passenger.

She shrugged. "I know you said you were borrowing a car as yours was known to anyone looking for us, but this is quite a change. Do you think it will actually make Barcelona?"

"Do not worry. My friend may have let the outside deteriorate a little," he did not mention that this was deliberate. "But the engine is in perfect order."

She smiled before turning her attention to the passing scenery.

* * * * *

When they reached Barcelona, the capital of Catalonia, they had a little time to kill so Manuel took a scenic route through the city of bright colours and unusual shapes ranging from the elegant to the grotesque. There was obviously too much to see everything so Manuel picked out a few of his favourites.

"I would show you a little of Barcelona, a city for us to be proud of," he told her and went on to point out some of the famous architecture such as Antonio Gaudi's Milá House, with its abstract nature of wavy lines reflecting the mountains and sea around the city, and his Batlló House with its crusty exterior and balconies shaped like fancy dress half-face masks. He showed her La Plaza del Rey behind the cathedral and Catalonia Square with its fountains and sculptures—probably the busiest part of the city—and the Plaza Real with its fountains surrounded by palm trees and Gaudi lamps. They went past the

Town Hall with its famous mixture of gothic and neoclassical facades and the statue of Christopher Columbus, looking out over the port, that marked the end of the famous Las Ramblas. Anita had seen pictures and television programmes of these sites and been impressed, but in the flesh or stone, as it were, they mesmerised her, their impact overwhelming.

"I am sorry we have not the time for us to stop so I can show you the city properly."

"Never mind. Perhaps one day I'll come back and do the whole tourist thing."

He looked intently at her for a moment before saying softly, "Yes, we will come back together."

Her face swung towards him as he looked ahead again, letting the clutch out and moving smoothly away from the traffic lights. Shortly afterwards, with the car parked, they entered the bustling Estació de Sants from where their train to Madrid left at midday for the three and half hour trip to the capital. Manuel had found some English magazines to help her pass the time.

At the Puerta de Atocha station in Madrid, he parked her on a bench. "I need to confirm arrangements for our travel to Portugal. Please stay here, or I will not be able to find you again." He winked. "And I cannot risk losing you now!"

"Why can't I come with you?" She did not like the feeling of being left like an inconvenient parcel.

"Please, I would like you to wait here. I will not be long." He was firm.

Bowing to the inevitable, she shrugged.

"You will wait for me here?" He pressed.

"Yes."

Giving her an uncertain look as she was clearly not happy about it, Manuel hesitated before turning and striding off.

Anita passed the time people-watching. Making up little histories about the passing travellers to amuse herself. Suddenly she stiffened. Then leapt up, calling out, "Luke! Luke South."

The man she had spotted stopped and turned to stare at her in disbelief. "Anita? My God, I can't believe it." He came towards her. "What are you doing here? I was sure that you would be back in England by now."

She opened her mouth to speak, but he carried right on. "You've no idea the trouble you caused by coming out here. I told you not to get on the plane without me."

The sheer effrontery nearly struck her speechless, but not quite. "Well, I like that! Who was it who had a personality transplant? Who handed out orders with no explanations? Who dropped me right in it here?"

"Ah no," he sliced the air with his hand. "You got on the plane against my instructions."

"Instructions! Yes, instructions. No thought of talking to me, telling me what was going on . . ." she was now building up a good head of steam, fuelled by the stress of the last few days mixed with self-vindication.

An announcement caused Luke to glance at his watch.

"God, I haven't got time for this," he muttered. "Look, just tell me, quickly, what you're doing here—please."

Her anger subsided slightly. "I'm fine, I'm being looked after." She looked up at him, "It's been really frightening, but I'm being looked after now. In fact, he'll be back here in a minute."

"Good," he looked at his watch again.

"He took me to a house belonging to a Señor Bolaño." She glared at him. "I think you know him. He certainly wants to meet you."

That certainly got his attention. "Christ, Anita, what the hell have you got yourself into? What's his name, your great protector?"

"Manuel Ortega."

"Ortega! He works for Bolaño, doesn't he?"

"Yes. Sort of. I don't know exactly."

Growling something under his breath, Luke made a quick decision and took hold of her arm.

"You'd better come with me. I'll arrange for your return home."

She pulled herself free. "You're in a hurry. I'm okay with Manuel." She said with dignity.

"He's not safe," he began.

"Oh, and you are?" Her resentment bubbled up again. "They're all looking for you and they're not happy you didn't keep to your side of the deal with them."

He looked directly into her eyes. "Things aren't always as they seem." He checked the time yet again before coming to a decision. "Well, if you don't want my help, I haven't time to persuade you now. Just be careful." He kissed her cheek before moving off. Then turned back briefly. "Don't say anything about seeing me to Ortega."

When she just stared at him, he sighed. "Please Anita, just trust me."

She looked at his appealing face for a long moment, they had seemed to get on so well before this ill-fated trip. She nodded reluctantly. He smiled in thanks and was soon lost to her sight in the crowd.

At the sound of her name she spun round.

"Who was speaking with you?" Manuel returned to her side.

"Oh, he was just looking for something. I couldn't understand very well, I'm afraid. My Spanish just isn't good enough." She kept her eyes on the hubbub of activity in the station concourse.

Manuel viewed her flushed cheeks thoughtfully for a nerve-racking moment before smiling. "We have some time, I thought we could look at a little of Madrid and have a meal?"

Relieved he had let the matter drop, she took his arm. "Sounds wonderful."

CHAPTER SIX

First he showed her the old front of Puerta de Atocha station that had been converted into a sort of botanical garden. A unique combination she was sure, but inspirational. They had wandered round the city centre before finding a tapas bar where they enjoyed a meal *al fresco*.

"You are enjoying this?" Manuel smiled as her eyes never seemed to stop moving, taking everything in around her.

"Oh, yes," she turned her attention back to him and, lifting her glass, she tilted it at him. "It's great. Thank you, Manuel. I just wish we could take more time to 'stop and stare' as the poet said."

He nodded. "Again perhaps we will come back, like with Barcelona, to look round with leisure."

"I hope so."

Their food arrived and they tucked in. Towards the end of the meal, Manuel leaned back and observed her for a minute. "Anita? The man you spoke to at Barcelona . . ."

"I told you, I couldn't understand what he wanted." She sipped her wine and returned the glass carefully back on the table. "Just leave it, Manuel. It was nothing."

He hesitated, then backed down with a dip of his head. "As you say." He glanced at his watch. "Perhaps we should go. We need to get the Metro right across Madrid to the Charmartin station, and we must not miss the train."

She agreed with alacrity, relieved the topic of Luke talking to her had been dropped. She wished he had not asked her to keep it from Manuel. He'd already been out of sight by the time Manuel had returned to her, so it was not as if he would have given chase. Still, she felt guilty and was irritated with both herself and Luke.

It was evening by the time they arrived at the Chamartin station having boarded the Lusitania Hotel Train which was to take them to Lisbon. Manuel had told her that was where the trail led. After leaving their luggage in their cabin, which proved to be surprisingly spacious, even including an en suite bathroom, they made their way to the dining carriage.

After they had selected and ordered their meal, Manuel leant back and rested his eyes on her face. "So, a busy day, yes?"

"It's funny isn't it? When travelling you spend most of the time sitting yet it's really tiring."

He nodded. "Anita, about the man you spoke to in the station . . ."

She interrupted before he could finish. "I told you, I couldn't really understand what he wanted." She adjusted her folded napkin avoiding his eyes.

"Anita," he tried again. He knew there was more to the incident. She would not be so adamant in refusing to talk about it otherwise.

"Look, leave it. I'm really tired." She hesitated a moment and then, assuming attack to bolster her defence, said, "Anyway, I think I need some answers." Her voice gained some belligerency. "I'd like to know more about what all this is about. Where exactly do you fit in? Who is Señor Bolaño? And don't say he's a business man."

Manuel held his hands up in surrender. "Perhaps it is best if we forget our problems. You are right, we are both too tired."

She subsided. If she pushed it, he would go back to asking about the chat she had had with Luke at the station, although she could not resist a final nudge. "I can't think how you got involved with him. He's really creepy. Those teeth."

"Anita, stop." He gave her his seductive smile, but she could see the iron determination behind it. "Tell me about your life in England. Your family."

Their food arrived and after the waiter had left them, she stared at him a moment. "Okay, okay. But don't think I won't get some answers sometime."

"I have no doubts," he assured her, adding, "As will I."

She smiled and dug into the delicious meal as she gave some potted insights into her life BM (before Manuel).

Later, back in their cabin, Anita got undressed and slipped into the lower berth, while Manuel, after giving her a brief kiss, climbed into the top one. She must have appeared slightly surprised because, once settled, he said, "I would like very much to continue on from last night, you must know that. But when I look at your face, I see you are too tired. Also we will have a busy time in Portugal. But do not worry, we will be together again soon!"

"I'm not worried," she huffed. Then she smiled to herself, all those sizzling good looks and consideration too. He was like a dream.

Her smile died away as she thought over the day. It was true, she was exhausted. They had been up early. Then there was her encounter with Luke. That was puzzling. He had not behaved in a guilty manner. In fact, the more she thought about it, the more he appeared to have been projecting justified annoyance with her for not obeying him. He certainly had not expressed any remorse over her experiences, which after all were a direct result of his actions. Now that she had time to think, there were a number of questions she wished she had asked him. He and Manuel were clearly on opposing sides yet she could not help feeling there were strong similarities between them.

She sighed. Well, she was with Manuel now and would have to hope she had made the right decision because she was rather afraid her emotions were growing deeper the more time she spent with him. He had given her a great time this afternoon sightseeing. Sleepily she wriggled, getting more comfortable. He might be a bit anachronistic, but she was finding it enjoyable being treated to his old fashioned courtesies. Perhaps she was not the epitome of a modern equal rights type of woman but they made her feel special.

They were up early in the morning to disembark at the Santa Apolonia station in Lisbon at eight o'clock. Walking briskly towards the exit, Manuel raised an arm in greeting and steered her towards an elegant man, smartly dressed and beaming in welcome. The two men embraced before Manuel turned to her.

"This is Marco Azenha, an old friend and also a policeman here in Portugal, who will help us. Marco, this is Anita Wright from England." Judging from the total lack of surprise on Marco's face she realised Manuel must have already told him about her. They took a taxi out of the city, along the coast to Cascais where Marco led them to a flat in a stonewashed old house down a narrow street.

"This belongs to a friend of mine," Marco explained. "He is away for now, so I have the keys. I know he would be pleased to help you in this way."

After briefly showing them round the comfortably furnished, high ceilinged rooms that included a large sitting room that led out on to the balcony, three bedrooms, a bathroom and a surprisingly spacious kitchen where he explained that he had bought a few basic groceries for them, Marco looked at the time.

Immediately picking up on the cue, Manuel turned to her. "I have to go out for a short time with Marco. You will be all right here."

She nodded, feeling slightly bereft. "Of course."

"Good," he started to follow Marco to the door. He turned halfway there and caught her eye. "You will not leave this apartment, no?"

She laughed. "No, I won't leave. In fact I think I'll have a nap. I didn't sleep all that well last night."

"Good," his lips parted in a devastating grin before he continued out of the flat.

* * * * *

It was late afternoon before Manuel returned. Anita heard the front door opening as she sat in the shade on the narrow balcony and enjoyed the luxury of not feeling afraid, just relaxing in the balmy atmosphere.

"Anita? Anita, where are you?" Manuel did not sound as benign as she felt. "Anita!"

"I'm here," she stood and moved to the French window connecting the balcony to the interior of the apartment. As Manuel appeared her contentment dispersed. He looked furious.

"Come inside," he ordered, fixing her with hard eyes. Automatically she obeyed as he continued, "Why did you lie at the station?"

"Lie?"

"Yes, lie. The man you spoke to was South."

There was a momentary silence while she weighed her options. "Why do you think it was Luke?" she tried.

He swore, interrupting her. "Do not attempt to deny it. He was being followed, his conversation with you was observed."

He stared at her, a muscle ticking in his jaw revealing the extent of his anger. "Imagine how I felt, when everyone but me knew about it. Especially after I just explained who you were and how you know nothing about this whole business."

Her gentle protector gone, Anita crumbled.

"I'm sorry. Yes, it was Luke, but it wasn't an arranged meeting, I promise. I was stunned when I saw him, I could hardly believe it. I called out his name, even then thinking it was just someone who looked like him, but he turned and . . ." she waved her arm expressively.

"If so, why did you lie when I asked who you were talking with?"

"He asked me not to say anything about seeing him," her voice was small.

"Oh, so that makes everything okay? I thought you trusted me."

"You don't understand. At first I was angry with him. Then he said he would take me with him, he would get me back home. But he was in such a hurry, I felt . . . I don't know how I felt. I just didn't want to go with him, I wanted to stay with you." To her mortification she felt tears well up and turned away.

Manuel sighed. "Fine, calm yourself." He moved to an armchair and dropped in it. He ran the fingers of one hand through his hair as he considered. "So, now you will tell me, yes? Everything you talked about."

She sniffed as she sat in an accompanying chair and nodded. Taking a deep breath to steady herself, she related her conversation with Luke, everything she could remember including Luke's concern over Manuel and his association with Señor Bolaño. This made Manuel smile grimly, but he did not interrupt her account.

When she had finished there was a long silence while Manuel considered, leaving Anita to fret inwardly.

"Well," she finally broke. "You believe me, don't you?"

He looked at her abstractedly. "Yes."

"It's all so confusing. You work with Señor Bolaño, who's a crook. Luke was also involved with Señor Bolaño. Both of you now seem to be in Señor Bolaño's bad books. He's after both of you. Luke got me into this, now you're angry with me. I just don't know any more what to think, let alone do."

He laughed softly, "Come here." He held out a hand.

She flew across the room to be drawn onto his lap and enfolded in his arms.

"*Pobrecita*, poor Anita. You are right. A lot has happened to you, and nothing that you asked for or expected, eh?"

In answer, she snuggled closer to him, inhaling his unique aroma.

"But," his voice took on a sterner note. "You must not lie to me again." With a lean finger under her chin, he raised her face to look into her eyes. "You are not good at it. I knew you lied and I should have made you tell me the truth at the station, or at least later, on the train. But," he carried on with a sigh, "I just thought maybe it was a man wanting to get to know you and I thought you did not wish to tell me in case it upset me." He ended wryly, "Perhaps in future I should not be so vain!"

She raised a hand to cup his jaw. "I'm really sorry."

He nodded. Then, looking down at her, he lowered his head until their lips met. What began as a gentle, conciliatory embrace soon flared into a burning conflagration. Her arms reached behind his neck, her hands threading through his hair as she held his head close. His hand swept from her face, over her breast and hip to reach the hem of her skirt. Sliding beneath it, his arm lifted it as his hand crept up her thigh. His hand cupped her while two fingers traced lightly up and down her sex.

They were both panting with desire when Manuel suddenly withdrew his hand and pulled both her arms down. Her eyes opened, cloudy with confusion as she stared up at him.

"Not here," he managed. "We could be seen from across the street."

She giggled and pushed herself from his lap. "I had no idea you were so puritanical!"

He growled as he followed her, "If that means I like to make love privately, then yes, I am puritanical. Although," his voice lightened in teasing, "once in private, as you know, I do not act puritanically at all!"

In the bedroom both rapidly divested themselves of their clothes before falling first into each other's arms and then on the bed. Soon the only sounds were the rustling of sheets accompanied by low moans, whispered words leading to sighs and eventually gasps of satisfaction.

When she woke up the next morning it seemed natural to hear the shower running, followed shortly by the low buzz of an electric shaver. She was still hovering pleasantly between sleep and wakefulness when the door opened and Manuel appeared, silhouetted by steam with only a towel knotted loosely low on his hips. Her body woke up, sharply reminding her of the night before as he greeted her.

"You are awake, good." He came over, leant down and engaged her in a mind-bending good-morning kiss, before pulling away to get dressed with economic efficiency.

"I will make breakfast while you rise," he said as he left the room. She could definitely get used to this, she thought, as she left the bed to start her own ablutions.

* * * * *

After some coffee to jolt her system fully awake, Anita looked across the table at Manuel.

"What are we doing today?"

He took a few moments to reply, but it was the way he avoided returning her look that first warned her.

"I have to meet someone who can tell me more of what is happening about South and the auction."

"Fine," she said as she slavered butter and jam over a piece of toast. "What time are we seeing him?"

He smiled wryly. "Not we, just me. I will go alone." As he saw her about to interrupt, he continued quickly. "This is an unpleasant business, not a nice game and I wish to keep you away from it as much as possible."

She straightened, seriously affronted. "I'm very much aware that this isn't a game, but as I am already involved, and by accident I would remind you, I don't see why I'm being side-lined now."

"Anita, be reasonable," he began.

"Reasonable? I've been more than reasonable. How many people do you think would have kept their cool after being kidnapped, taken to some God-forsaken place, dragged across one country, then into another, all the time having to hope they've chosen the right man to put their faith in?"

She held up a hand as he started to answer. "Then you expect me to sit here alone, I suppose, while you go out to save the world, just like yesterday. This is not the nineteenth century, Manuel. Women are not sitting, sewing a fine seam, keeping the home fires burning while the brave men enjoy all the action!"

Manuel covered her hand with his on the table. "I know you have courage Anita, I have seen it," his relaxed tones calmed her somewhat. "This morning the meeting will be very unexciting," he smiled hopefully at her. "When I took you from Bolaño's reach, he cut me out of the loop, as you say. I no longer know what he is planning. Also, my meeting will be in Portuguese, do you know the language?"

She shook her head as she mulled over his words.

"So, you would not understand what we were saying anyway. You would be better here—perhaps some sunbathing on the balcony?" he lightened his tone. "Pretend you are on holiday!"

Distractedly she smiled in acknowledgement before grasping his hand in both of hers.

"Taking me away has ruined your plans, hasn't it? I'm sorry, Manuel."

He grinned. "Do not be sorry, *chiquita*. I think it was one of my best ideas. As for the nuisance, you are worth it!"

She laughed as he wanted her to, and held up her hands in surrender.

"Okay, okay. You go to your rendezvous and I'll see you later. You can tell me all about it then?"

"Yes, I will." He came round the table and kissed the top of her head as she finished her coffee. "I hope I will not be too long." Shrugging on his jacket, he checked for keys and wallet before leaving the apartment.

Anita cleared away their breakfast while she mulled over the previous evening. No matter how she arranged it in her head, the real question was with which of the two men she should throw her lot in. Taking a gut reading, she really felt both would look after her even though it could not be denied that their associates were rather damning! Was she being recklessly influenced by her burgeoning feelings for Manuel?

She hung up the tea towel to dry and shook her head. Enough. If she stayed here, she would just go over and over the same things. She would probably go mad! Instead she decided to go for a wander to pass the time, explore the immediate neighbourhood. Manuel had not told her she had to keep inside the apartment, so it must be all right. Anyway, who knew she was even in Portugal?

Feeling lighter of heart, she collected her handbag from the bedroom and the key to the front door from the kitchen just as the doorbell pealed, making her jump. Muttering remonstrances to herself, had she not just decided she was safe here? She put her bag down and went to the front door and pulled it open.

She had been expecting a neighbour or delivery man and so the impact was considerable. Seeing her shock at his appearance that held her immobile and speechless, Señor Bolaño flashed his white teeth in a patently insincere smile.

"*Buenos dias*, Señorita."

CHAPTER SEVEN

His words released her temporary paralysis and she immediately tried to slam the door shut. But he easily stopped it with his hand, his smile never wavering.

"Not very kind, Señorita. Especially after I opened my house to you." Pushing the door wider he stepped inside, forcing her to move out of his way.

Leaving the door ajar, she trailed after him into the sitting room while maintaining a healthy distance. After a cursory glance round, Bolaño turned to face her.

"You have caused me much trouble," he began. "And surprise. I did not think Ortega was one to be led astray by a pretty face. I wonder, was it him, or perhaps you, I underestimated?"

Anita crossed her arms and stared back at him. "What do you want?"

Bolaño shrugged. "I hoped to find Ortega here."

"He's out."

"Yes, so I see. Where is he?"

"I don't know, he didn't tell me."

"When do you expect him to return?" his voice remained calm, unmoved with his smile still intact, so at odds with his cold black eyes.

"I don't know, he didn't tell me."

This produced the first sign of frustration. His smile dimmed as he hissed on an indrawn breath. "You are repeating yourself, Señorita." He took a moment to regain control of himself while Anita continued to stare at him defiantly.

"Ortega seems to be acting on his own now, or perhaps for someone else." He shrugged. "In either way it is clear he no longer feels loyalty to me. So, I ask myself what has changed. Have you, perhaps, recruited him to work with South? Or maybe he is working with you, or just for himself, eh? You see my dilemma." He gestured eloquently with his hands.

Anita made no answer, so he continued. "I think you are important to him. Either for his plans or emotionally. Maybe even both. I regret, Señorita, as you will not want this, but I must take you with me to see how he will act."

She raised her chin. "And you think I'll just go along with you?"

He shook his head mournfully, "No Señorita, I am not so optimistic." His hand slid to his jacket pocket and reappeared holding a small black gun.

The light glinted off the shiny metal as she stared at it in shock. Her heart pounded so hard that it shook her frame as she tried to speak, but her mouth was dry and unco-operative and only a few strangulated sounds emerged. She inhaled deeply and slowly as finally her brain kicked into gear and she drew again on the danger training she had received as a child.

Bolaño motioned to the door. No trace of his smile remained. "Come, there is no need to waste any more time."

With no other option available, Anita turned and preceded him out of the apartment. Any faint hopes she may have entertained on using people on the street to make her escape from him died as she saw two men at the top of the stairs who straightened up as they saw her and Bolaño approaching. One she did not know. The other, however, was Scruffy from her first port of call in Spain. She had no choice but to continue co-operating, at least for now.

Outside, Scruffy unlocked the waiting car and opened the rear door for her to enter, followed by Bolaño. He then got behind the wheel while the stranger sat beside him. As the car pulled away Anita looked back at the building. She was in a real mess now and how would Manuel know where she had gone?

Soon they were on the coastal road travelling at a frightening speed considering its seemingly unending blind bends and sharp curves that faithfully followed the ins and outs of the coastline.

By some miracle they arrived unscathed outside an attractive blue-washed building. Outside the door, Bolaño spoke to both men in Spanish. Scruffy then left, while the stranger followed them inside and took up his assigned post on the landing beside the door of an apartment. Bolaño opened it and ushered Anita inside. The hall was dark and she walked in the direction he indicated towards some light which turned out to be a sitting room. It was not empty, though.

Isabel looked up from a magazine, saw Anita, then her eyes moved over her shoulder as she smiled at Bolaño. "You've been quicker than I thought."

"Unfortunately, Ortega was not there. But I think the Señorita here offers us a lever to control him."

Isabel looked back at Anita. "You certainly seem to get around! No chance you knowing where Luke is, I suppose?"

Anita found her voice at last. "Isabel! What are you doing here?"

"Come now. You can't be that stupid," Isabel sneered at her. "Luke was supposed to deal with me. I always intended to come with him. I don't know what went wrong, but instead he attached himself to you. I can't think why, unless he thought you were so bland that no one would notice you and provide a sort of cover for him."

Anita seethed, partly from Isabel being Isabel and partly because she was afraid there was more than a bit of truth in her words.

"What about you? You're obviously very involved in all of this."

"So?"

"So? You stole from Crown Industries!"

Isabel and Bolaño smiled at each other over her naiveté.

Incensed, she continued, "Why? You had a good job . . ."

"Why?" Isabel interrupted, smile gone. "Well, for the money, of course. What else?"

Anita stared at her, bereft of words. She had never liked Isabel, but this cold calculating person was a revelation. Isabel shrugged and addressed Bolaño, "She's too stupid to be able to help us and now she's a hindrance. She's just in the way."

Bolaño's voice was very quiet, but there was an element in it that was unnerving. "As I said, she will be useful to manipulate either South or Ortega, or, perhaps, both."

Both women felt the menace that physically paralysed them for several moments. Then Isabel shrugged with an insouciance obviously feigned. "You're in charge."

"Yes," Bolaño agreed before warning. "Do not forget it again, Isabel, if you do not wish to make me angry." After a pause, during which he ensured Isabel had absorbed his message, he gave a slight nod that included both women. "I will leave you for a short time, I have some important calls to make."

He left them together and entered another room off the hall, closing the door firmly behind him. From the brief glimpse Anita got, it appeared to be a study. She swung her gaze back to Isabel who had picked up her magazine again.

"I just can't believe you're a part of all this," Anita dropped into a chair opposite the other woman. She felt dazed, rather as if she was a character in a film, but no one had given her the script leaving her to improvise.

"Why not?" Isabel flicked over a few pages, pausing to examine one more closely.

"For heaven's sake, Isabel, you're doing something illegal. It makes you a criminal. It's not like taking a bit of stationery. You'll go to prison if you're caught."

"The trick is," Isabel slanted her a cold smile, "not to be caught."

"Well, obviously. But when you're dealing with the likes of him," she flicked a hand towards the study door. "You're at risk from that side too."

"I can handle him. In fact it was me that found him. It was my idea to get hold of the prototype, and I approached him."

"How did you find him? I'm sure he's not listed in Yellow Pages!"

Isabel ignored the sarcasm and looked out of the window, but not as if she was seeing anything outside. "You have no idea of who I am. None of you in the office did. You all come from secure homes. You know where you come from. If any of you, say, lose your job and income and then find it hard to get another immediately, you know you can always go home to your families. Well," she turned to Anita. "This sort of security doesn't exist for me."

"But you had a good job, nice clothes and car and, I'm sure, a nice place to live. If security was such an issue for you, I'd have thought you would have done all you could to preserve it."

"God, you are so obtuse! It took every penny of my salary to maintain that style of living. Any problem and my life—the life I had worked so hard for—would dissolve." Her face tightened as if even the idea of it was frightening. She leaned back, eyes looking inward. "Taking Minutes at meetings for Mr Franks, I got to know things. Things like this new gadget. I also heard of the need for secrecy because of the danger of people like Bolaño." She focused on Anita again. "So there you have it. That knowledge and the need for financial security combined and I saw a way to permanent financial security. I would have been a fool not to take it!"

Anita wondered if Isabel truly believed that or if she had had second thoughts, after it was too late to pull out, and was now trying to convince herself as much as her.

After a few moments of contemplation while Isabel flicked over a couple of pages, Anita looked at her. "Isabel, if things went wrong between you and Luke, how did you get here? I mean, why didn't you go to Spain?"

The other woman raised her head. "I had to get out of the office, things were heating up with investigators being brought in. To be honest," she gave a tight smile, "Old Mr Franks was beginning to act oddly and I decided it was too dangerous to wait around for any fingers to be pointed at me."

"Wouldn't your absence imply complicity?"

"Oh, probably. Although I did book some holiday time in the hope it may deflect, or at least slow them down, from looking in my direction."

"I see. But why are you here and not in Spain?"

"Once I realised Luke had stiffed me, in more ways than one, my only chance was to follow him out to Spain. When I got there I contacted Señor Bolaño who picked me up on his way here. There," she returned to looking at the magazine. "Now you know. Hope you're satisfied!"

Anita did not answer. She was busy trying to sort out what Isabel had said and trying to match it with Luke's actions. It was all getting much too complicated for her and, in any case, she ought to be thinking of ways to get away.

"Isabel, you were right. I am in the way here," she paused as Isabel paid attention. "I could go now quickly, while he's tucked away."

She stood up. Isabel immediately caught her arm. "Oh no. What do you think he'd do to me after his 'lever' was allowed to escape?"

"Well," Anita thought quickly. "I know. If I seemed to knock you out . . . ?"

She trailed off as Isabel snorted. "Right! As if I'd go along with that!"

"I wouldn't really knock you out. Just hit you slightly so it would look as if I'd overpowered you."

"No, no and absolutely no. Bolaño wants you for now, so here you must stay. Anyway, I'm sure he's left someone watching the door or outside."

Anita dropped back in her chair. She had forgotten Scruffy's friend outside the apartment. Well, it had been worth a try, especially as Isabel did not seem to wholeheartedly trust Bolaño. But it appeared she feared his possible retribution more and, for the moment at least, was not prepared to go against him in any way.

The two women were sitting in silence, occupied with their own thoughts and schemes when Bolaño returned. He addressed Isabel. "We will soon have a guest," he paused to nod significantly to her. "Matters are progressing, even if not as fast as we would wish. However, I would not like him to know we have extra insurance." He inclined his head towards Anita. Her heartbeat increased dramatically as he continued. "There must be no chance he finds out about her."

"What are you planning to do with her?" Isabel's cold voice caused Anita to stare at her in disbelief.

Bolaño chuckled warmly at Anita's apparent terror. "Do not be alarmed, Señorita, I intend you no harm but I must make precautions, just in case you decide to be foolish."

Anita felt some relief that she was not apparently to be disposed of in any permanent way, or at least not yet. Yet she was well aware that Bolaño was not to be relied upon.

He continued, "I will put you in one of the bedrooms. Come."

Seeing no alternative, she rose and followed him into the hallway as he led her to a door, opened it and ushered her in.

"Isabel," he called. "I must ask you to help me."

He drew an upright ladder back chair from beside the bed into the centre of the room. "Please," he gestured at it. "Please, Señorita, come to sit yourself here."

She did. There was no other option. Better to play along now and hope for an opportunity later. From a chest of drawers, he extracted some rope and soon, with Isabel's help, Anita was securely attached to the chair. He stood back to check their handiwork.

"She can't free herself from that." Isabel sounded impatient.

"No," he answered slowly. "But she could make noise."

Isabel swung round and met Anita's eyes. "Perhaps we should knock her out. Not to hurt her, just to keep her quiet."

As Anita gave her an icy stare, she laughed. It was the first time, Anita realised in astonishment, she had ever heard Isabel laugh.

"No, that will not be necessary." Bolaño soothed with his trademark smile and dead eyes. He withdrew a scarf from the dressing table and expertly used it as a gag.

Anita soon found herself alone, trussed and gagged. She breathed slowly to calm her racing pulse. Cool thoughts were needed. Plans to be plotted. And where was Manuel? Had he returned to Marco's friend's house yet? Did he know she had been abducted? Her heart rate began to pick up again, so she consciously worked at calming herself. Training, training, she chanted like a mantra in her head. Keep calm, play along and be prepared when a chance presents itself.

CHAPTER EIGHT

The sound of the doorbell interrupted her thoughts. Bolaño's visitor had arrived. She heard male voices and the front door closing, followed by footsteps over the tiled hallway. The voices faded as the sitting room door was closed.

The visitor did not stay long. After his departure, Bolaño went to his study, next to the room she was in. She heard the clink of glass and liquid being poured. Anita frowned. It was very distinct. Looking up she realised the window was open. The one in the study must be likewise and that was why she could hear so clearly. She listened to the creak of a chair as it accepted the weight of a person sinking onto it, shortly followed by Bolaño's voice. By the interspersed silences Anita realised he must be talking on the telephone. To her surprise the conversation was in English.

"He has been here just now and, like me, he is not pleased. This should already be finished."

Silence as he listened to the person at the other end of the line.

"Yes, she is here, but it is unnecessary to worry."

Another pause.

"I am aware she is in the way. I thought at first she would be useful, but now I am not so sure. Perhaps you are right."

Another pause that he broke in an annoyed tone. "Of course I know what to do. Who do you think I am? A novice in this game?"

Obviously his respondent strove to appease him as the next time he spoke, his voice had relaxed. "Fine. Now I will deal with my problems. But you must deal with your side of the bargain." There was now a clear threat of menace in his tone. "So far you have not kept your side of the bargain."

Another longer pause, then, "Good, ensure that you succeed."

Anita heard the receiver snick back in position, accompanied by irritated mutterings she could not distinguish. She felt slightly nauseous and her blood pressure must be sky high. So now she was a hindrance he would deal with. Somehow she did not think he intended to return her to the house in Cascais with an admonishment to keep quiet about him and Isabel. How permanent a resolution was he considering? One thing was beginning to niggle in her brain. The prototype everybody wanted. Yes, she could see its commercial value, but to the extent they were going to? It seemed unlikely. There was more to it than Manuel had told her. What did that say about his openness with her? She closed her eyes, the realisation of his lack of trust in her really hurt.

The sound of arguing broke into her self-pity. She had not noticed Bolaño leaving his office, but clearly he was now in the sitting room and, from the sound of it, he and Isabel were not seeing eye to eye about matters. She could not distinguish the words, but the tones of both voices were becoming louder and increasingly vociferous. Perhaps Isabel, although hardly a compassionate woman, drew the line at physically harming her. Stealing, after all, was one thing, murder a totally different kettle of fish. Not that she thought Isabel's wishes were likely to deter a man such as Bolaño, she despaired.

Gradually she became aware that the voices could no longer be heard. Had they come to an agreement? Had Bolaño

71

simply imposed his will? As the silence lengthened, she felt her nerves stretching ever tighter. It was more ominous than their angry shouts. Where was Manuel? She needed him to do something now. She needed him, full stop.

CHAPTER NINE

It was some time later when the sun was starting to lower in the sky that Bolaño re-entered the bedroom. Anita's eyes widened in terror as she saw the wicked-looking knife he carried.

"There is no more time to be wasted," he said as he walked round to stand just behind her. Anita tensed, expecting at any moment to feel the cold blade slice into her neck, but instead she felt a sharp tug and then the pressure on her arms eased. He had cut her restraints. She brought her arms round slowly in deference to the pain of the sharp needle points in them as her circulation slowly resumed its normal flow and removed her gag.

"I go to ring South, now. He is good friends with you, no?" Bolaño wound the cut rope with the casual ease of experience.

"Yes." Anita realised she was to be used as some sort of bargaining chip. The relief was enormous. Slowly her natural optimism crept back. At least she was not to be killed immediately. She had to take comfort from that and who knew what opportunities might appear. "Do you know where he is?"

"*Naturalmente.* At least I have a telephone number." He opened a drawer in the bureau and placed the rope inside tidily. "Come, there is coffee made. You must be thirsty."

He had obviously fallen back into the 'good host' persona. That appeared to her quite surreal considering he had taken her by force and tied her up for God knows how long. But surely it was a good sign? She preceded him back to the living room where a tray with a coffee pot and two cups sat on the centre table. He indicated she was to do the honours. There was no one else in the room.

"Where is Isabel?" She began to pour.

"Gone," Bolaño turned towards his study. "She is no longer needed here." At the door he faced her briefly. "Do not attempt to leave the apartment. I can see the front door from my office and I have a guard outside, as you know. If you cause me trouble, I will have to tie you up again."

Anita lifted the cup as she returned his stare as coolly as she could manage. "I won't go anywhere. I'll just wait here."

"*Bueno*," he grunted and left.

Anita sipped her hot coffee as she glanced round the room. She felt rather more relaxed. Obviously Bolaño had plans for her, but they seemed to involve her co-operation, which could only be to her benefit, in the short term at least.

She stood and walked round to stretch her legs and back after their earlier confinement. Passing a door standing slightly ajar, she paused to back track. What was that she had seen? She pushed the door further open, then froze in shock. It was an arm. An arm she realised that was attached to a body. A dead body. A body dressed in the clothes Isabel had been wearing. It had to be Isabel. After a fleeting initial glimpse of her face, Anita studiously avoided it. She noticed one shoe had come off and was lying forlornly a few feet away. Some buttons too had come off the front of the dress. They were probably somewhere on the floor too, if she looked, but her gaze seemed transfixed on Isabel's dress and legs.

Gradually the silence of shock lifted. She became aware of traffic noises outside. She could hear Bolaño's voice, he had obviously reached someone on the telephone. Bolaño, what was it he had said? She is no longer needed. My God, had it been Isabel he was referring to earlier when he said he would deal with his problems? When would she herself become a problem to be dealt with? It looked as if his way of solving problems was radical and a pretty permanent one.

Bolaño calling her name released her stasis. Galvanised, she pulled the door nearly closed again and sped towards the centre of the room.

"Yes," her voice came out an octave higher than usual. She cleared her throat before trying again, "Yes."

Bolaño appeared. "Come, you must talk with South so he knows I do not try to trick him, that you are with me in truth. You will tell him to co-operate, no?"

Swallowing, she placed her cup on the tray and walked towards him. Act naturally, she thought desperately. Avoiding his eyes she entered the study and with a shaking hand picked up the receiver, noticing peripherally that Bolaño had not followed her into the room.

"Hello."

"Anita! Are you all right?" Concern laced Luke's words and, for a moment comforted her. Then her situation overcame her.

"I'm having a great time with your friend here!" It had suddenly occurred to her that this fiasco could also be laid at Luke's door.

"Look, I know you're upset," Luke began.

"Upset seems such a mild word to describe how I feel."

"Okay, you're furious. But at the moment the main aim is to keep you safe."

She would not argue with that. Her anger dissolved in the resurgence of fear.

"Luke, Isabel is here . . ."

"I know," he interrupted. "That's not important now. We need to concentrate on you."

Thinking of Isabel's body lying a couple of rooms away, Anita had to agree. There was nothing that could be done for the other woman now.

"What's your plan?"

"Bolaño wants a meeting with me. He wants us face to face, not over the phone. You're his ace in the hole, he thinks I'll agree for your sake."

"Yes, I had gathered that." A brief pause as she assimilated his words before she continued. "'He thinks you'll agree', what does that mean? You will agree, won't you? My God, you must. You have no idea what he's capable of." Her voice had risen as her panic grew.

"Anita! Control yourself. Don't worry, I'll get you away from him."

"Yes," she took a deep breath to compose herself. "So what are you going to do?" She saw Bolaño appear in the doorway and approach her.

"I'll fix a place and time for a meeting with him. It won't be today, I'm afraid, as there's a small problem I have to deal with first."

"What problem? How small? Now is not the time to go all cryptic!"

She would have continued, but the receiver was pulled from her hand and Bolaño began speaking into it. "So, now you know she is with me and unhurt. Now you will co-operate, yes?"

She could hear Luke's voice, but not all the words. He was so calm. How could he be like that? What was the "small problem"? Did it affect the extent that Luke would be prepared to go to rescue her? Damn, she should have told him to let Manuel know what had happened even though the two men clearly disliked each other. And not just because of her. Their objectives, or at least the way they went about trying to achieve them, seemed so very different. A wave of self-pity hit her as she acknowledged she had far more faith in Manuel. He would not have "dealt with a small problem" before helping her!

She noticed Bolaño had ended his call to Luke and was again dialling quickly. Soon he was speaking in Spanish—it sounded like instructions, at least the person on the other end did not say much until the very end. Bolaño scribbled on a pad before abruptly ending the call. He tore the paper off as he turned to her.

"We leave now."

"Where are we going? To meet Luke?" She knew that was a forlorn hope. After all, Luke still had his 'small problem' to deal with first.

"Tomorrow South comes with the device," he flashed his white teeth while his eyes remained cold. "At least I hope so, for you."

She shivered as she preceded him from the apartment. She also hoped Luke would come for her. However, she had to remember his behaviour at the airport. She did not know him at all really. No, she would be stupid to totally rely on him. She would have to help herself. She was determined she was not going to end up like Isabel. She must seize the first opportunity to escape from Bolaño.

CHAPTER TEN

Manuel let himself back into Marco's friend's apartment. He was tired, still he looked forward to a relaxing drink with Anita. As he entered the sitting room, he stiffened. The place was empty, he could feel it. *Dios*, could that girl never do as he asked? He looked around for a note telling him where she had gone. Nothing. He went into the kitchen, but that too was devoid of any message. He started out to try the other rooms when his eye caught sight of her handbag by the cupboard. He pulled it open. The usual feminine clutter was there, including her purse. He checked inside. It still contained her money and cards. Putting it back, he closed the bag. She must have left in a hurry. A big hurry if she left her bag behind. Not only a hurry, after all to carry a bag was ingrained in the female psyche, so it looked increasingly as if she had been taken by force.

Berating himself for leaving her unprotected—*estupido,* no one knew how high the stakes were better than him. He had not even told Anita all the facts. Manuel left the apartment and started knocking on neighbouring doors. At the third, he struck lucky.

"*Sim*, Senhor," the elderly woman nodded. "I see her leave with an older man, well dressed, and two others. She did not look happy. I thought perhaps they bring her bad news?"

Manuel nodded. "Something like that. Did you hear them speak?"

"*Não*, Senhor." She began to close the door, then paused to add, "Perhaps you should try Senhora Javier at *Numero* 2.

She sits by her window looking out at the street most of the day now. She may be able to help you more." The door clicked shut.

He had some trouble getting past the over-protective maid at *Numero* 2, but finally was shown into the front room where her mistress was settled in a wheelchair in front of the window.

"I saw her leave, yes. Poor child, she looked so . . . scared. Yes, scared." She fell silent, contemplating.

"The men she was with, can you describe them?"

The old lady closed her eyes as tried to remember. "They were very different. One, the one that was holding her arm, he was slim and not so tall. Smartly dressed. He was the one in charge, I think. Another was the opposite, a bit fat and his clothes were untidy and perhaps not so clean. The third man was tall with a bald head." She was silent a moment then opened her eyes. "That is all I can recall."

"That is good. You are very observant," he smiled and drew on his reserves of patience that were now wearing rather thin. Time was passing and it was now apparent that Anita was in real danger. Every minute could count. "Did you hear anything? The name of a place, a person, perhaps."

Senhora Javier blinked as she brought her attention back to him. "I could hear little, only some words." She thought hard for a few seconds before continuing slowly, "I heard Colares mentioned. Perhaps they went there? I cannot tell for sure."

"You have been very helpful, and kind in talking to me." He knew he was lucky to have got this much.

"She is in danger, no? I did not realise it at the time. Stupid of me," she fretted.

Manuel covered the twisted arthritic hands lying in her lap. "What could you have done that you have not done now. I am very grateful."

"*Que cavalheiro.* What a gentleman. You will find and save her, yes?"

"I will certainly find her. And you have helped greatly."

She smiled and nodded once. "Good."

As he left apartment *Numero* 2 Manuel used his mobile phone to call Marco. "Colares. Please see if you can find any place there that connects with Bolaño." He brought Marco up to date quickly as he went out to catch a taxi. "I am sure it was Bolaño. The description fits. Anyway, who else knew of Anita's connection." He thought a moment. "I am just not sure why he took her. He knows she has no knowledge to give him. Whatever the reason, we must find her, and find her quickly."

Within an hour, Manuel and Marco were in Colares and outside the yellow building Marco had found was listed in Bolaño's name. They gained entrance to the apartment with the help of the *conserje* and stood still a moment listening. It was too quiet for anyone else to be there.

"I will start with the bedrooms, you look in the sitting room." Manuel moved off quickly.

Moments later he called out to Marco. Silently he widened a door opening to reveal the body of a dead woman.

Marco hesitated, "This is not . . . ?"

"No. I do not know who she is. But it is bad, a very bad sign. The stakes have been raised considerably."

Marco nodded before using his phone to call in the murder.

Meanwhile Manuel carried on searching. Finally, in the study he found something. Holding a pad of blank telephone messages to the light he could make out impressions. Using a soft pencil from the desk he rubbed over it gently to reveal an address.

Marco knew the area. "It is across the river. We must cross the 25 de Abril Bridge to the Setubal Peninsula."

They had to wait for the police team to arrive, but then left as soon as Marco had promised his written report by the end of the day. Manuel could not forget the dead woman. She increased his sense of urgency to find Anita. He just wished he knew if Anita was better off not knowing the whole story, or if he should have explained it all to her. Bolaño had never really believed she was involved, so he must plan on using her in some way and, surely, for that he needed to keep her alive and unharmed. If she knew all about the prototype, there was always the danger she would blurt it out while facing up to him. He smiled faintly, she was definitely one to act first then think later!

A couple of hours later the two men arrived at the Quinta de las Flores. It lived up to its name with an impressive number of blooming shrubs and trees as well as flower beds to provide cover for them. Manuel thought back to Bolaño's garden in Spain. The man did love properties that were beautifully landscaped. It was a weakness in a man with seemingly few other frailties and, given his occupation, rather an odd one.

It was dusk but only two windows were lit. Marco had slipped up to a ground floor window and peered in. He rejoined Manuel. "Just Bolaño and two men. No sign of Anita."

"No," Manuel motioned to the upper floor window. "She must be in that room. I saw a silhouette, a woman, walking past the window."

The two discussed plans, eventually deciding to wait for a little more darkness before attempting to rescue Anita. After all, as Marco pointed out, if she was walking about, she had not been harmed. Manuel reluctantly agreed and they settled down to wait.

A quarter of an hour later, Marco suddenly gripped Manuel's arm. He was staring up at the house. "*O que uma mulher,*" he whispered.

Manuel followed his line of sight. Oh what a woman indeed. His emotions fluctuated between pride and admiration for her courage mixed with fear of her coming to harm. Also, he was a little annoyed that she did not appear to need rescuing!

CHAPTER ELEVEN

Anita had been ensconced in a bedroom on the first floor immediately they arrived. Scruffy had been the one to escort her there and she had been terrified that she would be tied and gagged, as in the previous apartment. However, after a cursory glance round, Scruffy had left her alone, locking the door after him.

There was another door, behind which she found a small bathroom. Quite a relief as one way or another she had undergone a lot of stress today.

Once back in the bedroom, she looked out of the window. Too big a drop to jump safely. There was a tree, quite substantial but not close enough. She looked at the wall, but it was too smooth. No trellis or conveniently strong vines to enable her to escape that way.

Hearing a heavy tread approaching along the hallway, she shut the window quickly and by the time the door was unlocked, revealing Scruffy with a tray containing a glass of water and a sandwich, she was standing nonchalantly beside the dressing table. By concentrating hard on keeping her breathing as even as possible, she managed to hide the thundering of her heart.

Placing the tray on the dresser, Scruffy left without saying a word, but not forgetting to lock her in again. She staggered to the bed and sank down. She had to think. There must be a way out. She certainly did not want to spend the night here. Bolaño's meeting with Luke was tomorrow. Morning or afternoon, she didn't know. But there were only two possible outcomes: Luke met Bolaño's demands and she was then handed over to him—always supposing he kept his word. Or Luke did not meet his demands or even failed to keep the appointment and Bolaño then had no further use for her. Thinking of Isabel's fate once she was surplus to requirements made her shudder. She straightened, pulling herself together. The real question was Luke. So far in this debacle he had not shown himself to be a shining light of reliability. Would he be prepared to jeopardize his own agenda to rescue her? She smiled ruefully. It seemed unlikely. Deep down she could not help believing that he would do whatever he could to help her even though, of course, he did seem to think it was her own fault she was involved! She was confident Manuel, on the other hand, would put her safety first. Just as she was sure he was doing all he could to find her now. Unless, an awful thought suddenly occurred to her, he believed she had gone out just to thumb her nose at him. No, even then he would look for her, if only to tear a strip off her. She was sure about that! She hoped. However, it was unlikely he would find her here, so she needed to escape and try to contact him

She crossed to the window again and looked out. More time had passed and dusk was gathering momentum. She had to make a move. Who knew when someone would decide to restrain her for the night. The tree was her only option. She would have to jump and hope she caught the nearest branch and that it was not rotten and would hold her weight. She just wished it was a couple of feet closer. The last thing she needed now was a broken limb.

Taking a deep breath for courage and trying not to think of how many variables she was relying upon, she opened the window wide, clambered onto the sill and, not giving herself time for any more procrastination, she said a quick prayer before launching herself at the tree.

Landing heavily on her stomach across the branch she took stock of her situation as she dragged air back into her lungs. Exhilaration filled her, she had done it. For a moment she stayed still, letting her heart calm slightly and checking there was no sound from within the house that indicated discovery of her absence. Then she agilely climbed down the tree. Just as she reached the bottom an arm slid round her waist while the other covered her mouth.

"It is me. Quiet." Manuel's low voice in her ear turned her full blown panic into relief as she sagged against him.

"I have so much . . ." she began.

"Quiet! *Dios*, can you do nothing I ask?" He took her hand, "Come, we must leave this place."

He led, or half pulled her, depending on your point of view, through the garden, taking advantage of the failing light and shrubbery. A few yards along the road was a car with Marco in it. Manuel bundled a disgruntled Anita into the back before taking his place in front.

Marco grinned at her. "What a jump! My heart stopped beating for you."

She smiled slightly. "I'm glad someone appreciates my ingenuity."

Marco glanced at Manuel who pointed at the road ahead. "Drive. We have no time to sit and talk."

Marco shrugged, gave Anita a wink and started the engine.

Anita leant forward. "I can't believe you two managed to find me. How ever did you do it?"

Marco waited, but when it was apparent that Manuel was not going to answer, he explained the stages they had gone through to end up at the Quinta de las Flores.

"Wow," Anita was impressed with their detective skills. "It all seems so logical when you say it, but it's like the unravelling at the end of a mystery novel to me."

"We are detectives," Manuel muttered, obviously still cross.

"I know that, I was only . . ."

"Silence." Manuel broke in. "I cannot think with you talking all the time."

Anita stared at him in disbelief. Even Marco gave him a startled glance. She slumped back into her seat. Fine, if he needed silence to be able to think, he could have it. Maybe even permanently as far as she was concerned. He could at least have shown her some sympathy, even if he could not bring himself to admire her ingenuity in getting out of the house.

The rest of the journey back to Cascais was silent. Once indoors, Manuel turned to Anita, but before he could say a word, she exploded.

"I can't believe you. I've had a day of traumas that you would not credit. I escape—by myself, I might add—and all you can do is give me the fright of my life and then order me to keep quiet!"

"It was not the time to talk there. We had to get away before anyone realised you were gone." Why he was on the defensive, Manuel was at a loss to understand. He looked into her mutinous face and sighed. "I am sorry, Anita, for shouting at you. I was angry that you were in danger—angry that I did not keep you safe, also for your jump. Marco and I, we had a plan to rescue you."

"And I was supposed to know that—how?"

"You could not, of course." He ran his fingers through his hair in frustration. "I am sorry. I should not have shouted at you, but I needed to calm myself. Also it was important to get away before they came looking for you."

"I know that. I was just going to say I . . ."

"You know that! You heard me say to be quiet, but still you started to speak!" He threw his arms in the air to express his disbelief. Marco's head was swinging between them as if at a tennis match.

She turned away, the fight gone from her, like air from a popped balloon. "I've had the most awful day of my life. I may never recover from it."

Her disconsolate voice deflated his wrath, although he had to smile inwardly at her dramatic words. It was only a matter of time, a short time he was sure, before her indefatigable optimism returned. He took her hand and pulled her into his arms.

"Yes. Forgive me, *pequeña*. You frightened me with your leap for freedom. And all afternoon I worried where you were, and who was with you and if you were all right."

She leaned into his warmth, relieved the old Manuel was back. "I never want to go though anything like today again. I was so scared. And then there was Isabel."

"Come sit with me here," he settled them onto the sofa. "Tell us everything now. Who is Isabel?"

"She works . . . worked for Crown Industries too. Oh, Manuel, he killed her."

"*Calme, pequeña*. Start from when you were alone here in the apartment."

With some stops and starts, Anita eventually finished her account from when Bolaño appeared at the door in Cascais to her escape from the Quinta de las Flores. At the end, Manual looked very serious as he cupped her face in his hands.

"You will not be left alone again." His mouth suddenly kicked up on one side. "You get into trouble always when you are on your own!"

His mouth covered hers but before she could fall totally under the spell of his kiss Marco's laughing voice broke them apart.

"Later, please. We still have the problem to sort out."

"*Si*, you are right," Manuel regretfully released Anita and faced the other man. "From what we know South must have the prototype. Anita's account also makes this seem to be so."

Marco nodded while Anita frowned. "I just don't get what all the fuss is about. Even if it is such a breakthrough for information storage, surely taking out a patent would cover it?"

A small silence was ended with a sigh from Manuel. "Yes, it is a new storage facility, but it has other uses as well." He glanced at the other man, "She deserves to know. She now is involved very deep."

Marco hesitated then gave a resigned shrug, "*Sim*, you are right."

Manuel turned back to Anita, "There are two elements that make it valuable. It is able to hold much memory, as you know, and it is made so each has its own physical key that must be connected to it for the memory to be added to or read from. So long as these two parts are separate, it is locked. If any attempts are made to hack into it, while they are apart, the device will self-destruct. This is the value to the commercial and private users." He paused to make sure Anita was following his explanation. "The other element, I do not know exactly how it works, but the real importance of it to Bolaño and our governments is the use it can be put to for remote espionage. Set up in a certain way, it only needs one person to place it where required. So anyone who can get into the place to be spied on, for instance, someone dressed as a cleaner, can put it in position and then it can be monitored remotely from many miles away by a person who can not only hear but see what is happening in the vicinity. It has a property that makes it undetectable by sweeping devices and it has other possible uses as well. So, potentially it can be a very powerful weapon. Now you understand?"

She nodded seriously while considering the possible ramifications. She understood its value now, and the urgency felt by all sides to have the device under their control. But she couldn't help feeling put upon and used. The hurt joined a cocktail of emotions that found an immediate outlet in anger.

"Why wasn't I told this before?" She slashed her hand for silence as Manuel opened his mouth to speak. "You didn't have to go all the way. You could've said it was of national importance, official secret or something. That would have been enough. Not claim it was just a commercial theft!" Tears glistened in her eyes, causing Manuel to draw her, despite initial resistance, back into his arms. "God, Manuel," she thumped her fist against his chest. "God, I still can't believe Isabel is dead!"

Over her shoulder Manuel jerked his head at Marco who rose, murmured something about coffee and went into the kitchen. Manuel held Anita, murmuring soothingly as she released some tension through her tears. He berated himself for being so insensitive. She had been through a lot over the last few days, culminating in a day in which she was kidnapped again, found someone she knew murdered and then making an escape by putting her life and limb at risk. Altogether it was enough to break the spirit of the most stalwart character, and of course his treatment of her at the Quinta and in the car returning here would not have helped.

By the time Marco returned with a tray of steaming cups of strong coffee, Anita had gained control of herself, blown her nose fiercely on a handkerchief supplied by Manuel and wiped her face. Her reddened eyes spoke of her temporary collapse, but her head was high as she thanked Marco for her drink.

"What now?" she prompted.

Keeping her close to lend her strength, Manuel answered. "We must concentrate on the lost prototype. The next thing we must do is find Luke."

"Yes," Marco nodded. "And *rapidamente*, to be sure Bolaño has no chance of getting hold of it."

The two men began brainstorming some ideas as Anita finished her coffee and placed the empty cup back on the tray. She cleared her throat gently, drawing the attention of both men.

"I know where Luke is."

CHAPTER TWELVE

With gratification she saw both men stare at her, rendered temporarily speechless. After a few seconds she modified her statement.

"Well, perhaps not just where he is at the moment, but you know I told you how Bolaño made me talk to Luke?"

Both men nodded.

"Well, when he got back on the phone obviously I was standing right beside him. I could hear their conversation, not just Bolaño's side. Luke must have been talking quite loudly as I could hear him quite clearly."

She paused to savour her moment. "Anyway, I overheard where they're going to meet. So you won't need to stake out and follow Bolaño, you can get there first."

"Where?" Manuel's voice was very soft.

"A place called something like Cervaria Trindad, at twelve thirty tomorrow." She caught sight of the clock on the mantelpiece, "That's to say, today now, I suppose."

Manuel looked at the other man in query. Marco nodded, "The Cervejaria Trinidade on the Rua Nova da Trinidade. It is a popular *restaurante,* many tourists as well as Lisboans go there to see the Masonic murals as much as the food and drink. So it is a good choice for South to make. Many people around for safety."

"*Bueno*," Manuel turned to Anita. "There is nothing to do until later. After your day you must be tired, you will go to bed, yes?"

91

"I am tired. Exhausted actually," she admitted. "But I'm too hyped up for sleep. With my luck, I'll probably crash just as the excitement starts!"

"Of course, it is natural. Why do you not have a bath, it will relax you perhaps."

She considered briefly. "Good idea. I need one anyway after throwing myself out of windows at trees!"

"Do not remind me," he took her hand and drew her out of the room.

"See you later, Marco," she called over her shoulder at the man preparing to take the tray back to the kitchen. He smiled, giving her a small salute.

In the bedroom Manuel left her to undress while he ran her bath. It spoke volumes of her state of mind that she felt no embarrassment in her nudity as she entered the bathroom and clambered in the steaming water.

"Oh, that's good," she leaned back and closed her eyes. "I can actually feel my muscles unknotting!" She smiled up at him.

Kneeling by the bath he locked her eyes with his, holding her attention. "You frighten me. You are too impetuous. Please, for the sake of my nerves, do not get into any more trouble. Let me look after you."

"Today really was not my fault," she began.

"I know. It was mine, to leave you unprotected."

"No . . ."

"Yes," he overrode her. "Relax and enjoy your soak. Try to make your brain slow down and rest as well. I am going to talk with Marco—just to decide how we will use your information." He smiled at her as he rose to his feet.

Her eyes immediately widened. "Wait. I don't want to be left out. After all that's happened I deserve to be included!"

He contemplated her for a long moment and she did not realise she was holding her breath until she released it in an audible gust when he spoke.

"No, perhaps you are right. Certainly I will be able to keep you safe more easily if we are together. But," he tacked on as her expression revealed her satisfaction. "But you must follow my instructions. If you do not, you may put not just yourself in danger."

She nodded. "Okay. You're the boss. I've had enough excitement for the time being anyway. I'm ready to take a rest from the worry and planning for awhile."

He shook his head, smiling ruefully as he left the bathroom.

Half an hour later, clean and feeling mellow Anita, wrapped in a full length white towelling robe she had taken from its hook on the bathroom door, returned to the living room.

"So," she said brightly sitting in a deep chair. "What's the plan?"

Marco didn't appear to approve of her inclusion but refrained from actually saying anything as Manuel replied. "Now we know where South will be, and the time, we plan to intercept him. Talk to him before he makes his reunion with Bolaño."

"That's it?" She looked at each man in turn. "You're just going to talk. No violence, right?"

"No, there is no need. We will only talk, either on the spot or in the police station."

"You mean to arrest him?"

Manuel sighed. "If possible, no. It would be better if he agreed to co-operate. But if not . . ."

"I see." She supposed that was the best she could expect. She just wished she had a firmer grip on things. There seemed to be so many loose ends. So much didn't add up. Frustrated, she ran her fingers through her hair, if only she could be sure she was being told everything. She could not help feeling that Manuel would keep some things back—no doubt in his mind it would be for her own safety! As for Marco, he obviously thought the less she knew the better!

Marco stood. "So, I will return about nine thirty. *Boa noite*, Anita. I am pleased you came to no harm."

"Good night, and thanks for coming to my rescue."

He acknowledged this with a formal nod although his mouth tilted slightly as Manuel accompanied him to the door and locked up after him.

Returning, Manuel took her hand to help her up from the chair. "Come. It is late and we are both tired."

Shortly afterwards they lay spoon-fashion in the dark. Anita tried to fall asleep. She really did. Closing her eyes she allowed her mind to drift. Then she tried the method of imagining one part of her body after another being weightless, touted as a sure-fire way of relaxing and sending the body into a torpor, then slumber. It was no use though, her brain would not co-operate and was racing from one topic to another. Abandoning all efforts, she concentrated on Manuel. Was he asleep? Would she disturb him if she got up?

Suddenly his arm tightened round her. "Chiquita, I can hear you thinking. What is the problem?"

"I keep going back to Isabel. How she looked." She turned to face him. "Do you know what's happened to her?"

"She has been taken care of through liaison between the Portuguese police and Interpol. You do not have to worry."

"What will happen to her body?"

"I think they will try to find some family. But, you say, she has none, so I believe she will be buried here, eventually."

Anita considered this. "It seems so . . . so lonely. Almost as if she never existed. Do you know what I mean?"

He pulled her closer. "I understand. But do not forget she chose her actions. She knew the risks."

"I know, but still."

"Also do not forget that she was not worried about Bolaño's possible plans for you. If you were the one dead and not her, do you think she would be thinking of you?"

"No," she sighed. "You're right, of course."

"You are kind-hearted and, too, you are not used to the sort of happenings you have experienced since leaving England. It is not strange that you should be affected."

She snuggled closer, inhaling his familiar scent, a mixture of musk and his own unique smell. She was positive she would be able to recognise him now through his aroma even if blindfolded. Their talk in the dark and her feeling of security with him wrapped around her finally allowed her body to win over her mind as she slipped gently into sleep.

Pobrecita, was Manuel's last thought before he too succumbed. She was in so far over her head, but he would do all he could to ensure that no further harm befell her.

CHAPTER
THIRTEEN

The next morning the three of them were positioned so they could easily cover all approaches to the restaurant.

"Do not forget, Anita. You must do as I tell you. This is not a game," Manuel warned.

"I know, I've grasped that fact." She turned her face away mumbling, "I'd have to be deaf as well as stupid, the way you keep going on about it."

Marco grinned privately while Manuel pulled her head round to face him. "I am worried. You act on impulse and get into trouble." He sighed, "I should not have brought you here. I should have left you locked up somewhere safe until this is all over!"

Her heart swelled at the emotion she could read in his eyes, she placed her hand over his. "I told you, I've had enough excitement. I'll do exactly as you tell me."

He stared into her eyes for a long moment before giving a groan as he placed a quick hard kiss on her lips. Suddenly Marco stiffened and quietly said, "South, he comes now. You are right, Manuel, he comes early for security. He does not want Bolaño to be here before him."

Manuel put Anita behind him and followed Marco's gaze. "Good we came early too or we would have missed him."

Marco stepped out from the doorway sheltering them to intercept the approaching man. Catching sight of him, Luke hesitated a second then, as if recognizing the danger facing him, instinctively he turned to run. Immediately Marco took off after him. Manuel paused to exhort Anita. "Wait here. Do not move until I return."

As soon as she nodded he raced after Marco. They had discussed the area last night and Marco had shown the best possible ways to trap a fleeing person depending on the direction they took. It was only a moment before all three men were out of Anita's sight. She leant sideways against the wall and closed her eyes. She had no intention of moving until Manuel came back for her and, besides, she was still so tired she wondered if it was possible to nap while in an upright position. The muted traffic sounds, the warmth despite the early hour and the faint smell of dried fish all contributed to her drowsiness.

She was rudely jerked out of her soporific haze when, with no warning, a hand covered her mouth, a hard arm circled her middle and she felt herself being half lifted, half dragged into the street and almost immediately round a corner out of sight of the Cervejaria Trinidade. Her heart pounding fit to burst she struggled, her hands on the arm banded round her for purchase while she tried to kick backwards. Once round the corner, with her efforts apparently having no effect on her abductor, she sagged in defeat. Despairingly the thought crossed her mind that Manuel would not believe this. In fact she could hardly believe it herself.

CHAPTER FOURTEEN

Marco and Manuel walked back towards the shop doorway where they had left Anita. Both were annoyed that South had managed to elude them somehow, Marco in particular was disgusted with himself. This was his city. How had the Englishman escaped them?

Manuel gave him a friendly slap on the back. "It is not your fault."

"But . . ."

"No, not your fault. It is clear South took time to learn this area. He was alert for a problem to his plans and had made plans for escape if it proved necessary."

Marco shrugged fatalistically. "Yes, you are right, I know. But still I feel he should not have been able to get away from me." He smiled at the other man, "Next time, yes?"

"Yes!"

As they drew level with the doorway where they had left Anita, Manuel realised it was empty.

"¡*Dios*!" he checked the street in both directions. "*Dios mio*, she is unbelievable. Next time I *will* tie her down so she cannot move." He ran his fingers through his hair distractedly. "Why can she not do as I tell her? She promised to stay here."

Marco, who had been examining the doorway area, grasped his arm to halt the rant. "*Mira*, look," he pointed to the dusty ground. "Look at the scuff marks. Someone else was here and took her. She did not go willingly."

Manuel stared at the irrefutable evidence. "Yes, you are right. *Dios*, I should not have left her unprotected. Again. Only last night I promised her I would keep her safe. It is my fault." He considered a moment. "Who took her? Who could know we would be here?"

Across the road an unusually harried-looking man approached the Cervejaria Trinidade. Manuel gesticulated. "It was not Bolaño, he is there for his meeting. It was not Luke, we were chasing him and he had no time to return here to abduct Anita." He groaned in despair. "I should never have brought her to Portugal. I should have sent her to her home in England."

"She would have been in danger there too. Her connection with South was known." Marco spoke distractedly as he scanned the area thoroughly.

Manuel would not be appeased. "I should have sent her home with bodyguards. They could have protected her and kept her under control!"

Marco grasped his arm. "*Calme*, Manuel. We need clear heads if we are to find her again."

Manuel drew a deep breath. "You are right, I know, but . . ."

"*Sim*, I understand. Look, Bolaño knows you, so I will go into the Cervejaria Trinidade, see who he meets and, if possible, listen to their conversation. You can see if anyone noticed when Anita was taken."

Manuel nodded. "I will ask that news vendor at the end of the street."

As they parted ways, Marco grinned at him. "She will probably extricate herself and we will find her waiting for us at the apartment!"

Manuel smiled half-heartedly in acknowledgement of the sally, but he felt sick with self-condemnation. Again he had let her down. She had courage, yes. She was resourceful, yes. But, and it was a big 'but', she was too impetuous, acting first before planning properly. He shook his head. It was a mystery to him that she had survived intact so far to reach her present age.

CHAPTER FIFTEEN

Anita's abductor did not have to drag her far. Just to a non-descript beige saloon car into which she was bundled over the driver's seat to the passenger side despite her renewed struggles. As she straightened in the seat she saw her abductor for the first time. Of course, she thought, you would think she would be becoming inured to shock, but somehow events kept proving her wrong. Mr NextSeat climbed in after her and started the engine.

"I'm sorry for the abrupt method, but speed was of the essence," he smiled at her as he fired up the engine and pulled the car out into the street.

Anita stared at him with disbelief. He was acting as if they were pals on a friendly outing instead of him having kidnapped her. The whole incongruity of it snapped her out of shock.

"Who are you? Why do you keep popping up?"

He smiled congenially at her again before returning his eyes to the road. "Frank Searle."

"What?"

"My name. It's Frank Searle. As for "popping up", as you call it, I've been trying to catch up with you to make sure you're all right."

She shook her head in confusion, but before she could speak he continued, "I work with Luke South."

Startled, she considered this for a moment, then said, "I've never seen you at Crown's"

101

He tutted gently. "We both know Luke never really worked at Crown Industries. He was just there undercover."

Silence fell as he concentrated on his driving while she thought hard. Undercover. In a way it made sense. The big question now was who they worked for. Either cowardice or an element of caution held her back from asking Mr NextSeat-Searle. The answer would also tell her if her knowing her kidnapper, or at least his name and what he looked like, meant she would be killed once her usefulness was over or if she would be safely reunited with Luke.

She looked over at Searle. "Where are you taking me now?"

"To safety."

Well that cleared that up, she thought. She only hoped it was her safety rather than his at the expense of her life. She turned her face to look out of the side window. She should concentrate on where they were going. Note landmarks and directions for when she had an opportunity to escape. And she would escape. If she could get away from Bolaño and his goons, she certainly could elude Mr NextSeat-Searle. She shifted uncomfortably, she was developing new bruises from her present companion's treatment. Well, she thought philosophically, they would match those gained from the tree yesterday. God, her life had spiralled totally out of her control.

Shortly, the car whipped into a car park and Mr NextSeat-Searle and Anita got out. Taking her arm in a firm grip he led her towards a hotel with four large columns fronting the revolving door entrance.

"Do not make trouble here," he warned. "You would be very sorry."

Anita did not deign to reply. She already knew his strength, but what was keeping her in line for the moment was what she saw as he undid his jacket giving a quick glimpse of a shoulder holster complete with revolver.

Once in the lobby, he manoeuvred her smartly across to the bank of elevators allowing her only an overall impression of shiny tiled floor and predominately wood furniture with red accoutrements. They rose to the fourth floor and she was briskly marched to one of the identical doors barring their numbers. Once in the room, he released her but maintained an alert eye on her. She crossed to the window drawn by the sound of muted traffic and pulled the curtains apart a little. She stood there awhile, absently rubbing the spot on her arm where he had gripped her while she looked out over a large plaza. Yet another bruise, no doubt.

Finally she turned to face him, "Well, what now?"

"Nothing. We wait. Won't be long." He paused, then, "Would you like a coffee?"

"No." Pulling a face she turned back to the view outside. God, she hoped Luke turned up soon. Her head tilted slightly while she considered her total lack of fear of Luke. Was it because he was English, like her? No, she had known him for some time—okay for a short time—but for longer than anyone else in this fiasco, enough to feel sure he wouldn't harm her. Oh, of course, she knew criminals, particular murderers, did not have a warning sign on them. The sweetest face could front an evil character, everyone knew that. Still, in her gut she was sure he would do his best to prevent her coming to grief. And she believed he was working undercover, as Searle had said. The question was: undercover for whom or what? The police? If so, which police? The British or an international agency? Another factor to consider was that he apparently worked with Searle, who also was English and he definitely did not make her feel safe. The opposite, in fact.

Eventually the scrape of a key card at the door announced a new arrival. Anita turned, her pulse raising a bit. To her unbounded relief Luke walked in. As he saw her, he smiled and tossed the key card on the desk.

"Good, you got here okay, then."

Her burgeoning answering smile fell away. "Got here okay?" she began ominously. "No. I got here. But not okay. I was kidnapped off the street and manhandled here—by him." She pointed at Searle, at ease in an armchair, who nodded congenially in return. "I'm sure I've got bruises all over." She pulled up her sleeve to display a growing imprint of a hand on her upper arm.

Luke looked at it, then directed his stare at Searle raising a brow.

Searle shrugged. "It was unavoidable. Speed was obviously of the essence. I did not have time to discuss the situation."

Luke looked back at Anita who was staring at Searle. Although he clearly was working with Luke, and he appeared so unthreatening sprawled in that chair, she could not throw off the continuing conviction that he was fundamentally dangerous. She gave a small sniff, of course she could be adversely biased by him snatching her off the street and by the gun at his shoulder.

"Look," Luke put his arm round her shoulder to steer her into the second armchair before plonking himself on the edge of the bed. "Anita, we've got to talk."

That she agreed with wholeheartedly and raised her eyes to meet his expectantly.

He obliged. "I'm really sorry you've been involved in all this. I realise it's my fault—at least to some extent." At her rapidly changing expression, he continued quickly. "You got on that plane against my expressed order."

She waved her hand. "Forget that, we've already been through that."

"Okay," Luke paused to arrange his thoughts. "We had to get you away from Ortega. I knew it wasn't going to be easy, somehow he's gained your confidence." His expression was one of reproach, which she ignored. "But he's mixed up with Bolaño, no doubt about that, and Bolaño is not someone you want to get involved with."

"You're right about that," she hurrumphed. "I was in his flat when he killed Isabel. I'll never forget what she looked like, it was horrible."

Realising both men were staring at her attentively, she went on to explain everything Isabel had told her. The men appeared to communicate silently, then Luke leaned forward and grasped her hand. "You see, then. Ortega and Bolaño—they're the same."

"No," she contradicted. "Oh, at first I thought so, but he isn't. In fact he rescued me from Bolaño twice—well, once and a half really. The second time I'd already made my escape when he turned up, but . . ."

"Anita," Luke broke in. "Anita, he was just trying to gain your confidence. It was an act. Look at this morning's events."

"This morning he was hoping to catch you before you met Bolaño. He wanted to get that nano thing from you before you could hand it over to him. He knew where and when you were meeting because I told him about it."

Luke shook his head. "He was there as back-up for Bolaño."

"That's ridiculous." She thought a moment. "Right, if that's the case why were he and Marco—who's a policeman by the way—trying to intercept you? Why not let you make the meeting with Bolaño?"

Luke sighed with frustration and looked at Searle who just shrugged as if to say you're on your own here, mate.

Luke released her hand and leaned back. "Let's get this morning straight. I was going to meet with Bolaño, to ensure your safety, if you remember?"

She flushed slightly and bit her lip.

He continued, "Anyway, as I said, he's not someone to underestimate, so yesterday we scoped out the area again. We'd previously checked it out pretty carefully before I suggested the venue to Bolaño. As an added precaution we decided to turn up early. That was when we saw you arrive with Ortega and someone else."

"Marco," she clarified. "A policeman."

"Or at least that's what you've been told!" He saw her gather steam and waved an arm to disperse it. "Regardless, it was a chance too good to miss to rescue you."

"What about your rendezvous with Bolaño?"

"Our plan on the fly was that, with luck, we'd get you away before he arrived and I might still be able to keep the appointment. If that wasn't possible, our priority was getting you to safety. Anyway, our plan was for me to decoy the two men, leaving you alone—of course there was the danger that only one would follow me, but we banked on their determination to finally get me into their clutches."

He raised his hands expressively as he concluded, "As it was, it all worked out perfectly! At least, nearly perfectly." He glanced meaningfully at Searle who straightened abruptly in response.

Missing this by-play, Anita treated it with the contempt it deserved by sniffing as she tossed her head away. Facing him again, she watched broodingly as he turned to Searle and began talking in a low voice. Not being able to hear clearly she retreated into a reverie, ignoring the two men discussing new plans while she considered both Luke and Manuel. Both maintained their intention was to protect her. And, to be perfectly frank, she believed them—both of them. At the same time each claimed the other was manifestly working with Bolaño who terrified her.

The two men left her to her ruminations and conversed quietly until lunch arrived courtesy of room service. They all served themselves and began to eat.

Anita finally felt the need to break the silence. "So, what happened when you saw Bolaño?"

Luke looked at her. "Nothing. I had to wait until Ortega and friend gave up, and they waited until Bolaño left. So I didn't have a chance to talk to him. I have to say he did not look pleased."

Anita shuddered at the thought of a Bolaño even more angry than before. Seeing it, Luke covered her hand with his. "Don't worry, you're safe with us. Anyway, on the bright side, it gives us more time to try to locate the gadget."

Anita was astounded. "I thought you had it. You were going to exchange it for me!"

"A bluff." Luke smiled disarmingly. "I never had it. Nearly did at one time, but then it disappeared again." He shrugged as if to say that's life.

Anita, however, was speechless. Luke was demented if he thought he could have tricked Bolaño successfully. After they had finished eating, Searle wheeled the trolley out into the corridor for collection on his way out.

"Where's he gone?" Anita asked.

"Just running a few errands. He'll be back in an hour or so." Luke settled comfortably in the armchair vacated by the other man.

"Good. While we're on our own, I have a question for you. And I want an honest answer."

Luke pulled himself out of the comfort zone into which he had been sinking. This sounded ominous. He needed to be alert. "Okay. Shoot."

"Back in England, when we started going out, what was it about me that attracted you?"

Luke blinked. This question he had not anticipated. He opened his mouth, trusting an answer would occur to him that would not upset her, but Anita hurried on. "What I want to know is, did you want to get to know me? Or did you think I was average enough to make a good cover for you while travelling to Spain?"

Luke stared at her expectant face. In her eyes he could read her insecurities despite her efforts to hide them. He sighed, "Truthfully?"

She nodded.

"At the beginning I was drawn to you and, in normal circumstances, I would have asked you out. But, I was working undercover which made personal relationships like that a no-go area." He grimaced. "Then things started going down the pan. The prototype disappeared, but not according to our plan. Anyway, to cut a long story short, I needed to get to Spain and contact Bolaño—as had been part of the original plan—to try to track down the missing gadget. I wanted to be in situ and make the appointment on my own terms." He paused a moment before continuing more slowly. "That's when I decided to travel 'on holiday' as part of a couple."

"That's when you first asked me out." It was a statement, not a question.

He half-smiled, "Yes. But I would remind you I was strongly drawn to you from the beginning! And that was why I approached you. Not because I thought you'd be a good cover, but because I needed a cover which gave me an excuse."

He stared earnestly at her. He had told her the truth, but would her lurking insecurities let her believe him?

She looked deeply into his eyes for a long minute. She read his sincerity, or was that what she wanted to read? What about Manuel? Closing her eyes, she shook her head to clear the conflicting thoughts.

"Never mind," she sighed.

Luke grasped both her hands in his. "Look, I never intended you to get involved in all this. It's true I hoped that travelling together would get me into Spain under Bolaño's radar. He would have been watching for a man on his own, not a holidaying couple." He looked at their clasped hands for a moment as he tried to sort out his chaotic thoughts.

"The thing is, Anita, from the worry and, at times, outright fear for your safety, I've realised how deep my feelings for you really are."

Anita's jaw dropped as she assimilated his words and the exposed emotion on his face. Then she straightened, withdrew her hands from his and looked away.

"Good grief, this is hardly the place and time for getting maudlin."

There was a short silence with absolutely no movement from either for a minute. Her stomach tightened with nerves before she let out a sigh of relief as Luke cleared his throat. "Quite right. I must be more tired than I thought."

CHAPTER SIXTEEN

Relieved, Anita sank back into her mediations. She needed to get back with Manuel. Although she felt reasonably confident Luke wouldn't harm her, she definitely did not have the same feeling about Searle. He still frightened her. And what made her present position untenable was Luke's trust in the man. She could not afford to find herself left in Searle's control again. No, more than that, she would not let herself be alone with him again.

The other pressing reason for contacting Manuel was more personal. She wanted to make sure he knew she had not left him voluntarily. Her big fear was that he would decide to wash his hands of her, deciding he had not the time to keep chasing and retrieving her from whatever situation she found herself in. Particularly as he knew she could not help his investigation materially.

She considered her options. First priority was to get out of this room. Luke and Searle were not likely to leave her alone in it. The trouble was, between the en-suite bathroom and room service, she could not immediately see a pressing reason to leave it. This meant she was trapped, unable to escape or even to telephone Manuel unless she was lucky enough for both men to succumb to exhaustion and fall into a deep sleep. Unfortunately matters never seem to oblige her like that.

Searle returned and he and Luke had another low-voiced short conversation she was unable to hear and had to content herself with giving them a supercilious look, simultaneously broadcasting both her censure of their rudeness and her complete disinterest. At the very least she hoped it camouflaged her anxiety.

After long evening shadows crept across the floor, room service reappeared with their evening meal. Although not really hungry, Anita ate. She needed to keep her strength up so as to be ready for escape when an opportunity presented itself—as it would, she was determined.

Later the two men rearranged the chairs to afford Anita some privacy so she could lie down and sleep. It took her a long time as her mind would not stop racing from one pressing concern to another, and she seemed to have plenty. But, eventually, sheer exhaustion won and she dozed off.

The following morning, to her surprise, the men decided they would all go down to the restaurant for breakfast. Whether this was because they thought she had now decided to stay with familiarity—Luke—or whether they felt a bit stir crazy themselves, she did not know and had no intention of questioning. A frisson of excitement caused by hope ran through her and, keen to leave the room, which for all its comfort, had been no more than a prison, Anita quickly tidied herself and was ready to go.

The restaurant operated on a self-service basis and the three of them collected a tray each and joined the short queue. Anita's brain was buzzing, this was her opportunity and she had to take it before finding herself stuck back in the room upstairs. There was a vast choice from full English breakfasts to traditional Continental ones along with an appetising variety of local specialities. The two men set to filling their plates with gusto. It was only when she noticed Frank giving her a peculiar look, she realised she was standing in a trance holding up the growing line behind her. Quickly she selected a couple of items at random along with a much-needed deep cup of strong coffee. Taking their laden trays to a table beside the vista of window, they settled down to eat in silence. Having finished her coffee and half-way through her fruit compote, Anita raised her napkin to her mouth before looking over at Luke.

"I'm sure I saw a Ladies in the corridor outside. I won't be a moment." She rose and quickly left the table before they could prevent her without causing a scene.

Opening the door to the Ladies, she glanced behind and saw Searle had followed and was now leaning against the opposite wall. He gave her a rictus smile that she ignored passing through the door leaving it to swing shut. She was relieved to see her supposition was correct, there were two large windows. The room was deserted, so in no time at all she had climbed onto a basin and from there onto the window sill and slithered out dropping onto the grass outside. She ran for the street, heart pounding expecting Searle to have divined her escape and be in pursuit at any moment. Soon she was protected from sight of the hotel by a tall vibrant bush before it gave way to other buildings. Feeling safer for the moment, she slowed to a brisk walking pace so as not to draw any untoward attention. She knew where she was going. She remembered seeing the Rosario railway station on the journey with Searle the previous day. God, it might only be a day past, but to her it seemed a life-time ago!

At the station, finding a public phone, she called Manuel's number. He answered immediately

"Ortega," was his succinct response.

"Manuel, it's me. I . . ."

"Anita? What happened? Where are you? You are okay?"

"I'm fine. It's a long story but . . ."

"Where are you?"

"At Rosario railway sta . . ."

"Stay there. I will come to collect you." He broke the connection.

Anita stared at the dead telephone. Well, that was brief. Still, at least he was coming for her. Perhaps she had worried needlessly that he would be tired of tracking her down, she thought optimistically.

In a remarkably short time she saw him enter the station and look round in search of her. A sudden flood of a mixture of emotions propelled her towards him at a run. As she ran straight into his arms, he pulled her into such a tight embrace she emitted a surprised squeak. Immediately he held her off to look her up and down.

"You are not hurt?"

"No, Manuel," she snuggled into his body again. "I'm fine. I admit I was scared when Mr NextSeat dragged me off to his car, but . . ."

"Mr NextSeat? The man who followed you to my village?"

"Yes, anyway, it turns out he works with Luke."

"South!" The way he spat out the name it sounded like a curse.

She laid her hand on his arm. "Manuel," her voice soft.

He looked into her anxious face and groaned.

"Come," he turned, drawing her hand through his arm. His voice calm again. "Come, Marco is outside with the car. We will return to the *apartamente* and talk over all what has occurred in a civilised method. Yes?"

She grinned back. "Good idea."

Marco smiled at her as Manuel guided her into the rear seat before crowding in after her. He took her hand, gave it a squeeze then rested them both on his thigh as the car fired up and was soon skimming away from the station.

Manuel spoke to Marco briefly, but too rapidly for Anita to pick up anything apart from Luke's name. Marco's even more brief response conveyed surprise. When she began to put her two cents in, Manuel hushed her.

"Soon we will be at the *apartamente*. You will tell us all your story then?"

She subsided. "Yes, of course." The rest of the trip was completed in silence.

Once in the apartment, to Anita's surprise, Manuel headed directly to the kitchen to make coffee. Apparently he was in no hurry now that he had her safely back. Finally they were all settled in the sitting room, armed with coffees, both men looking at her expectantly.

"So," Manuel started the ball rolling. "Where have you been and what have you been doing?"

"Well, you know Mr Nextseat grabbed and forced me to go with him to his car?"

Both men nodded.

"He took me to his hotel—his name, by the way, is Frank Searle." She noticed Marco making a note of the name. Presumably for him to check up on later, she thought knowledgeably. Who said she was not learning espionage skills? "Anyway, he took me to a room in a hotel and after awhile Luke turned up."

She frowned at Manuel's involuntary mutter and turned to him. "I'll have you know I was pretty relieved when he appeared. Although Searle said he was taking me to him, I didn't know if that was just to keep me calm. At least I know Luke doesn't want me dead!"

Manuel nodded. "I am sorry, you are right. Please continue."

She could not help feeling this apology would have sounded a lot more sincere if she had not observed the speaking look he had directed at Marco.

"Anyway," she said repressively. "Anyway, he was just as relieved to see me safe. He thinks you are a danger to me."

"It is not me who is a danger to you," Manuel was unable to let that slide.

"No," she soothed. "Of course not. I know that. But Luke is basing his opinion on you working for Bolaño."

"I was on loan from the police to go undercover for Interpol . . ."

"I know, you told me . . ."

"Marco is a policeman, you know that, and he is working with me. So you have proof that I am on the side of justice." He managed to sound both aggrieved and annoyed that he felt he had to reaffirm his position.

"Manuel, I know. You asked me to believe in you, and I do," she leaned forward as if to reinforce her words. "Luke is a policeman too, and he was also undercover when he came to work at Crown Industries and started to apparently make deals with Bolaño." Her brow furrowed, "Evidently Searle is a policeman as well, but somehow he still gives me the creeps."

Marco had been looking at each of them as they spoke, now he cleared his throat. "So South and Searle are police, as are we. That is settled now, yes?"

Manuel nodded. Marco continued, "So why is South planning to give the prototype to Bolaño? Did he tell you?"

She shook her head. "He doesn't have it."

"But he was to meet with Bolaño to hand it over," Marco looked at her sharply.

"I know that's what he said," she smiled grimly. "But he told me that was a bluff, part of his plan to rescue me from Bolaño's clutches."

"*Dios*," Manuel rolled his eyes. "The man is a lunatic. Bolaño is not someone to underestimate. Not a man you trick like that." He fixed her with a glare. "I cannot believe such a man, so stupid, is in the police—even the English police!"

"He was trying to do his best for me and, don't forget, he had to think up a plan on the spot. Anyway, he is in the police, Searle confirmed it."

"This Searle confirmed his claim, the one who works with him, abducting women off streets? This Searle, who you find creepy?" He leaned forward, adding weight to his sarcasm.

As Anita opened her mouth to respond, Marco beat her to the punch.

"Squabbling like children is wasting our time," both Manuel and Anita turned to him shamefaced. "We need to forget South and Searle, and plan for our next stage."

"You are right," Manuel fell back in his chair, but could not resist a final salvo towards Anita. "We will sort out who in truth rescued you from Bolaño when this is over."

Anita lifted her eyes heavenward but heroically turned her attention to the matter in hand. "So, where is this prototype? Luke has not got it. Bolaño obviously hasn't got it or he wouldn't be prepared to go to meetings to get it." She looked at both men, who nodded. "And Manuel hasn't got it. If Isabel ever had it, she obviously has not got it now. No one appears to have it!"

There was a silence while they all puzzled over the problem.

Finally, Anita shrugged her shoulders. "Look, I know none of you trust each other but I think you should meet up with Luke and Frank Searle to work together. Both of you say you are working for the law, so you have a common base to work from."

"No," Manuel was thunderstruck she could even suggest such an idea. However, Marco, when she turned to him, looked thoughtful. He was clearly the more level-headed one—at least in connection with Luke—so she decided to concentrate her persuasion on him.

Having won Marco to her side, it took a further hour of debate—both logical and unreasonable—before Manuel finally gave in to the two of them with bad grace.

"*Por Dios*," he threw up his hands in surrender. "I will no longer fight you both. I believe you are wrong but I am outnumbered and the two of you are too stubborn."

Marco and Anita gave each other a brief but speaking glance. However, they decided to quit while they were ahead. She rose to her feet and stretched, releasing tension from her cramped muscles.

"I'm going for a shower, it's been nearly two days since my last one and I need it!"

After a shower that was as therapeutic as cleansing, Anita wrapped the bath towel round herself, tucking in the end to secure it. She used the blow dryer to get most of the moisture from her hair before emerging into the bedroom. She was not terribly surprised to see Manuel sitting on the bed.

"Come," he held out his hand and with not a hint of hesitation she crossed the room to sit on his knee. Her arms went about his neck while he drew her close into his body. For a few moments they stayed like that before Manuel nuzzled her hair and began to speak in a low voice.

"I was so concerned for you. For what had happened to you. I thought maybe Bolaño, or some of his men, had got you again. Not knowing where you were. If you were frightened or hurt. I was angry with myself for leaving you with no protection again."

She shushed him with a hand over his mouth. "There was no way you could have anticipated it. Not your fault."

"But I . . ."

"No, just forget it. It's over, in the past."

"I was so scared for you," his grip tightened almost painfully for a moment.

"I know. I thought you would be—or at least I sort of hoped you would be," she glanced up into his face. "But I couldn't ring, all yesterday and last night I was not left alone for a minute."

"*Si*, I understand, but last night I could not sleep, and then when today you said you were with South . . ."

She straightened up and looked into his eyes. "Manuel, Luke is a friend, no more. He never was. Perhaps he would have been more if we'd come to Spain on holiday together as I originally thought we were. But that didn't happen." She smiled tremulously at him. "Instead I met you and the rest, as they say, is history."

"Not history," he murmured. "A beginning of something special, no?"

"Yes," her agreement was swallowed by his mouth as it took control of hers. Erotically reclaiming her. His hand travelled from caressing her back in comfort to her side where it hooked in the top of the towel to start loosening and easing it down.

Lost in each other, both were startled when Marco thumped on the door and shouted, "Come on, we must progress."

The spell broken, they leaned their foreheads together as they laughed a little, relieving the sexual tension gripping them. Anita got up to dress while Manuel also rose, straightened his clothes and moved towards the door.

"Do not rush, we will not leave without you. From now on you will be with me all the time." He smiled wickedly as he left the room.

For a second, Anita stared at the closed door. Whew! When he turned on the charm like that, he burnt all her brain sockets. Smiling she shook her head as she collected clean clothes to put on.

The drive across the city was silent, each lost in their own thoughts. Marco's expression was thoughtful; Manuel's growing steadily darker the nearer they got to their destination; while Anita's just seemed preoccupied. When they reached the hotel Anita led them directly to the elevators that carried them up to the fourth floor and then to the room she had been taken to previously. Luke opened the door in answer to their knock. He stared blankly at Anita in surprise.

"May we enter?" Manuel's voice managed to sound both threatening and cordial.

"Oh, of course," Luke stood back to allow them to pass. Then, after closing the door, he followed them into the main part of the room. "I wasn't expecting you to come calling, I must say," he directed at Anita. Then, lip curling slightly, added, "Nor your companions." He succeeded in imbuing a sneering intonation on the last word.

"For goodness sake, Luke, this isn't the playground. We've come to collaborate, pool resources." Anita plumped down into one of the armchairs. She pulled a face at the expressions on their faces—obstinate on Manuel's, incredulity on Luke's. "Look, all of you are in law enforcement of one sort or another, or you could think of it as keeping your enemies close" she paused to glance round. "Where's Searle?"

"He's gone to meet someone from the Department to report our progress or, more to the point, lack of it." Luke moved over to sit on the end of the bed. "I'm not sure what you're trying here, Anita, but remember what I told you—Ortega works with Bolaño, or at least," he tacked on quickly to forestall her interruption. "At least he was until very recently."

"Oh, for heaven's sake, Luke. You were working undercover and so was Manuel. Haven't you got some ID, or something, to prove who you are? You too." This last was directed at Manuel.

After a small hesitation Manuel produced a small black wallet that he opened to reveal a laminated ID card as Luke also displayed his own credentials. As they both put them away again, Marco, who had been an amused bystander so far, stepped forward.

"At the start I was unsure if Anita's idea was good. But now I think we should try it. At the moment, we are wasting much time and energy fighting with each other. It is better if we spend this time on the real problem."

"Exactly!" Anita felt vindicated by his support. She looked at Manuel and Luke in turn and could not help feeling amused by their almost identical grimaces.

"*Si*, okay," muttered Manuel while Luke gave a curt nod.

There was an awkward pause while no one seemed to be sure of the next move. Then Luke cleared his throat and moved to look out of the window.

"Right, well, I'll start then. Crown Industries approached the authorities, who then passed it on to us, for an undercover operation to find the breach in their security. No one outside the company was supposed to know about their new development, yet there were whispers. Perhaps more worryingly, they were even being approached on the Q. T. from several interested parties, some of whom were decidedly iffy." At the pair of blank looks, he elucidated, "they were suspicious. Then the government became involved. Anyway, the plan was for us to find the leak and clear it up before anything further happened.

However, my remit was to try to find the whole organisation involved rather than just the one player who was under suspicion—a player who was unlikely to be far up the chain of command. The intel we had was that Bolaño was acting on behalf of a third party." He looked round at his attentive audience. Assured of their complete attention he continued.

"Isabel was suspected, her position was such she was privy to all the necessary information. There were a couple of other possibles and naturally they were also kept under surveillance, just in case, but she was considered the most likely. Anyway, I started work there and dropped a few hints around that, to the person concerned, would imply I was working for Bolaño and in the market. Remember my remit was to expose the whole organisation, not just one of the players. So, with the scenario set up, we decided I should go to Spain to reconnoitre. It would have the added benefit of supporting my role as a trusted operator for Bolaño. As expected, Isabel did approach me. The original plan was for Isabel to get hold of the prototype and hand it over to me, then I would go to Spain to deal with Bolaño. She told me she would hand it over at the airport. What we had not anticipated was how Isabel would react when she found Anita was coming to Spain with me. After all, it was not as if there was anything between Isabel and me. When she didn't turn up with the gadget, I started to worry. Then, it was by pure chance that I saw her checking herself in at the airport. It put me in a real quandary: should I follow her? What about the plan in Spain? Not to mention, what about you, Anita?" He looked at her. She nodded thoughtfully.

"So that was behind your sudden jumpiness at the airport." She glanced at the other two men. "I thought he was nervous of flying."

Manuel and Marco smiled, but Luke ignored them and continued firmly, "I contacted Frank, who I knew was in one of the other terminals, and asked him to come pronto and keep an eye on you. That's why when you boarded the plane, so did he." He looked at Anita and snorted, "Nervous of flying? As if!"

"Well, what else was I to think when suddenly you underwent a complete character change as soon as we arrived in the Departure Lounge?"

Before Luke could retaliate, Manuel intervened to prevent them deteriorating into a silly wrangle. "*Bueno*, we now know your side. For me, my agency heard of this product as well as rumours of two separate terrorist organisations wanting to get hold of it. We did not know which was using Bolaño as broker. My task was to get close enough to him so I could prevent it falling into any of the wrong hands. Also to make sure it is retrieved and returned to the proper authorities."

"How did you get his trust so quickly?" Luke still harboured some suspicions.

Manuel smiled slightly. "I was already working undercover in his organisation on a different long-time investigation. That was why I was chosen for this job. It was not difficult to gain his approval. Just to study his interests and to flatter him." He shrugged as if it had been easy, but Anita could see the shadows in his eyes. What had he seen or, even worse, had to do to earn that approbation?

After a pause Marco cleared his throat. "So now we have returned to the start."

When Anita looked at him questioningly, he continued. "Where is this prototype? Manuel and South have not got it. Clearly Bolaño has not got it also, or he would not be trying to find it, as you said."

Anita was struck with this insight and, looking at the others' faces, realised with a sinking feeling what Marco had meant by saying they were back at the beginning.

CHAPTER
SEVENTEEN

Tossing ideas around and picking through the most likely for potential problems took several hours. Finally, Anita stretched.

"I vote for a break and getting some lunch. I'm famished."

Marco looked at his watch. "*Sim*, you are right." He looked at them. "If it would please you, I know a good restaurant close to this hotel?"

Full agreement was signified as they all rose to their feet.

"Hope it's a fish one, so we can boost our brains," Anita quipped.

Luke smiled while the other two men appeared puzzled. She took Manuel's hand.

"There was a famous butler in literature who had a very superior brain which was put down to his regular eating of fish."

Manuel grinned. "Then, of course, we must eat the fish to make us more clever. No?" He cocked his head towards Marco who laughed.

"Of course."

Luke scribbled a quick note in case Searle returned before he got back.

They had no trouble finding a table in the restaurant Marco took them to and were soon tucking into the complimentary baskets of shellfish and bread while they waited for their orders to arrive.

"So," Manuel looked round the table. "So, we agree that our only lead is Bolaño."

Nods and grunts all round.

"So," he continued, "We must be in contact with him. We must find a plan."

After a short silence Marco spoke. "It seems like I am the only one here Bolaño does not know, therefore I should make the contact."

Manuel shook his head. "No, he is very careful all the time. But now, after all that has occurred, he will be even more on guard. Especially with people he does not know."

"In that case," Luke spoke up. "It must be either Manuel or me."

"Yes," Manuel agreed just as the waiter arrived with their food.

The meal was eaten in near silence with each occupied with their own thoughts. Finally, with their coffees in front of them, Manuel cleared his throat.

"I think it must be me." He looked at Luke. "After you did not come to meet him yesterday, he will be very suspicious and will not think he can trust you to keep a new appointment."

"Well, he's unlikely to consider you a totally trustworthy colleague either after the last few days," Luke argued.

"No, that is true," Manuel acknowledged. "But I have two advantages over you. First, I am Spanish as he is and so more familiar, a compatriot, more easy to understand."

The other two men nodded thoughtfully as he took a sip of coffee.

"What's the other reason?" Anita asked when he did not immediately continue.

"So impatient," his eyes shared a private joke with her. Satisfied when she blushed slightly, he turned his attention to the others. "Second, I will say I could not control my lust for Anita, say it blinded my good sense." He ignored an embarrassed murmur from Anita. "He also is Spanish. He will understand, even if he does not condone it. It is the Spanish nature to be hot blooded, no?"

Luke and Anita stared at him while Marco laughed.

"True, so true," he said. "But it is the Latin nature, *verdad*? Really? Not just Spanish?"

Manuel gravely accepted the correction which proved too much for the English pair who burst into laughter.

Once the merriment subsided any remaining tensions seemed to fade away as well, and they brainstormed a plan involving Manuel contacting Bolaño first thing in the morning. Frank Searle, still not having appeared, they split up with Marco checking in at his office, Luke returning to his hotel while Anita and Manuel returned to the apartment. He watched as she wandered into the kitchen and started preparing coffee to percolate. She had been uncharacteristically silent since leaving the others, not responding to any of his attempts at conversation beyond an abstracted nod or hum. With an internal grimace he wondered if he should be worried. So far she had been nothing if not unpredictable.

She opened the fridge and surveyed the contents that Marco had thoughtfully arranged to be provided for their stay.

"What about steaks, tonight?" She looked at him over her shoulder. "If so, I'll need to put them to marinate now."

He came over and pushed the door shut.

"Forget the meal for tonight. Forget the coffee. Come and talk with me." He took her hand and led her out on the balcony, sat down and pulled her onto his lap. "What is causing you so much worry, *pequeña*?"

Anita looked at him briefly then out over the street below. "Nothing. I'm just tired, I suppose."

He ruminated on her answer as he examined her averted face. "Yes, you are tired. But that is not why you are so preoccupied. Is it your friend, Isabel?"

She shrugged. "I admit that is something I'll not forget in a hurry. But she was not a friend, exactly."

"So," he gently pulled her back until she was fully leaning against him. "So what are you thinking about so hard?"

He waited patiently as she finally sighed and peeked up at him again briefly before examining her hands lying over his on her stomach.

"It's silly," she murmured.

"Then tell me this silly thing," he murmured back.

"Do you only feel lust for me, Manuel?" Her eyes swung to his.

He expelled a relieved sigh as he relaxed. "Is just that your worry?" He tightened his grip as she straightened away from him. "No, stay where you are." He took note of her discomfited expression and flushed cheeks. "Anita, of course we do not only have lust between us. You know this. You are unlike anyone else I have known—I do not know from minute to another what you will do next. You cause me worry. Because of you, my plans concerning Bolaño have all been changed, making my work much harder. But, in spite of all this, I am very happy to have you in my life."

"Oh, Manuel," she managed. "I'm so happy to be in your life too."

"But," a smile slowly pulled at his mouth. "But, I think there is also lust, much lust, between us, no?"

126

Her giggle was cut off as his mouth covered hers. When he raised his head, he looked with satisfaction at her dazed expression.

"When we were talking with the others, I was using lust as a reason for my aberrant behaviour, an excuse I will give to Bolaño."

"I know," she began.

But he continued after closing her mouth with two gentle fingers. "Also, our feelings for each other are private to us, yes?"

She nodded smiling mistily before he lowered his head to kiss her again.

Later hunger propelled them to seek out some food which they prepared together and then ate in the kitchen before taking their coffees out on to the balcony. Once again snuggled together in one chair they quietly discussed elements of the day and went over the plans for the following day. Anita could not help feeling anxiety, that something would go wrong. Bolaño frightened her even when she was not in his vicinity. She was terrified Manuel would get hurt, or worse. He tried to reassure her that he knew what he was doing.

"*Querida*, there is no need for you to have so much concern. This is my job, what I am trained to do."

"I know, I know. It's just Bolaño. He's so evil, Manuel." She was twisting his shirt unconsciously in her hands as she tried to convey her fears.

He drew her more tightly into his body using it as added comfort. He soon realised she was not going to be convinced, her fear had too firm a grip on her so finally he resorted to a strategy of distraction with his kisses and ever more intimate caresses. Soon she was aware of nothing but him.

However the balcony was not secluded and peripherally both were aware of the limitations it placed on their actions.

Eventually by mutual, albeit unspoken, agreement they broke apart and stared in each other's eyes as they gained control of their emotions and tried to steady their breathing. They disentangled and while Manuel collected their cups and locked the balcony door, Anita retired to the bedroom to undress.

She was lying under the sheet when he entered the room and watched him unabashedly as he divested himself quickly and joined her in the bed. The short interval had given them both time to regroup and Manuel set himself the task of making love to her slowly and thoroughly, refusing to give in to her demands to hurry.

"No, *Querida*. I am determined that after this you will have no doubt ever again that we have much more than just lust between us."

His words filled her heart to the extent that she feared it bursting as she wrapped herself ever more tightly around him as he kissed her deeply. He caressed her with long languorous sweeps, rediscovering her most sensitive areas while his mouth left hers to nibble and stroke her neck, edging ever downwards until it wrapped around a taut, begging nipple, causing her to jerk then sigh with pleasure. However, it was not long before she was writhing and pulling at him again, trying to push him into giving her the release that he kept tantalisingly just out of her reach. He chuckled deeply but refused to be distracted from his aim to render her demented with pleasure. It was not until she had been driven nearly insensate that he relented finally and, placing himself in position, he tilted her pelvis and entered her in one swift thrust. She screamed as her climax immediately overtook her while he held her securely and murmured assurances. When she regained her wits, it was to see him still embedded within her but stationary as he watched the emotions washing over her face as she slowly recovered.

"You are okay?" he murmured.

She smiled. "Very okay. But what about . . . ?"

His mouth briefly brushed hers, cutting off her words. "Now, for me," he whispered, lifting his head with a wicked smile.

She held on to him as he rode to his culmination, his head back with neck muscles corded. To her amazement, the feel of his warm seed pulsing inside her along with the incredibly sexy sight of his extremis, triggered her shivering body into another series of contractions that stripped her of any remaining rational thought she may have had.

As soon as he recovered enough energy, he slipped off her on to his side, gathering her body close. Listening to her breathing as it slowed, his mind relaxed to match his fully sated body as he joined her in sleep, their entangled limbs reflecting their emotional attachment to each other on a plane almost separate from their physical needs.

* * * * *

The next morning Manuel finished his coffee and rose from the table.

"I will try to telephone Bolaño now." Seeing her expression he smiled slightly as he cupped her cheek gently. "*Querida*, I cannot put it off indefinitely."

"I know. I know," she waved him away. "Just don't expect to me to like it," she muttered to his retreating back.

She quickly cleared the table, rinsing the crockery and stacking it in the dishwasher. Giving a cursory wipe over the table she left the kitchen to go and lean against the study door. Manuel was still talking, but the Spanish was far too rapid for her to have a hope of understanding it. A few moments later he finished the call. He smiled wryly at her.

"He is not happy but has agreed to a meeting." He picked up the telephone again, "Now I must call Marco and then South with this information."

Looking down, he missed the moue she could not hold back. Only now when the plan seemed to be underway did she realise how much she had banked on Bolaño not falling in with it, so that Manuel would not have to meet with him. Still, she shrugged philosophically, if it had not gone as planned, God only knew what alternative they would have come up with. She walked over and slumped into a chair as Manuel brought Marco up to speed. She was waiting for his call to Luke, at least she would understand what he was saying and hear the details of the plan. Finally the call to Luke was made.

"South, Ortega here. I have contacted Bolaño and we have arranged to meet."

She could hear Luke's voice, but not well enough to know what he was saying.

"No, not much a problem. He was suspicious, as we knew he would be, but I am sure he believed me—although he is disappointed with my 'weakness'." Manuel chuckled as he saw Anita wrinkle her nose. "We arranged to meet at the Café Nicola near to your hotel. You know of it? He does not know you are staying there, because he agreed to the venue with no hesitation. As we talked about it yesterday, I will arrive there early and sit outside in a place you can observe from your balcony."

He listened to the reply, then, "*Bueno,* Marco will bring Anita with him. For safety, I do not want her on her own until this whole problem is finished." He disconnected the call and looked at her. "So now you know all the plan. No need to worry, yes?"

She groaned and he laughed as he stood up. "Come, we must be ready for when Marco arrives. There is no time to spare."

A short time later Anita was ensconced together with Luke and Marco. Across the Praça do Rossio they could see Manuel sitting at a pavement table outside the Café Nicola. It was old, built more than two hundred years ago, according to Marco's tour guide explanation, although its present art-deco front hailed back only as far as the 1920s. Nodding politely, Anita could not help wishing Manuel was here telling her this while Marco sat at the Café waiting for Bolaño. Luke was peering through binoculars for a close-up view. Regularly he swept the area looking for a sighting of their prey. Marco smiled at her.

"It is difficult, no? Only to wait."

"You're not wrong," she responded. Then, seeing his confusion, added, "You're not wrong, so you're right. It is hard." She was not exaggerating, she felt as if there were an army of ants crawling all over her skin. Added to this, adrenaline surges kept washing through her body. The quicker Bolaño arrived, talked, left and Manuel came to join them the better.

Marco rose. "I will collect some coffee for us."

She looked surprised. "We can order through room service."

"No, it is better if I fetch it so no one knows we are here. Also your friend with his *binóculos* may seem peculiar to a room service waiter!"

She laughed in acknowledgement of that truth as he left. Luke lowered the glasses and turned to her.

"Anita, I wanted to talk with you, about us."

"We already did. You explained about the airport and everything."

"That's not what I meant. I want us to talk about you and me quite separate from all this mess," he waved a hand in the general direction of the window encompassing the view of the frontage of the café.

"I think it's too late for us, Luke. If things had been different—we'd just gone on holiday together with none of this mess as baggage, who knows? We might have grown into love or it could have just fizzled out. In any case, I'm with Manuel now." She was not about to discuss the depth or certainty of her feelings for Manuel with Luke. Added to which she felt uncomfortable and was annoyed with herself. After all, Luke had been using her at the start of this whole debacle, not the other way around.

He looked directly into her eyes. "I'm sorry it was me that got you into this. But please believe me, I never dreamed everything would become so complicated."

She nodded acceptance and he continued, "Is there any chance, once this is over and we're back in England, of us starting over again?"

She was shaking her head before he finished speaking. "No, Luke, our chance has gone. I'm pretty involved with Manuel now. I don't know how things will turn out, particularly after I return home, but I couldn't just take up with you again. Even if things between Manuel and I don't pan out, it wouldn't work now with you. I'd constantly connect you to this trip and Manuel."

"I see. Well, it looks as if he's succeeded where I failed." He had an odd expression on his face. Regret? Sort of, but not quite. Before she could interpret it further, it smoothed away as he continued, "I'm sorry as I really think we would be good together. But I understand what you say." He turned to pick up the binoculars again as he added, "I just hope he is on the up and up and not just using you."

"That's pretty hypocritical considering your actions. And, for your information, Manuel has been honest with me from the start, and not let me down once." Her spirited defence broke off as the door opened to admit Marco bearing a small tray of coffees.

Anita turned back to Luke who gave her a small smile. "Pax?" he murmured.

Marco glanced at their faces as he moved to a table to deposit his tray. He could obviously feel the undercurrents in the atmosphere that were thick enough to touch.

"Everything is OK, no?" he began, then straightening quickly he pointed out of the window. "That is Bolaño, yes?"

Luke swiftly raised his glasses before confirming. "And it looks like he's not alone."

The three watched as Bolaño paused to say something to his bodyguard before moving on by himself to join Manuel at his table. They all looked on in silence for awhile, then Marco and Anita selected a coffee each as they waited for the meeting to conclude. Finally Luke put down the glasses and picked up the remaining coffee.

"It's over. Bolaño's gone and Ortega will be here soon." He took a sip, pulling a face as it was now cold, but finishing it nevertheless.

Shortly afterwards a knock at the door heralded the arrival of Manuel. Anita opened the door and flew into his arms. He gave her a squeeze and murmured into her ear, making her giggle. Coming further into the room with his arm about her shoulders he greeted the two men.

"It was good. We are progressing." He sat down on the sofa keeping Anita tight beside him as he started to recount what had transpired.

"Bolaño was especially perturbed by you," he nodded at Luke, "not turning up for your meeting yesterday. He felt, for sure, that you would come even if only to save Anita from him." He smiled slightly, "He made no mention of not having

Anita under his control any more. This makes me think he is not sure if you have her, I have her or if she got away on her own and nobody knows where she is!"

Anita pulled a face, "Makes me feel like a lost parcel!"

Manuel briefly hugged her closer, "But a very valuable one."

Marco cleared his throat meaningfully to bring Manuel's attention back to the subject.

"Ah, *si*. As well as South, he is also displeased with me, taking Anita away from his house against his wishes. I explained I had to get her apart from him as he clearly frightened her and she would not cooperate while he was around. Bolaño now is very wary of you, South. He wonders if you are a loose cannon, working for yourself or, even worse from his point of view, from a law agency. He told me he had a telephone call last night. He says he does not know who the caller is—that he only identified himself as a 'main player'. Manuel paused to let this sink in before continuing. "Anyway, this caller said that Isabel had taken the prototype and passed it on to him."

He looked at Marco. "Bolaño has ordered me to find the prototype and report to him immediately. He wants no more mistakes and warned this was my last chance."

CHAPTER
EIGHTEEN

A short silence reigned as they all digested Manuel's information.

"Who is this 'main player'?" Manuel directed them to the crux of the problem.

"Maybe he has direct access to information from Bolaño," Luke mused.

"You mean a spy in his camp?" Anita looked interested.

"Yeah, something like that. Although I have to say it seems unlikely," Luke responded.

"I agree," Manuel said. "I have worked with him for some months and I am sure if there had been another 'spy' like me, I would have known. Or, at least, had a feeling something was not right."

Marco looked at his watch. "From what I have seen, I also agree it is unlikely. I must leave you now to check in at the station, but will contact you later, Manuel, to learn your decision."

"*Bueno. Oiré de tu luego entonces.*" Manuel confirmed he would hear from him later.

As Marco left, Luke put forward another suggestion. "Could Bolaño be making it up—about this mystery caller?"

"Why? What would be the point?" Anita asked.

"To muddy the waters. Create confusion. Get us thinking in one area, while he moves in another."

"No," Manuel's voice was sure. "He does not work like that. Oh, he can be subtle and misdirect, only that this that you suggest is not his style."

"Just a passing thought." Luke looked at Manuel. "What about Marco?"

Slightly startled, Manuel counter-suggested, "I could ask about Searle."

Anita added, "I don't like Frank. He's sort of creepy."

Luke sighed. "You're biased after he brought you here against your will when collecting you off the street."

"Not just that. I found him creepy on the plane right from the beginning. Then there was when he tracked me to Manuel's village."

"Oh, for God's sake. He was acting on my orders."

"Still," her voice turned mutinous. "I'm telling you he gives me the willies."

"*Calme*," Manuel sandwiched her hand in both of his.

Luke sighed again. "Look, I've known Frank for over five years. We've worked together before on cases. He may not be my most favourite person in the world, but he's all right. Plus I can guarantee he is a member of the police working from Scotland Yard." His eyes rested on Manuel. "The problem is obviously more likely from this end, especially as they tried—and succeeded—in discrediting me with Bolaño."

Manuel cocked his head as he considered this carefully. Anita respected that he did not immediately defend against the accusation, but weighed it against his own conviction. It just increased her admiration and, what she was increasingly sure of, her love for him.

Finally he responded. "*Bueno*. I am confident in Marco, but also I have not known him for so long—a few months only. So, I agree to make enquiries. But," he looked hard into Luke's eyes. "But you must as well investigate Searle. He may be a member of your police, but that does not guarantee where his loyalties lie."

There was a brief silence as the two men stared at each other before Luke shrugged and turned to look out of the window. "Fine. I'll look into it."

The tension broken, Anita relaxed and let the two men discuss further on what Bolaño had said and what their next actions should be.

* * * * *

Manuel and Anita returned later to the apartment to find some food. They had missed lunch and the lack had caught up with them. They worked well in the kitchen, synchronising automatically as they moved about putting together a simple but filling meal of soup, hot rolls, poached fish with baby potatoes, cucumbers and some tinned peas. Finally, they sat down and applied themselves to it. Once the initial pangs had been satisfied Anita looked across the table at Manuel.

"I really don't trust Frank Searle. I'm sure he's in on it with Bolaño in some way."

"Do not disturb yourself. Luke will check him, as I will check Marco, even though I am completely sure Marco is not involved."

She cocked her head. "How will you go about checking him out?"

"At the police station. Do not worry, I know how to do this! You will come with me, yes? I must keep you close to me so I know you are safe."

She grimaced. "Honestly, it's not as if I go looking for trouble."

He smiled ruefully. "No, it finds you with no effort!" He raised an eyebrow, "You do not wish to accompany me tomorrow?"

"Of course I do. I can't wait to see how a clever detective goes about checking on Marco!"

He grinned and silence fell for a short while as they carried on with their meal.

Anita frowned. "Do you have any idea about where the prototype is? Who's got it?"

"No, I do not know where it is. I have some small suspicions, but I cannot be sure."

"Who? Where do you think it is?"

"I will not say until I am sure. I have to find out first."

"But, Manuel, just to me. You can tell me. I won't say a word to anyone."

"No, it would not be right." He smiled at her peevish expression. "Come, Anita, you know I would be wrong to tell you because I may not be correct."

After looking hard at him for a moment, she relented. "Okay, okay. But I think you're mean. Anyone would think you didn't believe I'd keep quiet about it until it was proved."

He laid his hand over hers on the table. "It is not that, *Querida*. Believe me. It is only a suspicion, not a fact."

She squeezed his hand in reply. "I know." She understood. It was linked to his notions of honour, which she was beginning to realise were very strong.

After they finished eating and everything had been cleared away and the kitchen was once again spic and span, the afternoon stretched before them with nothing to do regarding the case until the next morning. Anita was feeling the crash after the recent stresses, so they decided to take a couple of towels and some bottled water to the beach and replenish their reserves while absorbing some vitamin D along with UV rays.

*　*　*　*　*

The next morning after a leisurely breakfast on the balcony, Manuel prepared to keep his part of the bargain with Luke. Anita accompanied him partly because of his new "keep her safe with him at all times" policy and partly she was intrigued about how he would verify that Marco was as advertised. Added to which the mindless previous afternoon had done its work on relaxing her so well, she was now practically bouncing with enthusiasm. He could not help thinking that if such vigour could only be distilled and bottled for sale, it would make a fortune.

The taxi deposited them outside a nondescript building in the outskirts of the city. Manuel approached the desk near the entrance, gave his name and showed his credentials before asking for the use of a phone.

"Who are you going to call?" Anita trailed after him to the telephone sitting on the corner of the long reception desk. "And why can't you use your own phone?"

"It is possible my phone is compromised so it is safer if I use a different one to call my superior in Spain. I must ask him for the name of the head of the department that Marco works in. To check it is the same as Marco mentioned."

"And that's it? You could have done that with the phone in the apartment."

He smiled and tapped her nose gently. "No, it is not all." He paused while pressing out the number, then looked into her waiting face. "Once this is confirmed, I need to speak with Marco's boss, and that will be easier if my superior "introduces" me first." As the call was answered, he turned away and began speaking in Spanish. Anita sighed and turned to lean against the desk while she perused the depressingly bland pictures on the wall opposite as she waited for Manuel to finish.

Finally, he hung up.

"Everything okay?"

"*Si*," he smiled at her to hide an inner grimace. His *jefe* had made his displeasure crystal clear about Manuel's deviation from the previously meticulously planned operation, particularly in connection with Anita. It had taken some quick talking to assure him that leaving Bolaño had been a necessary strategy once her unexpected entry into the equation had occurred and that his boss should, in fact, be congratulating his initiative. He was pretty sure he had not succeeded completely in this endeavour, but at least by the end of the call cordial relations had returned more or less to an even keel. In any event his boss had agreed to contact Luiz Cordeiro, Marco's superior.

"We need to wait a short time, to allow my boss to contact Cordeiro here," he explained as he opened his small leather notebook and made a few notations.

Finally, with a gentle push he guided her back to the receptionist and asked him for an interview with Cordeiro. The receptionist made a call and Anita was not surprised when, with no delay, they were escorted to his office, where they were greeted politely and offered refreshment before Cordeiro got down to business. The two men spoke in English in deference to Anita.

It was shortly apparent that Marco was bona fide and had kept Cordeiro aware of events as they unfolded. Manuel brought him completely up-to-date, including possible suspicions regarding Marco and Searle. Coreiro had no hesitation in supporting Marco unequivocally.

"One of my best men. You should not worry concerning him. He will never betray you."

Following the cordial mutual thanks and pleasantries that Anita now recognized as an integral element of Latin etiquette, she and Manuel left. They found a bench to sit on while they considered what they had learned.

"Well," Anita honed in on the main objective of their interview. "At least we know Marco is exactly who we thought."

"*Si*, but in truth I never considered he was not." He smiled at her face-pulling. "But you are right, it is good to know for sure." Glancing at his watch he held his hand out to her. "Come, we will go to a café and relax with a coffee while we think of how to use our day."

Anita took his hand and fell into step beside him feeling her spirits lighten They were not meeting up with the others until the evening which gave them the rest of the day to themselves.

"I vote we forget about this whole damn business," Anita beamed at him.

He laughed.

They chose a café and were soon settled with drinks accompanied by a plate of ultra sweet pastries.

"You know the statue of Cristo Rei," Manuel sipped his coffee and relaxed back into his chair.

"The huge one that's lit up at night so Jesus appears suspended in the sky?"

"*Si*. If you like we can cross the river and go to see it very close up."

She nodded. "I could do with some sightseeing without worrying about this whole mess."

He leant forward to stop her talking by placing a finger over her mouth. "No. We do not speak of this at all for today. We are only tourists until this night."

She kissed his finger. "You're right. So, now we know what we're going to do today, what shall we talk about?" With care she selected a pastry stuffed with cream and covered in icing sugar to put on her plate.

Manuel looked startled before giving a surprised laugh. "Now we will not be able to think of any topic to talk about!"

She swallowed, savouring the rich taste from her pastry. "We can talk about you. Considering our relationship," she looked to see if this term discomposed him at all. But his face only portrayed interest, so she continued. "Well, I know very little about you. I know where you were brought up and that you work for Interpol. But I don't know your interests, what you like doing for fun. What music you listen to, the type of films you watch, your family, friends." She grinned. "So, tell me all!"

He shrugged with expanded arms as he considered where to start. "Music, I like many kinds, except perhaps the modern R & B. Books, I like the biography, yes?"

She nodded in encouragement.

"Films, I like action and sometimes the comedies. I have a big family, many uncles, aunts and cousins. We have many parties for birthdays, holidays, celebrations and I go when I can. They are noisy with lots of food, sometimes we argue, but always we love each other." He smiled. "They will like you."

A little discomposed, she flushed slightly and ducked her head. "Sounds great, although I imagine they're quite daunting to meet at first!"

He refuted this firmly and went on to entertain her with stories about some of the antics he and his cousins had got up to while growing up. Finally, he leaned forward and gestured to the plate holding the remaining pastries. "You have eaten sufficient?" When she nodded he continued, "I have talked enough about me, I think. Come, finish your coffee and we will go to be tourists."

Obeying automatically, for some reason this seemed natural and fleetingly she paused inwardly. Always it seemed to be Manual in charge. Then, pushing it to the back of her mind to be examined later, she glanced at her watch and frowned.

"Is this a good time? It'll soon be midday and too hot."

He shook his head. "Believe me, noon is the best time to view this statue close up."

They found a taxi to take them over the river on the 25 Abril bridge and on to the site of the towering edifice. Soon afterwards they were standing on the top of the pedestal.

"*Mira*, look up," Manuel put his arm round her shoulders. Craning her neck she immediately understood his insistence on coming here at the hottest time of the day. She had thought the night image of Jesus appearing to hover over the city was impressive, but now the sun, slightly behind the 90ft statue, imbued it with a celestial glow that was stunningly atmospheric.

He smiled at her rapt expression. "It is worth coming to see, no? Even with the hot sun?"

"Oh yes," she looked at him. "I just wish I'd brought a camera with me."

"There is no need. There are many post cards with pictures of Cristo Rei taken at all different times from different angles."

"Still, it would have been nice to have taken my own—proof I was here!"

Laughing gently, he directed her to look below. "This, too, is worth pictures."

She gazed down at the views of the Tejo River, the 25 Abril bridge they had just been driven over, and then over to see the city of Lisbon stretched out beyond, and could only agree.

When they came down to earth again literally they caught a bus to where they could return to the capital by ferry.

"Just to be sure you have the full tourist experience!" Manual teased her.

After a cold drink and a sandwich, they still had several hours before meeting with the others.

"Is there somewhere you would like to see?"

"I don't know what there is, but somewhere soothing and, if possible, cool. It's absolutely boiling."

Manuel thought for a moment. "We can visit a museum or," he quickly carried on as she wrinkled her nose. "Or we can go to Parque Eduardo VII."

"A park," Anita immediately had visions of cool grass, shady trees and gentle breezes. "Yes, that sounds good."

"*Bueno*," taking her arm he guided her out of the restaurant and shortly was able to hail a taxi.

"This *parque* was named for one of your kings," he informed her as the taxi sped through the traffic.

"Edward VII, I presume," she sassed. She was enjoying their day, even more than she had anticipated. Manuel was a terrific companion; interesting, surprisingly knowledgeable about a city that he did not live in, and best of all totally focussed on her. The only drawback was within her. She was increasingly sure she was falling in love. She snorted slightly. It was hardly an ongoing thing. If she was really honest with herself, she knew she was already in love with him—totally and irrevocably. Although he occasionally made comments that she interpreted as him intending to pursue a future with her, such as them returning to Barcelona together when this problem was behind them, he had not actually said so in as many words. For all she knew, he was always this intense during his many serial monogamous relationships. And, of course, there was his job. Not really a career tailor-made for connubial bliss in the long term, was it? She sniffed as she mentally pulled herself together. She was not going to let such lowering thoughts spoil the day, time enough for retrospection later. She smiled determinedly at Manuel.

"So tell me about this park."

"At night it has a very bad reputation, but in the day it is a beautiful green island in the middle of the city." His hand holding hers, began to gently stroke over her wrist. "Often exhibitions or concerts are held in it, although not at this time. But I will show you something special." He leant forward to give further instructions to their driver.

Soon they arrived and entered the north west area of the park and Manuel led her to an edifice.

"This is named the Estufa Fria." He paid their admission and they entered the huge greenhouse supported by iron and wood. "There are three sections, but this is the coolest," he explained.

Together they meandered along the gravel paths hemmed in by a wonderful variety of green foliage interspersed with small pools containing a variety of fish and statues, waterfalls and streams that they crossed over on bridges with uneven steps. They paused to examine some of the exotic plants that came from all over the world. The whole ambience was completed with strutting peacocks that disdainfully ignored them. The coolness in temperature intensified by the diverse greenery and sound of gentle water movements soon began to work their refreshing magic.

Manuel told her something of the work of Gonçalo Ribeiro Telles, the landscape architect whose work they were enjoying. She smiled inwardly as she listened, he really was a mixture of warrior and artistic aficionado—a real Renaissance man.

Most of the time, however, passed in an intimate silence, occasionally broken by one or the other to direct attention to a particular item of interest. By the time they emerged back into the stifling outside world, they felt reinvigorated, both spiritually and physically, and therefore more capable of dealing with their waiting problems.

CHAPTER
NINETEEN

They had returned to the flat to freshen up and change clothes. It was early evening as, hand in hand, Manuel and Anita strolled the tree-lined streets to the restaurant which was the venue arranged for meeting with the others. The fierce heat from earlier had gone leaving the evocative odour of salted fish drying ebbing as the soft light of encroaching darkness covered the city, throwing a cloak of romanticism over it to replace the bustle of business that filled its days.

In the restaurant they found Luke already seated with a beer in front of him. A waiter materialized, ascertained what drinks they wanted and provided them smartly.

"Where's Marco?" Luke asked.

"I gave him a little later time," Manuel responded. "So we could more easily discuss him and Searle."

"Oh, fine. Good idea." Luke picked up his mug. "So did you have any luck?"

Manuel succinctly gave him a run down on their activities that morning. "So I am sure he cannot be Bolaño's 'main player'. What about Searle?"

Luke hunched over the table looking unhappy. "I don't know what to think. First off, I can't find him. I even contacted his division in London, but they haven't heard from him over the last couple of days. They didn't appear worried, he was given a free rein for this operation. However, they had no hesitation in affirming full confidence in him. Apparently, he often disappears from the radar for short periods while working in the field. Plus they assumed, naturally, he and I were working together." He grimaced. "I have to say I also thought that." He looked straight at Manuel. "I'm afraid the combination of his continued absence and lack of communication is odd. I've been contactable, but I can't get any answer to my calls and he has not returned any of my messages. Still, I can't believe it's him, I've known him for years on and off and, of course, his colleague I spoke to said this "disappearance" thing is not that unusual for him."

He leant back in his chair. A short silence ensued until broken by Manuel. "I think we shall assume he is our problem, but," he continued with a raised hand as Luke shifted to interrupt. "We will keep our options open, yes?"

Luke sighed. Realistically, it was the best he could have hoped for as, to be honest, if it had been Marco who had gone AWOL, he was not sure he would have been so forbearing.

Silence descended again as they sipped their drinks, each immersed in their own thoughts. Finally, Luke engaged Anita. "So what have you been doing today?"

She perked up and described their visit to the Cristo Rei.

"Yes, I've been up there on a previous trip here. Very impressive. Did you go over the bridge that looks like the Golden Gate in San Francisco?"

"We did, but it's not the Golden Gate, it's the San Francisco—Oakland Bay bridge it resembles." She grinned at Manuel before turning to Luke again. "It's a common misapprehension."

Manuel laughed. "Good, you remember my teachings. I was thinking it was so hot maybe your brain could not work so well!"

Luke smiled as Anita gave Manuel a mock punch just as Marco turned up at their table. He pulled out a chair and sat down. Gesturing to their nearly empty drinks he asked, "I am late?"

"No, no. We were early," Luke assured him.

The waiter appeared on cue to take his order and soon the discussion resumed. Manuel addressed Marco. "We seem to have lost contact with Searle. Have you any ideas?"

Anita expanded for him. "Apparently this is not unusual for him. His colleagues are used to it."

Luke grimaced. "Still, I would prefer he kept us—or at least me—in the loop. It would be a right mess if we all played outside the box."

"Rather like," Anita could not help interjecting. "When you and Manuel were working independently, each wasting time and energy thinking of the other as the enemy, when you were both on the same track!"

"No," Luke snapped. "Not like that. Frank and I are supposed to be a team."

"No more arguing," Manuel addressed Anita directly, but included Luke. "We do not have the time for it."

After a short loaded silence, Luke sighed. "You're right. Okay, what do we do about Frank?"

Manuel looked at Marco who glanced at Luke with a shrug as if to say it was Luke's problem. Anita sipped from her glass as she stared pensively across the street. Just then Manuel's phone rang.

"*Sim*," he answered. As he listened, he mouthed the name Bolaño at the others. They all directed concentrated attention to Manuel's side of the conversation, but Anita soon retreated to her introspection as she could make nothing of it.

Finally, the call ended and Manuel, after scribbling in his notebook, addressed his avid audience.

"Bolaño has heard from a new contact, although he is not sure if it is a new contact or his "main player". Either way, this contact says he has the prototype. That he got it from Isabel Davenport. He wants to make an exchange for the prototype. His problem is he does not want to give the money—it is a lot of money, even for him—unless he is sure he is getting the real thing."

He looked round at all of them who nodded impatiently. It made him smile slightly, but he continued. "Bolaño has told me to negotiate with the contact, to get him the prototype with no more time wasted. The deadline for when he is supposed to supply it to his buyer is coming *rapidamente*. He has given me the number to reach the contact and I should do this now."

"Wait," Luke said quickly. He glanced at each of them briefly. "We should have some sort of plan in place, so we're not just following this other man's agenda."

Manuel nodded. "I understand. My plan is to arrange a meeting to exchange Bolaño's money for the prototype. I will try to choose the place." There was some doubt in his voice over the last sentence.

"Suppose he insists on somewhere else?"

"I do not think he will be difficult, although I am sure he will wish to take precautions. We know it is urgent for Bolaño—maybe he does too. But," he held up a hand to forestall interruptions heralded by drawn-in breaths. "But at least Bolaño has a buyer, and Bolaño is this contact's only possible buyer, at least as far as we know."

"What's to stop him going direct, cutting out Bolaño as the middle man?"

"He does not know the identity of Bolaño's buyer. As far as I know, Bolaño has kept this information to himself." He shook his head slightly. "Also, I think he must know of

Bolaño's reputation. I would not like to be the one facing his anger, his vengeance."

Anita shuddered. She remembered how he had dealt with Isabel, and that had not been in anger, but expediency. Just a piece of business to tidy up. What he was likely to do in a fury, she would rather not even attempt to imagine. A sudden thought crossed her mind. "I bet the visitor that came to Bolaño's flat to see him and Isabel is his buyer."

She had their undivided attention, and after a moment Manuel asked softly, "What can you tell us about him?"

She shrugged. "Nothing. I was tied up in another room."

Luke exploded. "What sort of information is that?"

She frowned at him. "It just occurred to me, so I told you."

Manuel sighed. "Please, enough quarrelling." He turned to Anita. "Although it would be good to have more information, if you had seen him it may have gone badly for you."

Luke slumped back into his chair. "You're right. Sorry, Anita, it's probably just tension, but I shouldn't have snapped at you."

Anita nodded acknowledgement and gripped Manuel's hand under the table. God, she might have joined Isabel. Another thought came to her, she would never have guessed that she could be grateful to Bolaño for being restrained and gagged as she had been. Manuel returned the pressure on her hand both to comfort and reassure her.

Breaking the short silence Manuel went on, "If Bolaño does not get the item in time to sell to his buyer, he will not want it—that means this man is left holding a stolen item with no buyer but still with the law forces of three countries and Interpol tracking him down." He leaned back in the chair with a rueful grin. "Of course this means Bolaño will also be coming after me!"

Anita jolted upright. "Don't joke about him."

He stroked her hand. "Do not worry, *Pequeña*, we will work to be sure this case is resolved with no one being hurt."

She smiled uncertainly. She was sure Isabel had thought she had everything under control too. Catching Manuel's eye, she stiffened her sinew. Of course that was Isabel, this was Manuel. He was experienced in this sort of work. Also he had back-up in Luke and Marco—also experienced. Her smile became more genuine. "You're right. We will all help you."

He squeezed her hand to convey his acknowledgement even as he inwardly shuddered at the thought of her being actively involved with either Bolaño or his contact at this stage of the operation. He turned his attention back to the others. "So, I shall phone to make the arrangements, yes?"

The other two men nodded and Manuel began to punch out the number Bolaño had given him.

Marco smiled reassuringly at Anita. "Do not worry. Events are moving to a finish."

"Yes," Luke added his tuppenceworth. "This will all be over soon and you'll be able to look back on it as a grand adventure. Plenty to tell your friends!" He winked.

She smiled as appreciatively as she could. They were only trying to be kind. She felt torn in two directions. It was just that once this whole episode was over, on the one hand Manuel would be safe. On the other hand, he would go back to Spain—he'd probably have to, so he could be debriefed or whatever they did. Anyway he would have to complete reams of paperwork undoubtedly and all this would take time. She would return home and get on with her life. At the moment her old life seemed unreal—with her present life full of excitement and colour and appearing more substantial; she felt more alive than ever before. Would she see Manuel again? Once he was free, he may only remember her as the girl caught up in his work, with whom he had enjoyed a pleasant time. She sniffed as she took herself to task. This was not the time to wallow in self-pity. She and Manuel were both still here together and there were more important matters to fret over at the moment.

CHAPTER TWENTY

Manuel's call was answered quickly and everyone fell silent. It was soon apparent the discussion was in English. Anita glanced at Luke, but his attention was fixed on Manuel, his own face giving nothing away.

"I am told by Señor Bolaño to make arrangements with you for the exchange." Manuel's voice was calm and unhurried. "If you wish to check with him, that is your choice. But I warn you he is not happy how things go. He is in a hurry for the item, did he not tell you so?"

A pause during which they could hear the buzz of a voice, but not what was said.

"*Bueno*. We progress." Manuel listened before agreeing perfunctorily and breaking the connection.

He looked at the others. "I am to meet him by the amphitheatre in the Jardim Gulbenkian and hold a copy of newspaper *Publico* by my face for him to recognize me." He shrugged slightly. "Of course, I must be alone, not tell anyone." He grinned. "He has watched too many movies, I think!"

"Was it Frank?" Anita inserted.

"I cannot be sure. Of course he spoke in English—but not good English. Still," his eyes became unfocused as he concentrated. "Still I would think he is English trying to disguise he is English." He looked at Luke. "If he was Spanish or Portuguese, I do not see why he wanted to talk in English. Of course he may be a different nationality altogether and using English as a *lingua franca*."

Everyone conveyed agreement by nods. "In any case, he is very nervous. He will check with Bolaño it is not a trap and I expect our actual meeting will happen someplace else."

"What do you mean?" Anita asked as the other two men nodded.

"He will ring me at the garden after he has checked I am alone." Manuel explained as he took her hand. "We will have a nice meal here, yes? Then tomorrow I will leave you in the apartment. You will stay there and promise to wait for the exchange to be over."

She glanced at the other two men. "I could stay with them," she began.

"No. Not possible," Luke answered. "We will have our parts to play and you'd just be in the way." The other two men winced at his tactlessness.

"I could help," she now appealed to Marco. "I could keep watch or something."

"Anita," Manuel's voice was soft but distinctly underlined with steel. "It is not an option. It is necessary for me to know you are safe, so I am not distracted. You understand?"

She held out for a few moments before caving in, although not without a final muttered, "It's not fair. After everything that's happened, I get to miss the end."

Relieved by her capitulation, he grinned at her disgruntled expression. "It will not be exciting. I will meet with him. We make the exchange. We get up and walk apart from each other. Boring, no?"

She chuckled. "I'm not stupid. He'll be followed and taken down, but," she continued hurriedly as it looked as if he were about to interrupt. "But I'll be good and do as you all seem to want."

"*Gracias, Querida*. I will make it up to you." He cupped her cheek as his eyes reinforced his words spoken in the low voice that never failed to set her body on fire.

The sensuous mood was broken as Luke opened the menu and heartily asked Marco if there was anything special he should order.

* * * * *

It was late when Manuel unlocked the door to the apartment before standing aside to let Anita precede him inside.

"You have been most quiet, Anita. This worries me!"

She turned as the front door closed and rewarded his teasing with a half-hearted smile.

"I feel a bit left out and at the same time I can't help worrying."

He pulled her into his arms. "Truly, there is no necessity. As I told you earlier, it will most likely be very boring."

"Yes, 'most likely'. What if it isn't so smooth? Oh hell, Manuel, nothing has gone as planned all along. Why would you think it will now?"

He rubbed her back soothingly while she let the steady beat of his heart against her ear add its calming influence. Finally he grasped her arms and moved her away so he could meet her eyes.

"In fact, the operation was going very well until a *problema* with brown hair and beautiful eyes arrived," his hands slipped down her arms until he clasped her hands. "She upset all my plans and continued to keep getting into trouble!"

She groaned. "It wasn't my fault. I didn't cause them!"

"No," he surprised her by agreeing. "Most of the time you were just in the wrong place. This is why tomorrow I wish you to remain here, so no trouble can find you."

She threw up her hands as she turned for the kitchen. "I've already said I'll stay here, but I'm going to want a blow-by-blow account of everything that happens afterwards," she warned mock fiercely.

"That I agree to," he followed her.

"Do you want a coffee or some brandy?" She hesitated by the cupboards.

He came close, took her hand and raised it to his lips. "What I would like is you. Now."

She was mesmerized by his eyes. God, he was sex personified when he stared at her like that while speaking in that low, compelling, slightly accented voice.

"Well?" he smiled.

Her breath left in a gust. "Lead the way." Not very romantic, but she felt it an achievement that she had managed any reply at all.

In silence, hand in hand, they moved to the bedroom. He undressed her with ease taking only a few moments to weigh her breasts as they were released from her bra. Leaving one hand to support a breast with his thumb flicking over the nipple, he let the other hand run down her abdomen to briefly cup her sex. Her heart pounded as her head dropped back against his chest. Immediately he removed both hands to gently push her upright.

"Get onto the bed," his voice was slightly hoarse which only excited her more as she stumbled to obey him. Lying back she watched as he quickly divested himself before coming to lie beside her. Propped up on one elbow, he did not touch her initially, instead his eyes devoured her body until at last he stroked from her shoulder down to her hip. As his hand touched her she jerked, as if being released from some spell of paralysis. She reached for his shoulders to pull him down so she could press his mouth with her own in a carnal kiss. He groaned as her whole body began to writhe in response to his caresses that became ever more harder and tantalizing. Soon it was impossible to tell where one was separate from the other. The warm air, being languorously stirred by the overhead fan, was for some time filled with groans, the sound of bodies shifting against each other, and whispered words of demand and encouragement.

Much later Anita lay with Manuel, who was fast asleep, wrapped around her. She stared into the darkness. She had no idea how she would ever be able to give him up. Not without losing a vital part of herself in the process anyway. She sighed. No use borrowing trouble, as her mother would say. Feeling some comfort from that thought, she relaxed completely and soon drifted off to sleep.

* * * * *

The next morning Anita saw Manuel off at the street-level entrance to the building. She forced herself not to whine, but all the time stretching ahead while he would be gone with nothing for her to do but wait was going to drive her insane. At the last minute she broke.

"Manuel, I've been think . . ."

His mouth covering hers stopped her. As he drew back, he smiled. "You will stay, please. This way I know you are safe."

Her shoulders sagged as finally she accepted defeat. "All right. But I expect to be rewarded for being left out like this."

His hand cupped her cheek. "I will reward you. I promise." The sultry look in his eyes backed up his words, mesmerizing her momentarily.

Stepping back, she laughed shakily. "I'll hold you to that!"

He grinned before turning to walk to the corner where it was easier to find a taxi. She watched until his figure disappeared out of sight, then turned to go back into the building and came face to face with a man standing in the entrance.

"Miss Wright, how good of you to make things easier for me. I thought for sure I'd have to break into your apartment."

Shocked, first by the use of her name, then by the realization he was English, and finally by fear. She opened her mouth to scream on the off-chance Manuel would hear, or failing that, to attract any attention that could help her.

A slight movement by the man, however, revealed a handgun before it returned into his pocket. The brief glimpse was enough though to force her to abandon that idea.

"Good choice." He gestured with his free hand towards a car parked across the street. "Over there. You'll drive."

"I'm not sure I'm allowed to drive here, or is an English licence accepted here?" She saw his face darkening. "Never mind."

They crossed the road and got in the car. He handed her the keys and she started the engine. She felt nauseous as fear and disgust churned within her. God, how could this keep happening to her? Then the thought of what Manuel would say nearly made her giggle hysterically. He would never believe it if he knew what had happened seconds after he had left her. But he didn't, no one did. Everyone thought she was shut up safely in the apartment until the action was over. To be honest, at the moment she wished she was.

"Turn right at the end of the road." Her captor broke up her whirling thoughts. She engaged the gear and started off.

"Do as you're told and, so long as your boyfriend doesn't try any tricks, you'll be fine."

She swallowed as she made the turn as directed. She had no faith in his assurances. She was going to have to extricate herself once again, and do it before the others arrested Frank Searle or whoever turned up to make the exchange. So much for worrying about Manuel, she had too much to do herself to have time.

* * * * *

Manuel made a brief stop to get wired up so Marco and Luke could hear what was going down and Luke could record it. Then the taxi took him to the arranged spot where one of Bolaño's men gave him a briefcase with the money to make the exchange. Finally, he arrived at the designated venue in the Jardim Gulbenkian, buying a copy of *Publico* from a newsstand at the entrance. He had only been there for a minute or so before his mobile rang.

"*Diga me,*" he answered.

"You are prompt. That is good." The voice still sounded disguised as it gave new coordinates for the meeting before abruptly hanging up.

* * * * *

Following instructions, Anita drove through Estoril on the serpentine coast road, finally stopping before a small run-down property. She killed the engine and turned to her passenger who held out his hand.

"Give me the keys."

She did and he got out of the car, came round and opened her door in an ironical show of manners.

"Come on." He grasped her arm and propelled her to the front door. She looked round. No one was near enough to help. There were plenty of people on the beach on the other side of the road, but it was pointless shouting for help. He still had the gun and she would be bundled inside the house before they reacted. And, in any case, it was unlikely they would hear from this distance.

Inside the building she was taken upstairs and pushed into a room before the door slammed shut. She heard the key locking her in. She stayed quite still until eventually hearing his footsteps retreat down the stairs. She looked round the small room, no other exit apart from the window. She approached and opened it. No helpful tree this time. She looked down. The ground seemed quite a way down, although there were some shrubs, of a vigorous nature her father would say. She could have used them to soften her jump. It was all academic, however, as the window was securely framed with iron bars.

Now what? she thought. There was nothing in the room she could use as a tool or weapon. There was nothing in the room, period. Not even a chair to sit on.

* * * * *

Manuel was becoming really ticked off. Twice more, on reaching a new venue, he was directed to the next. His phone rang yet again, he flipped it open.

"*Basta,* enough. I begin to think you do not have the goods."

"I have it. Go and sit on the bench opposite the ice cream vendor." The phone disconnected.

Manuel looked round, saw the bench and ice cream cart and headed in that direction. His eye caught a man sloping towards a tree to lean against, then opening and apparently reading a newspaper. He recognized him as one of Bolaño's henchmen. Pretending not to have noticed him he continued to the designated bench. He wondered with grim humour who Bolaño did not trust—the contact or him?

He sat down with his paper clearly visible. He did not have long to wait before, to no great surprise, Frank slipped onto the seat beside him. For a moment the two looked at each other in silence, broken eventually by Frank.

"I should have known. You certainly played me for a fool in that fishing village." He pulled a face while Manuel maintained both his silence and kept his face expressionless. After a pause, Frank sighed then continued. "Still to business, I know how these things are played, so I have insurance." Manuel arched a brow, so he elaborated. "I have Anita tucked up safely. In case you don't believe me, try ringing her."

Manuel maintained his expression with difficulty as rage swept through him, divided equally against Frank and with Anita for obviously not keeping her promise to stay safely in the apartment.

"You've got the money?"

Manuel gestured to the briefcase beside his feet. Frank hesitated a moment, then retrieved a small box from his pocket and handed it over. But when he stretched to reach the briefcase Manuel stopped him.

"Wait. I must examine this first, to be sure." He opened the box. A few seconds later he pushed the briefcase towards the other man. "You will let Anita go now."

Frank opened the briefcase slightly, just enough to see the money and flick a couple of bundles of notes.

"Not yet. In an hour, once I'm safely away and have had time to check the money properly, I'll send instructions to let her go and ring you with the address."

"If any harm comes to her," Manuel began.

"Yes, I know. Don't worry. I have no reason to hurt her, so long as all this is in order." He tapped the briefcase. With a nod he rose and walked away. Manuel remained seated. This was a signal for Marco and Luke to follow but not intercept him. They would have heard the conversation anyway. His emotions were making him jumpy. He desperately needed to do something, anything, to get Anita back safely into his care. The way he was feeling at the moment, he would tie her down and lock her in. It seemed only such measures would keep her under control.

His phone rang.

* * * * *

Anita leaned against the wall as she stared disconsolately out of the window into the distance. Her fingers betrayed her tension by drumming on the window frame. A sudden piercing pain broke her reverie. Raising her hand she saw a large splinter had become wedged under her nail. Quickly she grasped it and pulled it out with one firm tug. It was followed by a stream of blood and she stuck the throbbing finger in her mouth and sucked hard both to clear the blood and to try to ease the pain. She looked down at the wooden frame and realized it was old and rotten. Her spirits perked up as she pushed at the frame, easily crumbling bits off it. After several minutes of frenetic picking and fragmenting the wood she leant out to examine the iron bars. They, too, were old and rusty, but remained intact despite her efforts. Just as she was about to throw in the towel she saw, in the corner of her eye, movement. Peering more closely she realized the bar grille was attached to the wooden frame outside. With renewed hope and surges of adrenaline she set to picking and destroying the decayed wood around the metal.

After what seemed like hours, although a glance at her watch told her it had only actually been about twenty minutes, she had released one side of the grille and began to lever it away from the wall. At first there was little movement. Then suddenly the wood on the other side splintered and following a loud groan the grille swung away to hang drunkenly. She cringed at the noise and stood frozen, listening for footsteps to come or shouts. But there was nothing.

Gathering herself, she climbed out of the window and, trusting the shrubs to do their part in softening her landing, let herself drop. On the ground, relieved only to have sustained scratches and a couple of nasty grazes, and to have escaped any broken bones, she set off round the house. There was a lot of excited shouting but when she peered in a window it was to see her abductor nursing a beer as he watched television. No wonder he had not heard the grille screeching, she grinned. Running across the garden to the gate, she slipped through, crossed the road and reached the beach. There were lots of people and hopefully, if her absence was discovered, even if her abductor looked on the beach, she could lose herself in the crowd. Meanwhile she needed to contact Manuel.

* * * * *

Manuel looked at the display on his phone but did not recognize the caller ID. He pressed the button to answer. "*Diga me.*"

"Oh Manuel, it's me. You'll never believe what's happened. Have you met Bolaño's contact?"

"Anita," he interrupted firmly. "Where are you?"

"I'm on the beach," he heard her talking to someone else, then "Manuel, I'm not sure exactly where I am, but this man can tell you. It's his phone."

Before he could say anything else he found himself talking to Anita's new friend. He obtained their position, asked him to keep Anita with him until he could get there and thanked him with genuine gratitude for his help.

Disconnecting the call he went to hail a taxi as he spoke into his wire. "Anita is found. Pull Searle in."

The journey seemed to take forever, but finally he paid off the taxi and stalked over to the beach. He did not have to search for long as Anita saw him and started towards him waving her hand and calling his name. Her new friend trailed after her.

Once in proper earshot she began to talk excitedly until Manuel reached her and pulled her into his arms, squeezing her so hard she momentarily feared for her ribs.

"You have much explaining to do," he gritted in her ear. Then holding her with one arm, he held out his other hand to her friend.

"*Muito obrigado*, I am indebted to you."

The other man nodded as he smiled. "*De nada*. It is not often you can rescue such a beautiful senhorita! And really I did nothing but lend her my phone."

As Manuel quickly heard the man's account of what he knew and thanked him profusely again, Anita fairly shimmered with eagerness to tell him of her adventures along with wanting to know how he had got on. At last they turned to leave the beach.

"What happened? Was it Frank dealing with Bolaño? Did . . ."

"¡*Silencio*! *Dios mio*. I am very displeased with you. By not staying in the apartment you very nearly ruined the whole plan."

She pulled on his arm, forcing him to stop.

"No, this wasn't my fault. This man appeared just after you'd turned out of sight. I never had time to get back into the apartment!"

His eyes bored into her for some seconds before his face softened. His free hand rose to cup her cheek. He smiled ruefully. "Yes, I should have guessed. You have no need to look for trouble, it finds you quickly enough." She started to object but he continued. "If it was as you say, then the fault is mine. I should have left you in the security of the apartment. Do you forgive me?"

By the lights in his eyes, she knew he was half teasing, half serious.

"Of course. Manuel, I have so much to tell . . ."

"Yes," he again interrupted. "I wish to hear everything, but first I have to check the house before we go home, yes?"

She gave in as she could see she did not really have a choice. She was very reluctant to return to her place of captivity but could see he was determined to deal with her captor. As it turned out, the bird had obviously discovered her disappearance and flown the coop. In the taxi taking them back he told her of the exchange. "We will see the others this evening and they will tell us of all that occurred after I left to find you."

Finally, in the apartment he got them both a drink before seating himself in his favourite chair and pulling her on to his lap. "Now, *Querida*. Now tell me everything."

She burrowed into him, inhaling his familiar scent before telling him all that had happened to her. As her story unfolded he held her close realizing, as perhaps she did not fully, how close she had been to disaster. If her abductor, who she had blithely already told him was armed, had caught her escaping—he could hardly bear to think about it.

Hunger eventually drove them to the kitchen where they cobbled together some sandwiches and coffee. They had missed lunch and there were still several hours before they were to meet the others.

Marco rang to let Manuel know they had taken Searle in but he had no money on him. As both he and Luke could testify that he had met no one nor even got close to anyone, it was a mystery they were still trying to figure out.

Manuel and Anita spent the remainder of the afternoon quietly recovering after all the recent excitement. They talked about all that had happened. The missing money was a mystery and, of course, Bolaño still had to be dealt with. Anita drifted off to sleep and Manuel carried her off to bed. She did not wake even as he slipped her clothes off. Finally, looking at her peaceful form, he smiled slightly. She was not at all the type of woman he had always been attracted to before, either in looks or character, yet she had completely wrapped herself around his heart and he could not imagine a life without her by his side. He certainly could not conceive being with anyone else now. She needed a keeper, that was for certain. Sighing, he quickly stripped and joined her under the sheet pulling her back into him as he curved round her. In no time he also was fast asleep.

CHAPTER
TWENTY ONE

It was dark when they rose. Both felt mellow and the leisurely lovemaking she had woken up to had added its rejuvenating qualities. They showered, separately as they had no more time to waste, and got ready to meet with the others.

They were to meet at the Cervejaria Trinidade, the restaurant they had watched waiting to see Luke meet Bolaño just a few days previously. Only four days, yet so much had happened with a roller coaster of emotions it felt more like a lifetime ago. Marco had chosen the venue as he said she should not visit Lisbon without experiencing it. As they made their way there, she was amused when Manuel told her he had looked up its history and proceeded to regale her with it.

"It was a thirteenth century monastery where monks protected Christian prisoners from the Moors. It survived a fire and later an earthquake before it became the Trinidade Beer Factory with part of it turned into a bar and restaurant. I will tell you nothing of its interior, so you may form your own thoughts."

She smiled at him distractedly. She loved listening to the timbre of his voice even when he gave her a potted history lesson. However, she could not help being conscious of the fact that very soon all this would be over and she would be back in England, trying to pick up the threads of her life, and although Manuel was very affectionate and attentive, there was no getting away from the fact that he had never actually said he loved her or wanted a future with her. She didn't think she could rely on passing comments about showing her round various cities in the future, for all she knew he was just being polite or only meant that he would like to see her when she could return on future holidays. Her old life appeared so mundane now and, in an odd way, as if she had never been a part of it. Determinedly she threw off her depressing thoughts—she was not back there yet.

As they entered the famous restaurant, Anita immediately realised why Manuel had not wanted to tell her anything in advance of its interior. The vaulted ceiling and traditional tiles on the walls that featured mysterious Masonic symbols had to be experienced first hand for their full impact.

Satisfied with her reaction, Manuel guided her to follow a waiter to their table that had been previously reserved. They were the first to arrive and talked about the decorations until Marco's appearance soon afterwards. The three chatted, drinking Sagres beer while they waited for Luke and their food to arrive.

"No," Marco replied to Manuel's enquiry. "So far Searle is not telling us any information. In truth, I think he will not do so now."

Luke's arrival halted the conversation temporarily. He smiled at Anita as the waiter left with his order. "You've had an unexpectedly eventful day!"

She grimaced and reiterated her innocence regarding her adventure, before giving them the details of her escape. Both Marco and Luke expressed their admiration for her ingenuity despite Manuel's black look. Marco then carried on from her experience. "The police looked through the house but could find nothing to trace your abductor."

Luke's drink arrived along with their food, prawns and steaks for which the establishment was renowned.

"He is not very important, we think," Marco continued. "But he may have helped us to fill some holes in our investigation."

"But at least you've now got the prototype." Anita sipped her beer.

"Yes," Luke agreed. "But it would have been better if the case could have been closed complete."

"*Exactamente*," Manuel frowned. "For example, who was working with Searle? He is not the top man."

"How can you be sure?" Anita asked.

"The main reason is because he made the exchange and, so, exposed his identity. This has been too well carried out for the head organiser to make such a mistake."

Marco nodded. "Also, what happened to the money? We saw him leave Manuel with it then, when we arrest him, he has the case still but it is empty."

Luke agreed. "It's a mystery all right. He wasn't out of sight of either Marco or myself and neither of us saw him even talk to anyone, let alone hand over the money!"

There was a short silence as they all brooded on the problem.

"The only thing I can think of," Luke continued. "Is that he must have emptied the case at a designated spot for someone else to collect."

Anita looked up. "Wouldn't you have seen him?"

Marco sighed. "If it was done so that his actions were covered by a low wall or bush, whichever one of us was following him then may not have seen. We had to keep some distance behind, so he did not see us."

"You weren't both tailing him then?"

"Yes, we were. But I followed more closely then after a bit I signalled to Marco who took over. We would have switched again, but once Manuel messaged us that you were safe, then Marco took Frank into custody. That's when it transpired he no longer had the money."

"I see." Anita's gaze became unfocused as she absorbed and processed the information. The others turned their attention to their food.

Anita suddenly tensed. "What about the prototype?"

"We have it safe," Marco assured her.

"No, I don't mean that. I know you've got it. But that means Bolaño doesn't. Won't he come after Manuel for it?"

Again it was Marco who supplied the facts. "Bolaño left the country this morning and is back in Spain. He left someone called Garcia to pick up the prototype. We have arrested him. So Bolaño knows the exchange was made and that Manuel left the park. He will also know by now that Garcia is under arrest. He will realise we have the prototype, but think that we got it from Garcia. So Manuel is in the clear for Bolaño."

"Oh good." Anita relaxed.

Manuel leant over and spoke softly in her ear. "It is good you have the concern for me!"

She blushed and, picking up her fork, concentrated on her food, tuning out the others as they planned their next steps.

* * * * *

The next morning Anita saw Manuel off and returned to the kitchen for a second cup of coffee. It had been very late by the time they had returned the previous night or, more accurately, early this morning. They had both been weary after the long stressed-ridden day and had fallen asleep immediately. This morning she had awakened to Manuel making languorous love to her. She sighed. She only wished she could look forward to a lifetime of such wake-up calls. She finished her coffee and cleared away the breakfast things. Her flight home was tomorrow, arranged by Marco at Manuel's instigation apparently. It had taken her by surprise, although obviously she had to return home at some time, she wished it was just not yet. She ran over the conversation before he had left.

"Today I must go with Marco to finish the loose ends." He had smiled at her. "I will return as fast as possible. You will be okay, no?"

"Of course. I might have a wander and do some window shopping."

"*Bueno*. Perhaps also you pack your luggage ready for tomorrow?"

"Tomorrow?"

"Yes, a reservation is made for your return to England. But please keep out one dress for tonight. I wish to take you to a nightclub I like where you can hear traditional Portuguese songs. You would enjoy this?"

She had nodded vaguely through the numbness that had overtaken her at his casual words. It seemed now the operation was all but finished, he wanted her gone from his life without further ado.

* * * * *

Manuel returned to take lunch with her and brought her up to speed on the surprising events that had occurred during the morning.

"We waited for a long time for South to join us. We thought he had slept too much, no? But still he did not arrive.

When we telephoned his hotel they told us he checked out yesterday."

She stared at him. "Do you mean that when we were all together last evening he had already left his hotel?"

"*Si.*" Manuel watched as she processed the underlying meaning. She did consider South a friend, after all.

"He was in it with Frank Searle, then?" she said slowly. He nodded but said nothing further. Suddenly her head snapped up. "He must have been involved with that man that took me yesterday. My God, what a creep! When I think of his sympathy last night and his reaction to how I got away . . . what a hypocrite! Well, I hope you get him!"

Manuel relaxed. She was angry, not devastated. "Yes, he is already arrested. The police tracked and intercepted him. It is good, too, that Searle now knows South abandoned him. He thought before that South, as one of the policemen on the case, would arrange his release." He took a roll and broke it on his plate. "Unfortunately, this means I cannot be with you this afternoon as I must attend the new interrogation of Searle. He now is happy to talk with us."

Anita carefully rearranged the food on her plate. "No problem. As we're likely to have another late night, I might have a siesta. Then, if I'm feeling like it, I may go for a walk along the beach."

"I wish I could join you, especially for the siesta," he was rewarded with a smile. Inwardly he acknowledged her plan for the afternoon was probably a good one. Despite the way she had reacted, it must be a shock on top of everything else that had happened to her since her arrival in Spain and this would give her some down time to come to terms with everything.

He filled in a few blanks for her, including part of Searle's interrogation. When Manuel had asked him how he found them at his home fishing village where he had taken Anita,

Searle had replied, "Luke suggested I try Bolaño on spec, so I did. Bolaño knew you must have taken Anita from his house. He said that as you must have made the decision and acted very fast there was a chance you'd taken her to your childhood home to regroup while you made new plans. Obviously he was right." This last remark had been accompanied by a smirk that Manuel had been tempted to remove forcibly.

Manuel hesitated a moment, then decided she had a right to know the rest. "South, when we talked with him, knew it was all over for him. He was prepared to answer our questions. Isabel refused to hand the prototype over to him as they had planned, but he managed to get hold of it from her at the airport without her knowledge by using his credentials with the airport authorities to retrieve it from her luggage. By this time you had flown to Spain, so then he flew to Spain also. It looks like when she found it was missing, she contacted Bolaño directly and he told her to come to Portugal. You know what happened then."

She shuddered, she would never forget it.

"South claims he kept hold of it, instead of immediately making his deal and escape, in case he needed to use it for leverage in getting you out of the trouble that you found yourself in, as he felt a bit responsible." He smiled at her. "Of course he thought it partly your fault for boarding the plane against his advice." She pulled a face then returned his smile. Manuel continued, "He wanted to get you away from me as he thought I worked with Bolaño—a dangerous man, and so maybe I was also a dangerous man."

Anita nodded then asked, "Were they really policemen?"

"Yes, but when the possibility of easily making a fortune, the temptation was great, so then . . ."

"They joined forces and went for it!" she finished for him.

174

He looked at the pensive expression on her face. "He is a criminal but he does, I think, have feelings for you. He wanted to make you safe, perhaps especially as originally he thought to use you as a cover for him to enter Spain."

She nodded. "Yes, I see that." She looked up at him. "Go on, I'll be fine. The sooner you go, the sooner you'll be finished and back."

He kissed her gently on the cheek and left, hoping she would not brood too much. Also, he did not want her thinking of the other man, even though he was now completely out of the picture.

The evening spent in the small intimate nightclub was perfect. The food wonderful, the ambience as romantic as anyone could wish, while the songs, known as *fados*, added the finishing touch. The *fados* could be likened to blues songs, full of the plaintiff sadness of partings, abandonments and lost loves and lives. They perfectly suited Anita's feelings on the prospect of parting with Manuel the following day.

On returning to the apartment, by some unspoken agreement they went straight to the bedroom. Anita stood still as Manuel flicked on a small bedside lamp. He watched her a moment before moving across to take her in his arms.

"Do not be sad. We can return here another time, if you wish. Although I hope it will just be for holiday!"

Her heart lurched. 'We' he had said. Surely that meant he intended at least to keep in touch? Suddenly her spirits lightened considerably, he was careful and would not give her a platitude, not after all they had been through. She choked a small laugh.

"You're right," she looked up into his eyes. "Just the thought of returning home got me down a bit. What shall we do to cheer me up?"

The tenseness left his body, relieved to see his Anita back.

"First, I think we have on too many clothes." He gave her a slow wink as he eased the zip down the back of her dress. In no time they were both naked and stretched out on the bed. Manuel propped himself up on one arm while the other traced her contours as if imprinting them in his memory. Meanwhile his head dipped to allow his mouth to nibble the corner of hers before moving across to her throat and slowly making his way southwards.

Her arms went round his neck while her body arched to direct his attentions where she ached. He chuckled softly. "Not so fast. I want to savour our lovemaking." He dropped kisses in the hollow of her neck before continuing in a slightly strained voice, "I want that you never forget this night."

True to his word he took his time, bringing her near to her peak time after time before pulling back and then starting again until finally he pushed her over into the most explosive orgasm of her life.

By the time she woke she could tell by the angle of the sun streaming in the window that she'd slept later than she'd intended. She listened intently, but could hear nothing. Manuel must have left for the police station where he hoped the last bits and pieces would be settled quickly. She padded to the kitchen to put the coffee maker on before taking a shower. She found Manuel's note in the centre of the kitchen table.

> *"You looked so peaceful I decided not to wake you even though I was very tempted. I hope to be finished in time to accompany you to the airport. If I am too late, please do not wait for me. I will catch you up."*

She sighed as she ran water into the pot. "Where have I nearly heard that before?" she muttered. However, she reminded herself that Manuel was not Luke, in any way. He would not let her down.

Four hours later she was not feeling so sanguine. Manuel had not returned to the apartment before she had to leave for the airport. She had now checked in and should be in the departures lounge. Instead, she stood at the security gate straining her neck in an effort to spot him in the crowded concourse. The second announcement for her flight blared over the tannoy. She sagged with despair. She had to go through or she would miss her flight. She only hoped he would get in touch with her once she was back in England. She had left her address and phone number at the apartment, but the only contact details she had for him was his family's cottage in the Spanish fishing village, but goodness knows when he would be there again.

Dejectedly she entered departures and joined the now short queue for her flight. She pulled her boarding card out ready just as a hand clutched her shoulder. Startled, she spun round. Manuel stood there, wordless as he stared at her, breaths sawing in and out of his chest.

"I thought you weren't going to make it," she whispered as her heart lifted in joy.

"Almost I did not, but Marco arranged a police car for me." He pulled her close to his body.

"At least we can say goodbye," she hesitated before throwing pride to the winds. "You will write to me?"

He kissed her, taking his time. "No, I will not need to write to you, I will be with you."

She stared at him, ignoring the attendant asking for her pass. "You are coming to England? Oh Manuel, when?"

He turned her to face the increasingly impatient attendant. "Now. I travel with you." The attendant checked both their passes and ushered them through.

"Come," he draped his arm round her as they stepped into the tunnel. "I said nothing before as I was unsure if I could finish in time. But with Marco's help I can travel with you"

"But your job?"

"I have ten days holiday before I must return to Spain and finish the paperwork." He bent forward to look at her face. "You are pleased with this, no?"

She nodded vehemently. "Of course. I was so depressed not seeing you before I left, not knowing if we would ever see each other again. I was determined not to act as a limpet and make a scene!"

"Why did you think we may not see each other again?"

"Well, I know you said things that implied we'd be together in the future but, Manuel, you never actually said you loved me. I was frightened it was just your way—you know, sort of part of the Latin romantic temperament."

Manuel stared at her in amazement. "But every way I look after you whether rescuing you or making love to you, showed my feelings for you!"

"Well, women, or at least me, want the words," she advised him demurely.

He stopped and lifted her face on one hand and stared deeply into her eyes. "Anita, *te amo, eu te amo*, I love you."

She blinked up at him, momentarily overwhelmed with emotion. He released her chin and claimed her arm propelling them forwards again. "I have told you in words now in three languages, but still I wait to hear your words."

"Perhaps I should just let my actions speak for me," she teased, laughing as he growled his opinion of that as they continued towards the plane.

"You will introduce me to your family. Then you will come to Spain with me. My family will be pleased I now settle down."

"I can't believe you're coming home with me." She felt as if her face would split with the wide grin she could not control while she bubbled over with excitement. "I'm going to take Spanish lessons. Oh, and I've just thought, now we'll be able to work together as a team on other cases."

Manuel groaned. That just about described his worst nightmare. "This will not be necessary. My superiors are pleased with my work and I have been offered a promotion. I will be based permanently in Madrid. You are mine, no?" She nodded. "So, I must look after you. I must be with you to show you belong to me and to keep you out of trouble. Also, perhaps, to help you with our future children, yes?"

Overwhelmed with a surge of emotion, she could find no words to answer so squeezed his hand. He understood.

THE END

Lightning Source UK Ltd.
Milton Keynes UK
UKOW040822300912

199842UK00001B/7/P